NAADI PREDI

D1759005

A Mind Boggling Miracle

Wing Commander Shashikant Oak

FUSION BOOKS

© Author

Publisher:
FUSION BOOKS
X-30, Okhla Industrial Area, Phase-II
New Delhi 110 020
Phones: 40712200
E-mail: sales@dpb.in
Website: www.diamondbook.in
Revised Edition: 2021

Naadi Predictions
By : Shashikant Oak

Dedication

Humbly dedicated as a petal at the graceful lotus feet of Sri. Agastya, Sugar, Bhrugu, Kak-Bhujandar, Parashar, Vashishtha, Vishwamitra and many other unknown Maharshees whose incrediable predictive Naadi literature has been inspiring to the mankind.

Request to the readers

On reading my articles on Naadis, published in various periodicals, a number of readers have written to me enclosing their thumb-impressions along with other details about their lives, and the fees, requesting me to arrange for their Naadi readings. I understand their feelings, but due to my employment, busy schedule of work, possibility of transfer-postings etc, it is not possible for me to act as a go - between to pass on their thumb impressions to the Naadi readers, calling on them at the appointed time, waiting for hours till the Naadis are searched, taped or read etc. Kindly understand that it is also not possible for me to incur the expenses involved in forwarding those thumb-impressions etc. to Naadi centres. Readers are requested to note that.

Preface

In June 1994, when I called on the Executive Editor of Sahyadri, a Pune weekly and gave him the Marathi translation of Sri. Agastya Naadi prediction, he suggested to contribute an article for his weekly. Later I also inquired from some persons whether it was advisable to write a book on that topic. I received a number of letters from readers of my article published in Sahyadri's 1st August' 94 issue. I then felt that a magazine - article was too short. A number of other questions arising in the minds of readers ought to be answered. That led me to write the present book. Now, while presenting this book to the readers, I am satisfied that I have tried my best to answer a number of questions arising about Naadi Astrology.

For readers who would like to go to the South to obtain Naadi-readings, I have given detailed information about the titles of days, months, years, nakshatras etc. in the Tamil almanac. For undertaking recommended Shanti-Deeksha rituals, I have given the addresses of temples of nine planets. A map showing the route to reach there and some relevant information about lodging, transport, buses, and railways in Chennai is also provided. I am neither a chum nor a relation of any of the Naadi-readers. However, because I have been a frequent, inquisitive and interested visitor to the Naadi Centres in various parts of India, I have cordial relations with Naadi-readers and their staff.

I myself have not studied the science of Astrology. Consequently readers are requested not to involve me as their intermediary. Kindly don't send me your thumb impressions, other particulars about your life, money etc. with a request to obtain the English translations of your Naadi predictions. I don't undertake the responsibility of attending to correspondence of that nature.

It gives me immense pleasure to bring out the third edition of this book in such a short time. In July 2003, I retired from Indian Air Force service, after serving for long 32 years. I owe all the credit to

IAF for giving me the opportunity to get introduced to the amazing world of Naadi predictions.

The book presents the revised and updated addresses of more than 220 Naadi Centres operating throughout Indian states. The list is presented in alphabetical order for an easy search and is also updated till 25th Nov 2012. I am extremely thankful to my colleague in Indian Air Force, Group Captain Rakesh Nanda, for providing me information of many Naadi Maharshees' new work and centres.

In recent past, Uday Mehta had opened very informative website, <Nnaadiguruonweb.org> for the benefit of the persons far away from Naadi centres. They can directly be in touch with Naadi centres.

In last few years, many books mostly written for western audience, have been published on Naadi Predictions. Some of the prominent ones are by– Danish - Kim Paisol's (Naadi Palmleaf Astrology), British– Andrew and Angela Donovan's (The Hidden Oracle of India: The mystery of India's Naadi palm leaf), American–Johann Landis's (the future code–Find the mystery of your fate deciphered in palm leaf), Indian-American-Komilla Sutton's- (Naadi Granthas and Palm Leaf Astrology) German– Thomas Ritter (The Secret of Indian Palm Leaf Libraries), Japanese–Deepak Aoyama's (The secret leaves of Agasthya), etc.

Many websites and groups connected with Naadi Predictions are providing useful information on this predictive method. This is possible because of the extremely astonishing results to Naadi lovers have had from all parts of the world. Blogs maintained by me namely – 1.Workshop on Naadi Granths, 2. हिन्दी भाषिकों के हेतु - नाड़ी ग्रंथ भविष्य, 3. मराठीतील लेख व पत्रव्यवहार, 4. Naadi palm leaf study circle. And You tube a/c <shashikantoak> will provide latest information and developments. In case of difficulty send email to shashioak@gmail.com to get links directly.

I am grateful to Narenderji of Diamond Publication without whose encouragement and support the book in decent print and ebook form could not have been possible.

Wing Commander Shashikant Oak (Retd)
A4/404, Ganga Hamlet Society
Viman Nagar, Pune-411 014, India
Mobile: 09881901049
E-mail: shashioak@gmail.com

Indological Study- Naadi palm leaf Literature

Proposed Project: Naadi Palm Leaf Data Bank for Systematic Analysis of Forecasts.

Introduction: The ancient sages or Maharishis such as Agastya, Vashishta, Kausika, Shuka, Brigu, Kak Pujander and many more; whose names are often mentioned in ancient Indian scriptures; have written predictions for spiritual and material well-being of mankind. They have produced many grants in the divine sciences. Part of this divine science is related to Naadi astrology, which is one of the various Hindu astrological practices in India. It is rooted in the principle that in ancient times, various Maharishis foretold and recorded minute details of human life on palm leaves. Naadi predictions are consulted for a variety of reasons, mainly for general guidance of future events and to avoid and eliminate difficulties and complications in one's current life. Researchers have been studying the matter for years, systematically examining palm leaves from a variety of angles, including the non-astrological area.

In short, textual notes on palm leaves, rules of linguistics, evolution and modification of scripts, forms of poetry and presentation need to be studied in depth. Attempts have been made to preserve palm leaves that remain in bad condition and to test the true nature of palm leaves as told by carbon testing. The need to help hands arise when the boundaries of research exceed the restricted boundaries of the individuals involved. As can be seen, the tasks involved in the process of the afore mentioned research are enormous. The researchers involved in this project are mostly from non-Tamil backgrounds. Most of them do not really know Tamil. However, with great enthusiasm, they have succeeded in collecting and maintaining data such as handwritten notebooks, pictures, audio and video recordings. Now, it takes time to systematically organize the above data so that future generations of researchers and students of this course will benefit. It is hoped that the systematic regulation of the entire data will certainly provide an impetus for future generations and that more researchers will enter the space of current researchers and further expand the boundaries of that work.

Proposal : In the Data Banking project, at present, more than 1800 scans of Naadi notebooks have been offered to provide various personal notebooks for research purposes. These notebooks come with scans, photos of Naadi palm leaves and attached functions. Audios of several persons are included for ready reference of descriptions. Many Tamil-speaking people may come forward to translate these scans, and this may add some value to the source data. This facility is provided separately in this project to generate statistical data analysis of the accuracy of the predictions made. This feature can be verified by people involved in the future. Although, the data are systematically compiled for research-oriented students and experts in various fields. If this topic allows, it could attract PhD dissertations to linguistics and script studies. The poetic form used in the collection of verses requires special attention from the world of Tamil literature.

With this in mind, future assistance and guidance are requested:

1. Necessary assistance for future committees. Interested organizations and universities may share our Naadi literature data for research purposes.

2. They will select suitable candidates for a research study.

3. Develop appropriate procedures to oversee, moderate and report results, standards and certification in accordance with their current regulations.

4. Scholarships will be awarded to eligible candidates by the Naadi Lovers Group or any other trust or individual.

5. A copy of the research paper to be shared with Naadi Lovers Group representatives for the future.

6. Research articles to be published by his copyright by institutions, universities or faculty.

Time Frame: Data can be provided over the Internet or in any other way convenient to researchers and operators. The period for completion of the said project with the interested parties is initially for 3 months.

They should be provided to researchers:-1. Certified copies of handwritten notebooks.2. Copy Model software program specially designed for the purpose of this project. With operating instructions.

Conclusion: This project is primarily to explore the possibilities of digitally preserving the precious source of information compiled by sages and Maharishis, and it will be the subject of many future projects in the coming centuries.

Wing Commander Shashikant Oak. (Pune) & Shri Vishvesh Deshpande.(Hong Kong)

Please Note:

No specific educational qualification is compulsory if the applicant is a keen student of Indology and knows the scripts in the palm leaves. Anyone can apply on linked format, for free sample data of 100 scans, with biodata and photo.

He should not be a rationalist or member of any rationalist organisation. He will not despise any of the ancient Naadi (sages) Maharishis. Furthermore, he will not discredit any Naadi reading community or center or reader.

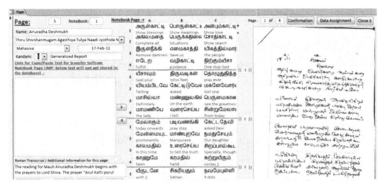

A sample of Databank project indicating notebook and its tabulated translation

A Unique Book

I am happy to introduce this unique and very useful book to all prospective readers. Its author happens to be my nephew. He has taken great pains, spread over a number of years, to inquisitively locate and visit unique astrological compendium centres in our country, from north to south where anybody and everybody may find his/her past, present and future accurately and astoundingly recorded for reference and enlightenment, if needed, by inquisitive or worried souls.

Those records of the past, present and future of all humans, anywhere in the world, born or yet to be born recorded by gifted omniscient sages, is a unique, unimaginable astrological treasury which any seeker may avail of.

This book provides the addresses of those Naadi Centres and introduces the reader to the procedure followed there.

Those predictive compendiums are known as Agastya Naadi, Shughar Naadi etc. in the south and as Bhrugu Samhita, Arun Samhita etc in the north.

On the persuasion of knowledgeable friends I have had occasion to have my own future read out to me both in North Indian and South Indian centres. The details narrated were astounding.

Those gifted souls of the very first generation of humans, multi-billion years ago (as per the Vedic cosmic time –schedule of six elapsed Manvantaras), were known as "Dravid" (द्रविड़) because "Dra" (द्र) is the first syllable of the Sanskrit word 'Drashta' signifies 'foreseers; while the second syllable; Vid' (fon~) means the learned . Therefore Dravids were basically those, gifted with a prophetic vision to record in writing the role that every human was to play in future generations, till the end of humanity.

Consequently the current notion that Dravids are Tamil, speaking South Indians, and the cognate assertion that though Dravidians initially inhabited the north, they were later pushed down south by Aryans, constitute a jumble of confused ideas.

All those following Vedic culture (and of course speaking Sanskrit) were known as Aryans. Therefore at the commencement of the Universe, all humans were Aryans. Among them those individuals gifted with a special prophetic vision and assigned the task of recording the future of all humans were known as Dravids. Therefore present-day Dravids are descendents of those Aryans who were initially assigned a special prophetic task of recording the future of all mankind.

Many persons, Laymen as well as scholars specializing in various sciences are habituated to dismiss Astrology as mere mumbo-jumbo misused by the crafty to rob the gullible.

To all such doubters I would like to narrate my own experience of an Indian astrologer's astounding prediction in September 1945, soon after British victory in world war II, that India was destined to attain independence from British rule, before December 1947, attended by a saddening national upheaval (viz. the India-Pakistan partition) which won't be a dubbed as a war.

It should convince anyone that Astrology is not only a science but a science of sciences, because it has the potential to foresee and forecast all the happens on our globe, because of divine computer-programming.

It follows therefore that all living beings play their assigned role in the cosmic drama, as noted by William Shakespeare and pointed out by Omar Khayyam in poetic lines saying:

"Tis all a checker board of nights and days
Where Destiny with men for pieces plays
Hither and thither moves, mates and slays
And one by one back in the closet lays."

2nd March 1917-   **–Late P. N. Oak**
4th Dec. 2007

Contents

Sri. Agastya Naadi Samhita – A Mind Boggling Miracle

In today's world of science, if just from the impression of your thumb somebody accurately tells you, your name, the names of your mother, father, husband/wife, your birth-date, month, age etc. what would you call such prediction? Would you regard it as an amazing divination or as black magic?

No, it is neither black magic nor a hand trick. Such prediction, which defies all logic and boggles one's mind, forms the subject-matter of the Agastya Naadi. Those predictions were visualised at different places by various ancient Sages, with their divine insight and factually noted by their chosen disciples, thousands of years ago, to be handed down from generation to generation. This great work makes us realize the limitations of human sciences. That great compilation predicting the future of all human beings born or yet to be born, eclipses the achievements of all other sciences put together!

Naadi is a collective name given to palm-leaf manuscripts dictated by ancient sages predicting the characteristics, family history, as well as the careers of innumerable individuals. The sages (rishis), who dictated those Naadis, were gifted with such a remarkable foresight – that they accurately foretold the entire future of all mankind. Many scholars in different parts of India have in their safekeepings several granthas (volumes) of those ancient palm-leaf manuscripts dictated by the great visualizing souls, alias sages such as Bhrugu, Vasistha, Agastya, Shukra, and other venerable saints. I had the good-fortune to consult Sri. Agastya Naadi predictions. It was an unforgettable experience. Perhaps I was destined to publish this book to share with readers the amazing information about the predictive expertise of the Agastya Naadi concerning the careers of persons born or yet to be born.

I was transferred as a Wing Commander to the Air Force Station, at Tambaram near Chennai (Madras) in July 1993. The Agastya Naadi Nilayam (Centre) was about 3-4 kms, from my residence. I got that information from local contacts. One day, I called at that centre in the morning. The attendant took my thumb impression on a piece of paper. I was called in after an hour. One Naadi- reader, holding 50-60 palm-leaf manuscripts, tied in a bundle and held between two wooden strips of footrule size, started conversing with me in superfast Tamil! When I informed him that I did not know even the A, B, C, of Tamil, the inmates asked me to call later that day. In the afternoon, my wife and a photographer too accompanied me. We had to wait for about 2½ hours as the reading of predictions of other visitors was in progress. The photographer who could not wait for long, took 3 snaps and left. When my turn came, I requested some of the visitors there to act as interpreters and the reading started. An interpreter should preferably accompany non-Tamilians. The Naadi-leaves are about 10-11 inches in length and 1 to 1½ inches in width. They are flexible, being made of palm-leaves used for making hand-fans, after due processing. The matter is written on them in 6 to 8 lines, leaving some margin, with a long thick nail held in the fist. The script is a running-continuum written without lifting one's hand. Paying homage to Sage Agastya, the reader started reading the matter etched on the leaves, inquiring from me whether my name began with consonants p, ph, b, bh etc., whether the name of my mother contained four-letters? Whether my father had expired? etc. Whenever the reply was in the negative, the reader used to discard that leaf and read the nothings on the next one. On that day he discarded about 200 leaves when my name was not found quoted in any of them. They then asked me to return after a month. Accordingly when I called at that centre after a month, I came to know that the leaves (Pattis) pertaining to my thumb impression had been received from Sri Lanka. During the intervening period, I had an opportunity to hear the predictions concerning other visitors. I thus got used to those predictive-readings. This time also the first bundle did not bear my name. In the second bundle, after 5 or 6 leaves, in one leaf, the reader read out the name of my mother – Mangala, father – Janardan, my name – Shashikant and wife's name – Alka; I have one son and one daughter and that I would come to seek the prediction at my age of 45 etc. Later followed the name of the Samvatsar, (Hindu calendar year) as Virodhi, Adi Maasam (the Hindu month of Ashadha), the 16th day, Sunday, Chitra Nakshatra (Star), Dhanu (Sagittarius) lagnam (Ascendant) and Kanya (Virgo) Rashi (Birth Sign) etc. A thick, 40-year Tamil almanac was lying nearby, which corroborated the above details as accurate to the minutest detail. My date of birth, 31 July 1949, as per the English calendar also tallied. The reading about my life continued. Facts such as my being the eldest child, my children's schooling, my being educated and working in the nation's defence services, in a high position etc. were all mentioned very clearly. Further on, he told me my birth-chart at the time of my birth. It matched with the one I was carrying with me. There was no doubt that my specific leaf (Patti) was located among millions of other leaves. That reading took a lot of time. So I was asked to return after 2 days. In between they were to jot down the matter from the leaf in a 40-page notebook. By that time a reader, Sri. Rajendran who knew English had also arrived. They read the notings in ancient Tamil from the notebook, explained the same in modern Tamil, and interpreted the meaning of 3 to 4 sentences together in English, which was simultaneously recorded on an audio tape. Finally, he bowed and handed to me the audio tape with my future recorded therein, in Tamil. For all that I had to pay Rs. 100 plus Rs 25 for the tape. So the total expenditure was only Rs. 125/-.

In that general chapter (which dealt with the Ascendant in my horoscope), Sage Agastya had directed me (the Jataka), to read the subtle and detailed information contained in other Kandams (Cantos). That aroused my curiosity to ascertain the predictions in other Kandams, which dealt with various houses in my birth-chart. The subsequent Kandams (chapters) revealed that each Kandam prediction was recorded in 15-18 verses containing 60-70 lines. The first chapter described the person whose future was being narrated and mentioned some horoscopic details such as, Dhanu lagnam, Kanya rashi, and my name- Shashikant. Every detail was accurate. There was no chance of any mistake. Thereafter, some important incidents of my life were read out from that chapter. After that, there was a clear mention of my earlier birth's sins and good deeds, and their effect on my current birth's good and bad deeds and planetary positions etc. About the future, there was a mention of a single year or a group of years.

In my case, at the beginning of chapter one, there was an accurate description of some incidents in my life, e.g. the undue delay in my promotion, break in children's education, my wife's skin disease (an allergy leading to itching) and mishap to my vehicle. (A few days earlier, a vehicle coming from the opposite direction collided with my car. However, due to my presence of mind the vehicle alone was damaged, while all the members of my family remained unscathed). Then there was a mention of a court-case! (Initially I could not believe, as to how I could be involved in any court case while being employed in the Air force?). But after racking my brains I recalled that I had indeed deposed as a witness in some case before a Court-Martial. The mention of those very graphic and verifiable past-events convinced me that my past was accurately recorded in those prediction-strips. A narration of that gratifying experience by me induced a number of my colleagues from the Air force to visit the prediction-centre. All of them returned highly impressed.

Those predictive texts also contain a chapter recommending certain pilgrimages or prayers, worship and charities at specific shrines, to atone for one's past sins. Whether all those suggested remedies are truly effective or they have any commercial angle, needs to be considered.

I got chance to read many Maharishi's writings about me. Latest being in Ravan Naadi in 2008 at Pune. Ramani guruji's astonishing readings in Pune. I was witness to the readings of Chandrakala, Suryakala and Nandi Naadi of highly spiritual persons in Vaideeshwaran Koil. In July 2009, I was specially called by Saptharishi Maharishi's Naadi reader Dr. Om Ulgnathan to be a witness in New Delhi.

❑

Wing Commander Shashikant Oak and his wife while observing their Naadi Patti.

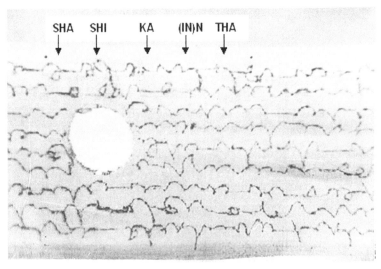

Enlarged photograph of the Naadi leaf

Structure of the Naadi Notings

This book aims at imparting information about Naadi Shastra (Science) and answering questions arising therefrom in the common man's mind. Such efforts have already been made earlier by a number of scholars and talented people. Compared to them, this author is a novice and totally lacks any knowledge of astrology. The author can't even cast a horoscope. However, this author is certainly curious and inquisitive about the Naadi shastra.

Among the various characteristics of man, one is "his obsession for probing things unknown. From ancient times, man is obsessed and eager for seeking more and more knowledge. He has succeeded too. It is an unending quest.

India's contribution to this search of the unknown is very important. India has a tradition that has always kept alive its link with the unknown. India is not just a nation, a country, or a piece of land. India is much more than that – something symbolic, poetic, and talent-invisible! The reason is that India is the only country in the world, which has concentrated on and devoted its entire talent and intelligence in the search of the truth. For thousands of years millions of people have been making efforts towards that single objective. For that, they shunned riches, adopted poverty, risked ill-health etc. But they never gave up their search for the truth. The divine, blissful vibrations of all those sages are always present in the atmosphere here. They include saints, mahatmas, rishis, munis, gurus, scholars, great poets, painters, and talented intellectuals who were the medium of Divinity. They have obliged mankind by opening up various avenues to divine knowledge. But to grasp that divine knowledge, it is necessary that one attain a certain high standard of moral behaviour, asceticism and knowledge.

Of the many aspirations that humans have, one is to peep into one's future. A number of sages (rishis-munis) have dwelt on that in a number of ways. One of its outcome is the science of Naadi.

Needless to say that these rishis-munis were experts in the science of Yoga, which describes the different states of one's being. If we grasp them, some light can be thrown on how the Yogis get or may be getting the knowledge of ascertaining and recording the future of every human being. That is just a small part of that vast store of cosmic knowledge.

How do they acquire that extra-sensory knowledge? In order to understand that, one has to know in detail the composition of the subtle body of man. Man's personality has seven facets.

First facet – one's gross body (Physical body)
Second facet – the subtle body – space body (Etheric body)
Third facet – extremely subtle body (Astral body)
Fourth facet – Manas Body (Mental body)
Fifth facet – Atma body (Spiritual body)
Sixth facet – Braham body (Cosmic body)
Seventh facet – Nirvana (Salvational body)

To grasp that arrangement one has to visualize them as one behind the other, or one within the other.

It is believed that for the first seven years of one's life, the stress is on the development of the gross body. Imitation is its basic characteristic. During that period, there is a lack of development of intellect, emotions and desires. There isn't much difference between such a being and an animal. The physical body of an animal is also developed, but its other facets remain undeveloped.

In the next seven years, the emotive body is developed. Youth attains maturity. In the succeeding seven years the subtle body attains development. That phase leads to the development of logic, thinking power, and intellect. After the development of the second facet there is some kind of adolescent maturity. But the third facet leads to the development of one's rationality, logic and intellect, because of education, culture and morality considerations. Probably because of this, the voting age throughout the world is 21.

The mental calibre of most human beings gets stuck up at that third stage till death. The development of the fourth, i.e. mental plane does not evolve in their beings. Experiences of the mental plane are very interesting and unprecedented e.g. mesmerism, telepathy, clairvoyance, reading the thoughts in others' minds, etc. In that state the visual reality is out of consideration e.g. it is possible to grip a thing in one's hand and then transcend its existence. Others' could be aware of the things in your hand, but to pull others into your transcendental plane of thoughts would be impossible. From there onwards one's own intellectual world begins. The rules of truth and falsehood of the material world begin to lose their significance. One is in a trance; unable to distinguish whether what is happening is real or just illusory!

A number of practitioners of black magic (Mantrics/Tantrics) get trapped in that state of their mind. They earn a bad name because of their black-magic power. In that state, one obtains a lot of power (siddhies), which is known as the awakening of the Kundalini. Modern Physiologists do not accept the existence of Kundalini, because they are not able to locate and identify it in the body. What is known as Kundalini is the development of the fourth state i.e. the mental faculty. One specific result of activation of the Kundalini is unprecedented, spiritual experiences as also the power to foretell the future of individuals.

The development of the fifth i.e. spiritual faculty (Atmic body) is a continuation of the development of the fourth state. Words such as 'house' or 'TV' are easily grasped because they connote concrete things. But when one mentions soul alias Atma that becomes incomprehensible. One has no experience of that and therefore one cannot grasp its meaning. Those who can comprehend the existence of the 'soul' are the persons in the fifth stage of development who stand on the threshold of the final spiritual liberation (Moksha) i.e. the final escape. However, some unknowingly stop at that stage, with a sense of total fulfillment.

For those in the sixth stage, there is a possibility of their crossing into Moksha, i.e. total liberation and merger into the divine soul i.e. 'Brahman'.

What is the distinguishing mark of the sixth facet of realization? Attaining Brahma means merging with the divine soul to feel "I am the Brahman". One step further, alias the leap forward is where there is neither 'I' nor 'Brahman', no 'You' and 'me', where there is Nothing. It is only a big zero – (total, absolute void), which is Nirvana, the seventh facet.

Stages from the fourth onwards are abstract, like a dream. The mind works day and night resulting in planning, imaging and dreaming. The imagination culminates into a concrete resolve and becomes one's will. When the ability to dream develops fully, it leads to extra-sensory vision. (Psychic vision)

To transform a dream into a vision, one need not keep one's eyes open since one can sense the things just by closing one's eyes where dreams seem to be the reality. One can see things beyond the wall, or one can read another person's thoughts. 'Vision' here means the ability to see things by contracting the distance between time and space and to notice or hear of things with the subtle inner cognizance. From that extra-sensory knowledge the Naadi authors must have been inspired to visualize detailed happenings of the future of generations, and note them down on palm-leaves demonstrating Divinity's mechanical, methodical and mathematical control of all happenings in the universe. That kind of service of theirs, to all humanity is invaluable. They undertook the task in the spirit of sheer inspired duty sans remuneration or reward.

How did all that happen? How many other sages were gifted with that prophetic insight? How many others volunteered to note down those predictions? How long did the task of etching palm-leaves take? What must have been the etching device? What could have been the duration of the task? Who encouraged them to read out the same to those for whom it was meant? What is the pattern of index used, so that the relevant noting about any person wanting to know his or her future could be quickly sorted out? A number of such questions arise.

While reading and discussing about the Naadi treatises so far, I have been able to sense the logic behind the compilation of these treatises. From whatever I have read or discussed, I dare deduce that there must have been Gurukuls (residential schools run by several sages and gurus) at various places under the supervision of Saint Agastya and other Naadi-recorders. While engaged in the meditative grasping of the Vedas for self-enlightenment and insight into the future of the Universe, the other subjects such as Ayurved (Medicine), Jyotirved (Forecasting), Dhanurved (Archery), Sthapatya (Architecture), Chitrakala (Painting), Nrutya (Dancing) and Sangita (Music) etc. must have been taught for relaxation from their concentration in divining the future of all human beings. Some disciples might have obtained expertise in those subjects. There might have been seminars at the royal courts, organised for these disciples to participate in the debates and discussions on those subjects. With a view to make use of these discussions for the benefit of humanity at large the Naadi- writing must have been undertaken under the guidance of the head of the Gurukul.

Besides, every morning the guru must have been guiding and leading his 200 to 300 disciples into collective mental sorties into humanity's future. Because of that, those disciples must have become adept at divining the past, present and future of all human beings.

Around every seer, there must have been about two to three other disciples, who might have noted down whatever was seen of the past and future about human beings. Since such a trance might have lasted for a few minutes, writing of only five or ten horoscopes might have been completed on any single day. While compiling all those rough notes and finalizing them, they might have been discussed, corrected and then noted down as final notes ready for recording on palm-leaves.

At the same time, the newly-joined disciples must have been engaged in collecting Palmirah (Tadpatra) leaves from the neighbouring farms or forests. Later on, classifying them, chemically processing them and readying them, like reams of paper, trimmed to a standard size and shape with a hole punched in their surface for tying them together in neat bundles must have followed.

Some hundreds of disciples – especially trained in the Tamil code script, must have etched the writings on palm-leaves with a sharp nail gripped firmly in their palms.

Some other disciples must have been engaged in sorting-out the palm-leaves into 108 sections, depending upon the variety of thumb-impressions, and packing them firmly into 50 to 60 palm-leaf bundles between two wooden strips, secured with a string. Those bundles of predictions must have been sent to big temples in the state for safe-keeping. That must have been organised through advance consultations with the kings of the region. It could also be possible that the ruler had been a past disciple at the Guru's hermitage. That noting-job must have taken hundreds of years, resulting in a compilation of millions of prediction-strips. **(While writing out this account, the author of this book had a strange feeling that a supernatural power was guiding him).**

Those palm-leaves alias Naadi Pattis are available even today, despite numerous social, political upheavals and natural disasters. Non-availability of palm-leaves, delay in drafting and finalizing the predictions correcting mistakes committed by the carvers in hurry, or those arising from some distractions etc. might have naturally hampered the recording task.

There must have been some plan, during different periods of history, for the safekeeping of these records in different places and regions to facilitate their perusal by the needy. Some of the disciples of the Gurukuls must have settled as citizens in different regions carrying those leaves with them. During the course of time some of that massive material must have got damaged in transit due to differences of opinion, power-struggle and such other calamities. A considerable portion of that predictive material must have been destroyed during the 1000-year-long Muslim invasions. Despite all such calamities, the Naadi patties are still available in our own day to foretell the future of all people.

Should it not then be our sacred duty to preserve that precious predictive record hereafter?

❑

History of Naadi Samhita (Compilation)

You might have read earlier how I visualize the compilation of the Naadi predictive strips by gifted sages and saints (Yogis-Maharishees) who possessed (Ateendreeya) extra–sensory powers to forecast the future of every human being. Now, let us examine what other well-known intellectuals and Naadi Shastris have to say on this subject.

I could get the opinion of the late Babubhai, Chhaya Jyotishshastri of Mumbai, who possessed the Surya (Samhita). According to him, the history of Naadi compilation was recorded in the Samhita itself. It is said that millions of years ago, the then Yogis who could visualize the Past, Present and Future, had gathered in the vicinity of the Himalayas. They foresaw the future of living-beings born on the Earth. They discussed among themselves and arrived at certain conclusions. Scribes from the South took notes of the dialogues held there. They knew the art of carving on palm-leaves. They etched the dialogues held at the seminar. The seminar must have continued for a number of years. At the end of the seminar, the huge material - the notebooks-must have been compiled. People of the South returned to their respective regions with that material. The decay and destruction of that, massive material might have begun in the third or fourth generations of those compilers due to natural and social upheavals, as also due to the breakdown of vehicles used in transporting those records. Knowing this, Maharishees such as Bhrugu, Kardam, Maitreya, Vashishtha, Brahma, Krishna, Prahlad and Bali communicated with each other on various occasions and redrafted those findings, which were later compiled once again by Rishi Surya. He endorsed nine compilations by different rishis. Later those scripts were divided each into three groups. However, over the millenniums, only the Surya and the Bhrugu compilations have survived to our own day.

The above account appears to be all jumbled and garbled. Several questions arise e.g. exactly when and where did the Yogis hold their Seminar? How have the rishis, who could accurately mention every individual's date, day, month, year, name and the place of birth, been so vague about the place and the period of compilation of Naadi literature, saying " Millions of years ago, somewhere in the Himalayas etc."! If the artisans of the south carried with them the etched forecasts to the South, (which are available even today in Telugu, Malyalam and Tamil languages), how come there is a confusing proliferation of what are known as Bhrugu and other versions in the North? And what are the classifications of those records? Questions like these remain unanswered.

Dr. R. Nagaraj Sharma has with him the " Saptarishi Naadi". He at times writes articles about it. But his writings are hard to understand being academic and conjectural, using astrological jargon. Beginners like me with only rudimentary knowledge get bored while reading those articles. For instance at one place, he mentions that the "Saptarishi Naadi" commenced with the dialogue between Parvati and Parashar". In Maha Shiva Vaakya or other mythological accounts, when Lord Shiva discusses the intricacies of life with his wife, Parvati and advises her on the omnipotence of knowledge, the rishis present are benefited by that divine discourse as though it were the Ganga stream of knowledge. However, in that Naadi (May be because Lord Shiva was more engrossed in practising the Tanadav Dance) it is sage Paraashar who enlightens Goddess Parvati about the future of mankind. At some places, Atri and 5 other rishis participate in the discussions and voice their individual opinions. We are already aware of the conflicting stands of sages Vishwamitra and Vasishtha. The same is reflected here too through their differences of opinion and arguments.

Sri. Sharmaji writes further, "from the style of the noting, it appears that Mother Parvati might have convened a meeting of all those rishis-yogis who had congregated to seek the darshan and blessings of Lord Shiva, the father of all. She herself must have chaired the gathering. Mankind is engrossed in its struggle for life resulting from their evil-doings during earlier births i.e. the individual's *Karma*, and the process of balancing of evil with good deeds. They might have thought of some possible remedies for man's sorrows so that man's burden of sorrows and worries could be somewhat mitigated through spiritual practices? They might have also thought it proper to prepare and encourage humanity for intellectual pursuits, with divine knowledge about their future and warn mankind of the dangers well in - time. That appears to be the main objective in compiling the Naadi forecasts.

The above surmise appears to be quite vague and mythical. But the purpose mentioned appears to be genuine. This same Dr. Nagraj Sharma has expressed a shocking personal opinion, in another article. He thinks that whosoever were those writers, Maharishees who compiled the Naadi texts, did not have anything to do with extra sensory perception alias divine vision. According to him, innumerable horoscopes were cast, based on the birth date and accurate information available from the then existing records from the positions of the Nakshtras (Stars). Their predictions must have been deduced from mathematical calculations of the planetary positions. But then how was it possible for them to mention the names of humans and the other details of their lives, merely from the positions of the stars and planets? Have we ever come across anyone from the roadside astrologer to the learned ones of the TV Programmers, who has stunned us with accurate predictions of names of people from the use of the same basic data, such as planetary positions at birth or from one's thumb-impression or by any other means?

In fact, the astounding accurate Naadi prediction and the names of present-day persons recorded in the Naadi Texts, were the main reasons I got drawn towards astrology. But for those records I would not at all have bothered to glance at the predictions appearing in newspapers and magazines!

In the Saptarishi Naadi available with Dr. Sharma, neither the names of individuals are mentioned nor are other details available. Those are typical predictions based on certain birth-Nakshtras and planetary positions. Dr. Sharma has deduced some predictions from the Saptarishi Naadi, which are very complicated. However, Dr. Sharma cannot satisfactorily answer the question as to how the Naadi leaves actually mention the names of individuals, besides predicting the important events of their lives.

Similar hazy predictions are available in Hindi and Marathi volumes of Bhrugu Samhita in the North. They all claim to be "Authentic." In those volumes, the first few pages cover a number of horoscopes of persons born in different years. Those horoscopes are numbered. One has to identify the one matching with one's own horoscope and read the prediction noted under the number recorded against it on the particular page of the book. Names of father, mother, husband, wife etc. are not mentioned in those books. Date of birth, month, and year are also not found in it. One can finish reading that standardized prediction in a trice. Thereupon one realizes that only some of the predictions match with one's own past or present situations.

Late Dr. Bangalore Vyankata Raman alias B.V. Raman, editor of the Astrological Magazine published from Bangalore, was once invited to deliver lectures on Hindu Astrology in London, during September-October 1970. In that series of his lectures, he spoke on 'Naadi Astrology'. Sri. Raman was an authority on astrology alias Fal-Jyotish. His emphasis was on individual predictions appearing in the Naadi records and on how to establish the relationship of various conjectures as per other methods in the science of astrology. He expressed the view that the Naadi Shastra is highly advanced and divine, as sages have written the same. He further said, " I am studying the Naadi Shastra for the last 20 years. I would be writing a book on the subject by the year 1972. (However, I have not yet come to know the name of the book) Naadi records are part of the great and unique literature of Hindu culture. Some Europeans believe that when the library at Alexandria was burnt, the keys to a number of scientific subjects were destroyed and humankind was deprived of that divine knowledge. Even if that is true, I feel proud to tell you that not only the keys but bunches of keys of a variety of such branches of knowledge are not only safe in India but are even successfully and silently serving mankind. Naadi records are one of them. After studying the Naadi records in depth, one realizes that the Naadi authors might have been benefited by the formulae and the yoga mentioned by Parashar Rishi. This vast literature could be conveniently saved because it is written briefly in the form of poetic stanzas. My grandfather, the late Suryanarayan Rao had read one Naadi about sixty years ago i.e. around the year 1910. The names of Naadi records I came across later are: Budha Naadi, Shukra Naadi, Saraswati Naadi, Satya Naadi, Chandra Naadi etc."

Sri. S. Kannan of Chennai wrote a very interesting series of ten articles in the Astrological Magazine. (I don't know where he is at present. I am looking for his address). He says at one place, "I discussed with Sri. Gopal Krishna Rao around 1952 about how the various Naadi's were formed and what could have been the method of their findings etc. Sri. Rao was the Meenakshi Naadi interpreter. According to him, there was a mention about this in the Budha Naadi. He was told by Budh Naadi shastri, Srinivasa Acharya, that some Naadi's come into the limelight only for a short period of time. Thereafter they become extinct. Whereas some of them in the hands of proper persons come alive with the glow of their predictions and become popular with people e.g. The Nandi Vakyam and Saptarshi Vakyam Naadi's do not predict the future of people now living. Not being of any use now they are stocked in the Chennai Government Oriental Manuscript Library, for inquisitive readers.

Sri. Kannan and Sri. B. V. Raman have conveniently avoided saying anything about the history and origin of the Naadi Texts. Some other names of Naadi's mentioned by Sri. Kannan and Sri. B. V. Raman are Sahadeo Naadi, Narad Naadi, Navgrah Samvad Naadi, Maharishi Siddhant, etc. In the Navgrah Naadi, the grahas (planets), themselves describe their benefic or malefic effects. That is how predictions therein are unfolded to the reader. In the Maharshi Siddhant, 18 Maharishees discuss the predictions. In one article, Sri. Kannan had mentioned that he started seeking Naadi-reading at the age of 15. He married during Rahu Bhukti. But according to Shukra Naadi, it happened during the Ketu Bhukti. He has eight children. However there was no mention of the last two children in the Shukra Naadi. In order to find out the secret behind these facts, he took interest in reading the Naadi. He also appears to have taken interest in becoming friendly with Naadi readers, helping them to get accommodation or a house, and also in getting them clients etc. If one looks at the names of Naadi-astrologers, one is likely to be astounded, because in Chennai (Madras) or south of it the number of Naadi centres may be more than the number of cycle-shops or hair cutting-saloons!

This author has also put in a lot of effort to trace Naadi texts and their custodians. Apart from Kannan and others mentioned earlier, I have seen Naadi treatises such as, Irrattai Naadi, Meenakshi Naadi, Vashishtha Naadi, Agastya Naadi, Kak Bhujandar Naadi, Ganesh Naadi, and Murugan Naadi etc. ❑

Naadi Texts Comprise How Many Leaves?

This chapter concludes about texts and leveles of Naadi's in the human beings. There are various misconceptions about the exact number of Naadi's. In different parts of country, several logics behind this.

Let us assume that currently the world population exceeds 6000 million. Earlier, innumerable human beings have lived and died during the course of thousands of years. If Naadi literature has covered all these people, then what must be the magnitude of that literature? So, a time may come when the relevance of those patties would come to an end and new patties would be needed. There are similar other doubts. A number of scholars have attempted to ascertain the number of pages of Naadi books. According to Dr. B.V.Raman, the Saraswati Naadi, comprised 1000 bundles with 50 Naadi Pattis in each bundle. That means there were predictions of fifty thousand horoscopes in that Naadi. In Satya Samhita there were 125 bundles, each consisting of 300 horoscopes. That means there were predictions of 37,500 horoscopes. In his book ' Naadi Granth – A study" written in Marathi by the late Sri. Shantaram Athavale in the late seventies it is stated that Nandi Naadi Shastri had once said that he had 1.2 Million palm-leaf manuscript horoscopes. In the same book, at one place it is claimed that Pandit Haveliram of Delhi had around 70 Million (7 crore) horoscopes, together weighing about 400 seers. (old Kgs.) In the forward to the book " Subodha Bhrugusamhita" published by Dhawale Publications in Marathi, the astrologer Prabhakar Narayan Dahiwalekar has cleared some doubts. He mentions that there are about 2,56,800 horoscopes per 100 years, and a number of centuries have already elapsed. This will give the reader a fairly good idea of the total number of Naadi horoscopes that may exist. I too have tried to calculate their number.

Two years ago, when the son of late Babubhai, Harshadbhai Chhaya Jyotishi of Mumbai was asked about this, he said his ancestors brought the patties from Kerala the southwest coastal province of India, in 20 bullock-carts. However, he left it to me to calculate the number of patties that could have been loaded in each bullock-cart. I leave it to the readers' imagination. The proprietor of the Sugar (Shukra) Naadi Centre in T-nagar of Chennai has thrown a different light on the topic. He has about 1000 to 1200 bundles of various Naadi's. Those account for in all, may be, 50 to 60 thousand patties. But probably he felt that number is too small. So he made an attempt to impress me through his translator saying that there are a number of other bundles in Tamil kept elsewhere.

In Chennai, there are some people who admit having 2 or 4 bundles in their possession. According to them they assumed that only those whose names are in these bundles would approach them for the predictions, so why keep other bundles, they think. But instead of telling the actual number of Naadi's they hold, they avoid the question saying, "We don't know"!

Perhaps they give vague answers out of the fear that whatever the number of Naadi's they mention that may not be large enough to impress the visitor. Nobody has showed willingness to say that he will count the bundles and tell me the actual number.

❏

My Experiences of Various Naadi Centres: Part I

Authors have visited various Naadi centres in the country and abroad. Telling his experiences about Naadi centres, such as Nilayam, Tambaran, the Irrettai Naadi Centre, Parashar Naadi, experience with Japanese, Chinese and other Naadi centres. Author also tells about Temples of Navagrah (Planets) which are located in the country.

Agasthya Naadi - Nilayam, Tambaram:

I paid a number of visits to that Naadi centre, it being near to my residence in a Chennai- suburb, first for myself, then for my wife, children, relatives and friends. I became familiar with the people at that Naadi Centre. The problem of language is a big hurdle. Everyone there seemed eager to speak to me, but they seemed helpless. I could not speak to them since I am not conversant with Tamil language, though I can read the Tamil alphabet.

At that centre, Sri. Shiva Shanmugam appears to be more talented. Another inmate, Sri. Rajendran, who has done his diploma in engineering, has taken to the Naadi profession because of family-tradition. He can convey his thoughts in English. Sri. Rajendran tape-records those readings. Another inmate Sri. Meenakshi Sundaram is adept in transcribing the old epigrammatic Tamil writings into modern Tamil. He transcribes the predictions in 40 page notebooks speedily. A Police Inspector has gifted him a pen-set, which he recalls gratefully. One day I sensed that he wanted to talk to me. When I said "Hello, Sri. Sundaram," he talked to me in Tamil for about 20 minutes! What he said was not as important, as the fact that he derived great satisfaction in addressing me.

Yet another Naadi reader is Sri. Nathan. "Swami", he said once addressing me "English kuncham-kuncham" (little-little). He tried to talk to me through Rajendran as the interpreter. Being encouraged, I said, "Look, I hardly know any Tamil. Yet I keep trying, so you too try to express yourself in English! Keep speaking, I shall try to grasp what you wish to convey." Thereafter, he started chatting with me! He had a strong desire to convey to me my future, because he was the first who, having searched through 3 to 4 bundles, had told me to return a month later. Once I took a Telugu person to have his future read. I requested that Sri. Nathan only to read it. Accordingly Nathan read out the Naadi. Thereafter Nathan thanked me. Though in fact it was Nathan who had obliged me!

Please wait !

People at most Naadi centres use the expression, 'Please wait' off and on. As per the joke narrated by the famous Hindi film-music-director late Kalyanji (Anandji), "Everywhere they say wait for 5 minutes", though actually the wait extends even to an hour!

"To wait" is a basic way of life here. All those who come for astrology, either keep looking at one another or glance over the Tamil newspapers there or sometimes chat in high-pitched voices. I used to get bored sitting like a dumb creature. So at times I used to pick up a conversation with fellow visitors. From them I came to know about a number of episodes. There was a gentleman, who appeared to be quite worried. I came to know from him that he had his Naadi reading ten years ago at Kanchipuram Naadi Centre. He was advised to "perform the Shanti Deeksha (ritual for obtaining peace) as there were bad times ahead." He did not pay any heed to it at that time and had totally, conveniently forgotten it, A number of unfortunate developments followed. He lost his job. A friend of his desiring to know about his own daughter's future called at the Naadi Centre. The friend's daughter had fallen in love with some boy. The father wanted to know whether the boy would cheat his daughter. It came out in the Naadi reading that, he was the groom who would marry his daughter. Accordingly that marriage did take place. That incident had made a deep impression on his mind and so he called again at that Naadi Centre to ascertain his future. In his Naadi reading at the centre he was directly confronted with the question "When you were told to perform the peace ritual, why did you not do it?" He was advised to perform it even now and was assured that he would be benefited. Accordingly he undertook the recommended ritual and now, after two months, he had called at the centre to inform the Naadi readers that his life had indeed been better.

Once a person told me that when he had called at the Naadi Centre accompanied by his pleader friend, the Naadi reading began. His name and other details were correctly mentioned. But then in the next line Agastya refused to say anything further, unless his pleader-friend was sent out of the Naadi centre. Poor fellow, had to go out! Later the Naadi-reader explained that, that man had insulted the Agasthya Naadi in his last birth!

Once, I met some Maharashtrian visitors from Satara, who were visiting Tambaram for a Naadi-reading. One of them narrated an incident that while his Naadi reading was in progress, a youth had come to ascertain his future. His proper Naadi-Patti was located. The Naadi-reader started reading but stopped midway advising the client to call some elderly persons from his family. Even after contacting his parents on the phone, none of them could come. After two days, the young man died all of a sudden. That explained why the Naadi-reader wanted the visitor's elders to be there. Similarly, when another gentleman-caller was having his Naadi-reading, it was mentioned therein, that his father was not alive. Other details tallied but he asserted that his father was very much alive, two days back when he had started from his hometown his father was alive. To his greatest shock, when he reached his hotel, he got a telegram informing him about the demise of his father. That proves the accuracy of the Naadi readings.

At the Tambaram Centre, once when the Naadi-reader left for a while to fetch a new bundle of Pattis, the Hindi translator Sri. Arulraj narrated to me some interesting episodes. He told me of an incident when there was a great commotion at that Naadi centre. It so happened that a woman had come to ascertain as to when and with whom would her daughter get married. The Patti of the daughter was located. When the Naadi-reader read out that the girl had been already married, the woman visitor got furious and started abusing the Naadi-reader. He requested the woman to ascertain the truth from her daughter. The daughter confirmed that the Naadi statement was true! When the daughter stated that she had in fact married somebody a month ago, her mother was furious with her daughter! There was quite a commotion. Peace returned to the Naadi-centre only when the quarrelling ladies left the Naadi centre.

In July 1996, I travelled to Tambaram for a few days' stay to take my family to my new place of posting in Kashmir. During that visit Arulraj of the Naadi centre said to me, "Oak sami, it is good that you have come personally. I want to tell you about a recent happening. Someone from Nagpur had come to find out the whereabouts of his friend. While his friend was sailing in a merchant-navy ship, the ship had capsized and the company had declared that all its occupants had been drowned and dead. They had even paid compensation to the bereaved families. However, the caller had come to ascertain what was recorded in the Naadi about his friend. The Naadi-reading stated that the ship in which his friend was sailing met with a mishap and also that the friend's family had been duly informed. He was also asked to call his relative within the next 15 days and perform some puja in a particular temple etc. After his brother performed the puja, it was revealed in the Naadi that his brother was stranded on some island but had lost his memory. However, he would manage to return home when his memory revived!"

Once I met an expert numerologist named "Kiro", by chance. He reads horoscopes and foretells the future based on his reading of the date of birth and names of relations. His mother had suffered chest-pain for about 2 months. He arranged for her medical investigation and treatment. But when he had his Naadi reading at Tambaram, and performed the advised ritual in his Shanti Deeksha Kandam i.e. Peace Chapter, the pain suddenly vanished! But a new problem arose! His mother was an insurance agent, and because of her chest pain, having been unable to transact any business for 2 months, she was nervous. She was not able to recover her lost self-confidence and wondered why was it so despite the performance of the recommended rituals, as per the Shanti Kandam? The son had come to inquire about the same. He was advised to seek the answer in the Prashna Kandam i.e. Question Chapter!

The Irrettai Naadi Centre Of Dr. Om Ulganathan:

He has an air-conditioned establishment; naturally the consultation fees there are Rs. 1500/-! which is staggering. I met a Malyali visitor, Sri. Ravindran there, who is fluent in both English and Sanskrit. Also he is an authority on black magic. He said that, in his young age, like other Keralite youths, he also dismissed all talk of gods and goddesses as pure humbug as per his Communist mode of thinking. He also insisted that religion and religious undertakings were nothing but a blind prop of weak-minded people. After his father's death, his mother advised him that, it was not a question about his belief or disbelief, the traditional calling had to be continued since he was trained in it and that it was as holy as the river Ganga. Ravindran studied the Tantrik ritual only to honour his mother's bidding. He added, "There are among these tantriks, people who cheat others and systematically make money. As far as I am concerned, I don't mislead people I charge reasonably". On my asking him he said he charged fees ranging from "nil" to Rs. One lakh! While mentioning this he had told me to select any two figures between 1 and 9. Then he asked me to count the letters in my name. Then he asked me to do this and that and finally opened one of his fists and showed me a number and asked me whether that was the number I had in mind? Then he showed me his other palm and asked me whether that other number was also in my mind? The two figures, which I had mentally selected, were 9 and 7, which he had accurately divined!

"What are you doing here in this centre?" In response to that question of mine he said, "I am invited by the centre to perform some black-magic rituals suggested in the Naadi."

I was very curious to know how did he guess the figures that I had conjured in my mind? When and how did he manage to note them on both of his palms? Agreed that he might have written them before he kept me engaged in conversation. Yet how were those the exact figures, which I had conjured in my mind? He evaded the answer saying, "I will tell you in our next meeting." But we never met later!

EXPERIENCE OF THE JAPANESE

In one of my visits to the Tambaram Naadi centre I happened to meet some Japanese visitors. An Indian interpreter, Miss Sujatha accompanied them. Through her I could converse with them. What was their experience? Did they find their exact names mentioned therein? How did they come to know about this astrological miracle? Were some of my questions to which I sought their answers!

Regarding the names, Miss Sujatha said, "Their names were exactly pronounced barring the Tamil accent. One of them was called Ke Su Ke Matsushita. The others were UA Matsu, and Jo Buo. The elderly lady's name was stated in the Naadi as To Me Ewajawa! Though the name of their country was not specifically mentioned, "Foreigner" was the adjective used. Their religion was not mentioned. On that the Japanese stated that they did not believe in any religion. May be that was the reason. Readers may be shocked to know that religions such as,

Christianity and Islam are referred to as "Jesus" and "Nabi Nayakam" respectively. The names of Lord Buddha and Lord Mahavir are stated to indicate Buddhism and Jainism respectively. When I asked the Japanese visitors as to what particular aspect of Naadi astrology did they regard as astonishing? After their mutual deliberation, through Miss Sujatha I was told that the, "Old lady, To Me's parents were divorced, whereas Jo Buo's wife was suffering from Asthma! Those revelations were truly stunning since only they knew those!

THE EXPERIENCE OF A CHINESE LADY

There is one Chinese beautician settled in Pune. She narrated her experience with great enthusiasm. She accompanied her friend to the Tambaram Naadi Centre. She was curious to see how ancient books of prophecy described a person residing in a remote region? That was one of the reasons of her visit to that centre. In her Naadi-leaf her name was stated as Mei Yung. The names of her parents were also recorded as, Che Ted her father and Chun Moi her mother! Her profession was described as expertise in hairstyling and makeup!

Sri. Natarajan Sharma of the Parashar Naadi

I accidentally came to know of that Naadi centre. My informer forewarned me that though the Naadi was authentic its reader was eccentric!

It was difficult to locate his house in the Icehouse area in Chennai. As usual the house was old. A small room therein contained old books and registers scattered all over, in bits and pieces. It would not be an exaggeration to say that the room was full of cobwebs, which indicated lack of cleaning, and dusting for long. A typical Tamilian old man, over 70 with a grown white beard, chewing paan was there. The hair on his half-bald head appeared uncombed and tangled. The upper part of his body was bare as per Tamilian tradition.

I had my uniform on. While removing my shoes outside the entrance I was watching what was going on inside the room. I guessed that the manner of the talk inside was rather audacious.

I decided to use a trick so that I could befriend the person, or else I would not get anything out of him. When I was called in, I straightaway prostrated before him. I got his blessing "Shubham Bhavatu!" Then I squatted before him. I introduced myself. Sri. Sharma then inquired, "What is your Gotra?" "Vasishtha," I replied. He said, " Good, you belong to the same Gotra as me, but I have no time. Come after four days!" But when I informed him that I was a Maharashtrian, Konkanstha etc., he asked me to show him my horoscope. He further asked me to look for the ephemeris of the year 1949. I got up and searched for it in the shelf in-front and handed it to him. "I don't believe in cleanliness, I am a Mangalik as per my horoscope", he remarked, exhibiting his betel-leaf-stained red-teeth. He declared, "your horoscope is wrong". In between, he suddenly asked me "Do you know where is Pardi?" Maybe, he thought I would say I don't know, and that he would remark sarcastically something like "what sort of a Maharashtrian Brahmin are you?" I felt he was about to say that but when I replied, " Yes, it is the place, where Pandit Satavleker wrote and published books on the Vedas and Upanishads. Earlier he had a scowl on his face. But now he seemed pleased that he and I had a common Gotra. He then added that Pandit Satavlekar was so great a man that every house should have his photograph displayed on the altar along with other deities.

Later, for a couple of months whenever I phoned him, I was told that he was sick and I should ring him up at some other time. When finally I said "I cannot wait any longer, and I am coming right away today itself", he banged his receiver saying, " You are a peculiar fellow!" Later when I met him in person he remarked that I was really adamant. That day he looked for my palm-leaf reading. When I asked him some questions about my future he remarked, " From top to bottom, you are full of questions!" Natarajan Sharma has the Parashar Naadi. It is in Sanskrit. When I wished to handle it, to ascertain its script, he silenced me saying "What for?" When I asked him if he could give me a transcript of it as well as a taped-reading, he exclaimed pointedly, "I am not like those rogues. At the most I will give you a pen, but you have to bring your own paper to make your notings." When I inquired why there was no mention of my name, birthplace etc? He said his Naadi was 'genuine', while those with others were 'bogus!' He then told me to leave if I did not desire a reading of my Naadi forecast! On inquiring about his fees, he tried to avoid a reply, but when I thrust a hundred-rupee note in his hands, he coolly accepted it.

A look at him, or his movements, reminded me of the character of 'Antu Barve' as delineated by the Marathi humorist the late P. L. Deshpande.

Sri. Mohan Sundaram:

He is a reader of Agattiyar Naadi. He stays at New Bungalow Street, Chennai. One is led to think from the name of the street that the locality would have a row of tiny, decent bungalows. But actually it is only a small, tunnel like lane, very difficult to locate, having a very old-styled tenement. In one of the small rooms of that house Mohan Sundaram reads out the Naadi's all alone. His small advertisement appears in the English daily, Hindu every Sunday. When I reached his house, there was some visitor inside. So I waited at the entrance. Outside, two persons were standing with motorcycles. They gestured to me to knock at the entrance door. But out of decency I just stood silently. Those two persons then approached me. One of them knew English. He told me that the reader inside couldn't speak English. No names figure in the Naadi texts there unlike the Agastya Naadi, and the fees are Rs. 100/-. By this time the door was opened and I was asked to return the next day, As usual. I insisted saying, "I have come from a great distance, so please examine my horoscope now itself". Then the person who knew English advised his colleague to look for my horoscope. Sundaram started shuffling 5 to 7 leaves, as if to put them in their proper sequence, and started to read their contents. I was ready with pen and paper. The Naadi reading lasted a mere 5 to 7 minutes and I was asked to pay Rs. 100/-. My name was not in the Naadi, but the details mentioned were obviously about my career. As I put my hand in my pocket I realised that I had hardly Rs. 60 to 70/-. Sundaram literally snatched that amount from my hands, put the money in his drawer and closed it! When I said I had no money to go back, he thrust back a tenner in my hands, and told me to remit the balance by postal money order. I was shocked to note the Shastri's greed and his scanty foretelling. I thought to myself that if, as per his prediction, I ever get 1 lakh gold coins, I would certainly send him Rs. 40/-

Please wait for 11 Hours !

Once again I experienced the familiar "Please Wait" situation, when I called at the Sugar Naadi Centre at Tyagraj nagar in Chennai It has nothing to do with the sugar we eat. That is the South-Indian pronunciation of Shukra Naadi. That in turn, is a modern name of the earlier Sanskrit name Shuk Naadi. At this new Naadi centre, which I had approached for the first time I thought I should work out some stratagem to avoid being turned away, saying, "Come some other time".

"Coming from Mumbai-Air Force-No time" I told him in telegraphic language and entered the tenement at 8-30 a.m. But it was 2.30 p.m. by the time my thumb impression was taken, and the General Kandam was chosen for reading. While I was waiting for my Naadi-reading someone suggested to consult the "Knowledge Kandam." The Naadi-reader went inside to search for the same and did not come out until 5.00 p.m.! Thereafter suddenly two Tamil ladies started shouting. One who was in modern attire, took the Naadi reader left and right, saying, " I have been sitting here for more than 3 hours. If you were to keep me hanging on, saying-"Please wait", why did you fix up the appointment for 2.00 p.m.? Those two ladies had come during their free-time during their working hours at the American bank. The poor Naadi-readers were totally confused. I felt impelled now to give vent to my own pent-up feelings too. I said to them. "You arrived here at 2.00 p.m., but I have been sitting in this room from 8.30 a.m. No one offered me tea or even water all this time. I had to forego even my meals. The people here don't cater to new clients until they have finished with the earlier ones. So I advised others waiting like me, for long "if you have no time to wait, please go away." But they continued to wait. Their Naadi-records were also traced. Later my Naadi-noting too was read out to them.

While returning by a local train that day, I cast a glance at my watch. It was about 9.00 p.m. I was thus at the Naadi centre for more than ten and a half-hours! After I commiserated with those ladies, the Naadi-reader ordered coffee and biscuits for me. But I was lost in my own thoughts, being thrilled by the unbelievably bright future predicted for me in the Knowledge Kandam. I wondered about my predicted future and whether I was supposed to strive for it?

Ramani Guruji and Kak Bhujandar (Bhushundi) Naadi

While searching for other Naadi books and places where Naadi reading is available, I came across one more Naadi centre in Tambaram. It was about 2 kms from my residence but in the opposite direction of the Agastya Naadi Centre. Those two centres are very near the Air Force Station, yet residents of the Air Force camps had hardly any inkling of Naadi astrology. I thought, may be the convention was that Naadi prediction and its discussion was permissible only among family members but not among Air Force personnel themselves. However, I started narrating my astounding experience about Naadi texts to everybody I met. Thereupon my friends started taunting and teasing me at our parties etc., Saying, 'Sir, which Naadi Kandams have you consulted this time?" On my informing a colleague about my experience in my office, (Squadron Leader Govindrajan) who left on his new posting after performing a Shanti Deeksha. About his experience, he said he wanted to give up his job. He had lost interest in life since he had no child. Naadi prediction had advised him otherwise. He was resigned to lead a childless life. But the Naadi predicted that he would have a child later. And indeed some years later, I received a letter from Sqn Ldr Govindrajan saying that he had indeed been blessed with a daughter in August 99! Thereafter he gave up the idea of resigning his job!

I kept suggesting to my colleagues to visit Naadi Centres nearest to their place of posting. In those days of my posting in Chennai, I had enrolled as a member of the Theosophical Society library. There I came to know of the ashram of Ramani Guruji. So I visited that Ashram one Friday evening. It was raining. The roads were muddy and my clothes were drenched. I was in half pants, my sports attire. That centre had a medium-size hall. Its walls displayed framed photos. Images of various Gods and Goddesses were also exhibited in that hall. Prominent among them was that of a sage, in the style of Lord Shiva Parvati. All those holy figures had Mogra-flower-garlands hung around their picture-frames. Lighted incense-sticks placed in front spread their sweet aroma. In the centre sat Ramani Guruji singing verses from the palm-manuscript leaves in his hands. His voice magnified by the mike had a pleasing sonorous enchanting tone. The singing was in the southern style. Guruji was totally engrossed in his chant. After a 25 minute rendition of that prayer, while the Naadi leaves were bundled up and kept away, someone delivered a short speech in Tamil and then 'arati' was performed. The devotees who had come about 60 to 70 of them were offered a 'prasad' of rice and curds. One or two south Indian snacks were also served to all, on banana leaves. Within 15 minutes people ate the prasad. The banana leaves were folded and consigned to waste-bins and the visitors squatted on the carpet there. Then the visitors called on the Guruji, one by one. Everyone bowed low to him, to pay deep respects and narrated own problems. Thereafter Guruji would cast his dice to devise a solution to the stated problem. Then he would fix his gaze in the mirror in front of him for a few moments, lapsing into a meditational stance and then spell out the remedy to the problem posed by the worrying devotees. When I was called in, I bowed down to him and mentioned that I was a non-Tamilian and a first-time visitor, seeking his blessing. So saying I bowed down to him, informing him that I had no problem as such. Thereupon the Guruji gave me a booklet in Hindi and a kumkam (holy vermilion powder) and advised me to call on him later at my convenience if I sought any information about Kak Bhushundi predictions. When I rose to take his leave, Guruji told me to feel free to call on him again. Before returning, I asked some inmate there about the Naadi which Ramani Guruji possessed. He told me that Guruji had the Kak Bhujandar Naadi and that the pictures exhibited in the hall are of "Kak Bhujandar and his disciple, Bahula". Every morning and evening between 7 and 7-30 Guruji casts the dice set of 9 cowries and sings songs noted on the leaf, indicated by the dice and then meets the visitors who call on him. He then suggests the remedies for their woes. Like others he doesn't give readings from Naadi-leaves. A special characteristic of this Naadi is that it is believed to be living (*Jeeva Naadi*)! Namely, it is the ancient sages who speak through the mouth of the reader of that Naadi. Among the visitors are doctors, surgeons handling complicated cases, who come to seek his advice. Advocates and engineers also at times come and seek subtle and special directions concerning their professional problems. Though Ramani Guruji has not studied any of those subjects, his advice satisfies all. Guruji doesn't charge any fees. All advice is free of any charge! There is another *Jeeva Naadi* called Shuka Markandeya Naadi wherein the reading is done from plain blank white paper!

Once while I was returning home a large painting of Yogi Ramsurat Kumar caught my attention! This Ashram is 6 kms from Tambaram railway station, located at an odd place opposite Bharat Engineering College in the remote Selayur area and yet surprisingly there is a crowd of cars and two wheelers etc. parked outside!

Once when, I felt drawn to the Ramani Guruji Ashram. I was worried about the health of my brother-in-law. My uncle, the famous historian, Sri. P. N. Oak suggested that I seek some remedy from Naadi readings, I also needed guidance on some mundane problems faced by one Joshi family. The Naadi centre at Tambaram is so crowded always that one can't even step in. Even those whose thumb-impressions, were obtained 2 to 3 months ago, haven't had their future read. Therefore I suddenly remembered Ramani Guruji's free-of-charge Naadi reading. One evening I called on Ramani Guruji with my wife. After the usual rhyme -singing by Guruji when it was our turn to speak to him, I reminded him of my earlier visit to him. To ensure that we don't forget the question to be asked, my wife had written the questions concerning her brother's health and about Sri. Joshi's problem on a piece of paper, and she handed over that chit to Guruji.

As usual, Ramani Guruji cast the dice of 9 cowries and stared vacantly at the mirror and started writing on the paper- pad there. I later sent those two answer-chits to the concerned parties. On that occasion I met an old colleague from the Air Force and his wife. He informed me that he had been posted there a year ago. Their daughter was in the 8th standard in the Central School. One day she failed to return home from school. A frantic search was undertaken. The Police were informed. He had arrived there on somebody's advice. Guruji predicted that the girl was safe and suggested that he look for her in the northern part of his native state. Accordingly when he searched for his missing daughter she was found in Haryana State! She explained that she had gone there because she did not like the atmosphere and friends at her school. Disgusted, she left for Delhi by train and thereafter proceeded to a place of his previous posting in Haryana all by herself!

From the Kak Bhujandar Naadi with Ramani Guruji I got guidance in many matters. That includes the scope of Naadi Pattis, the speed of Maharishee's flight into space with their Divine vision and, their ability to grasp in a trice everything about the lives of thousands of people. Common people's minds have been prejudiced regarding astrology because of the uninformed and biased opinions expressed about Naadi astrology by well known scientists, learned scholar and institutions who cultivate negative views about Naadi astrology. The Naadi's predict that I shall be instrumental in informing those who are anxious to know about Naadi astrology. A number of other things are also mentioned. It is also predicted that at the appropriate time my services will be used for the welfare of mankind.

Ramani Guruji celebrates Kak Bhujander's birthday around first-second week of April with pomp and gaiety, followed by AnnaDaan. A lot of people attend it in his ashram near East Tambaram. In that celebration, the marriage of Nandikeswara has special significance. When Guruji undertakes the *parikama* holding pitcher on his head and slowly dances as a marriage party, the atmosphere fills with elation and spiritual ecstasy.

Shankar ji, Guruji's younger son has the blessings of Maharishi Agasthya. He speaks through him. The beauty of his revealing – they are free, and are generally told after midnight!

TAMIL NAMES OF HINDI NAKSHATRAS

NAKSHATRAS					
Sl. No.	Hindi Name	Tamil Name	Sl. No.	Hindi Name	Tamil Name
1.	Ashwini	Aswini	15.	Swati	Swati
2.	Bharani	Bharani	16.	Vishakha	Vishaham
3.	Krutika	Karthihi	17.	Anuradha	Anusham
4.	Rohini	Rohini	18.	Jyeshtha	Kettai
5.	Mruga	Nirugashi/	19.	Moola	Mulam
6.	Aardra	Tiruk Tirai	20.	Purvashadha	Puradam
7.	Punarvasu	Punar pusam	21.	Uttarashadha	Uttaradam
			22.	Shravan	Tiruonam
8.	Pushya	Pusam	23.	Dhanishtha	Avittam
9.	Aashlesha	Aailyam	24.	Shatataraka	Sadayam
10.	Magha	Maham	25.	Purva Bhadrapada	Purattadi
11.	Purva	Puram			
12.	Uttara	Uttiram	26.	Uttara Bhadrapada	Uttarattadi
13.	Hasta	Hastam			
14.	Chitra	Citterai	27.	Revati	Revati

TEMPLES OF NAVAGRAHA (PLANETS)

In the Naadi Predictions, visits to Navagraha Temple are suggested in Shanti Parihar Kandam. If observed with extreme care and very high sense of devotion, Naadi Maharishees promise to overcome difficult situations. Those who believe in it, may plan their travel with the help of following information and the map of Tamilnadu.

Sl. No.	Planet Temple	Place of Town	Special Information
1	Surya/Sun	Suryanar Koil	Near Kumbha Konam 1 Km. from Aaduthurai.
2	Chandra/ Moon	Tingaloor	Near Tiruvaiyyar city.
3	Mangal/Mars	Vaidheeshwaran Koil	On the bus route from Mailaduturai to Sirakandi.
4	Budha/ Mercury	Tiruvenkadu	16 kms. from Sirakandi to Pum Puhar.
5	Guru/Jupiter	Aalangudi	15 kms. from Kumbhakonam to Needmangalam.
6	Shukra/Venus	Kanjanoor	Near Aaduturai.
7	Shani/Saturn	Tirunallar	On the way to Perumal near Karaikal.
8	Rahu	Tirunageshwaram	7 kms. from Koil Kumbhakonam.
9	Ketu	1. Perumal 2. Kalhasti	Near Tiruvenkadu. Near Tirupati.

❏

My Experience of Naadi Centres : Part II

In spite of the predictions there are several persons who condemned as a sheer hoax. After several invitations to them from time to time, they refused to visit any Naadi centre to convince themselves and other so many short comings of Naadi custodians. Author describes here.

My Book titled 'Naadi Astrology' in Marathi was published in September 1994. The response of the readers was very encouraging. A number of readers liked the book so much that they bought extra copies at various bus-stands and railway stations bookstalls and distributed them among their friends. Sri. Hirabhai Butala of Khed (Ratnagiri) made over 200 Xerox copies and distributed them amongst his friends! As a result a number of readers visited the Naadi centres. Many of them had in their hands my book. Some carried soiled copies indicating that many had handled the book. My enthusiasm increased with the response of the readers. Thereafter I wrote to Dr. Jayant Naralikar, renowned Astrophysicist and to the State organizer of the Blind Faith Eradication Committee for Maharashtra Dr. Narendra Dabholkar. They have been condemning Naadi predictions as a sheer hoax. But despite my repeated requests to them, to actually visit some Naadi centres to convince themselves, they have remained adamant and defiant. They seem to be more interested in mocking and scoffing at my fascination and admiration for Naadi predictions, while they themselves continue to firmly disbelieve both in any predetermined Destiny and infallibility of Naadi predictions.

In spite of my several invitations to them from time to time, they refused to visit any Naadi Centre to convince themselves. The pet reply of theirs published in their articles was, "there is no need to visit Naadi centres," which showed that they were avoiding the issue. Their intention was obviously to continue deriding my appreciation of Naadi Astrology as an unwarranted humbug. More details regarding that matter are provided in Chapter No. 23 & 24.

SHORT COMINGS OF NAADI- CUSTODIANS

Some readers of my book or articles are likely to conclude that my appreciation of Naadi literature is unwarranted. Though the Naadi literature is no doubt a very rich, rare treasure. Sri. Oak ought also to expose Naadi-readers as exploiters of Naadi-predictions as money-spinners. I have certainly criticized that attitude of theirs in this book.

Agastya Naadi Centre, Tambaram:

A number of people, especially from Marathi speaking areas such as Jalgaon, Pune, Sangli, Kolhapur and Satara, and from Hindi- speaking areas like Delhi and Allahabad have complained to me personally, or through correspondence, that even if payments are made in advance, there is considerable delay in the response and supply of prediction tapes, leading to clients getting fed-up of following up the matter. I have myself experienced the same. I discussed the matter with Naadi Centre staff, and others, but their reaction was, "Swami, you are right but what can we do? We cannot cope with the task of reading out the general and Shanti-Deeksha Kandams to people crowding here day in and day out. We have to cater to all sorts of clients every day. We have no alternative but to satisfy every new visitor who looks upon the Naadi-reading with suspicion or as something unimaginable great and marvellous. Therefore the fees have been doubled for people other than Tamilians, and Rs. 1000/- are charged from foreigners. You have yourself observed how the workload keeps us busy. You have observed how we keep working continuously from early morning till even midnight or past midnight. So the delay is certainly not deliberate. We have no alternative but to inform people by telephone to wait for 10-15 days. Can you suggest any remedy?"

I advised them to appoint a reader and a clerk to complete their pending orders, open a register to note down the demand of every client and follow it up till their requirements are met and they get a receipt from their clientele on their receiving the notebook and tape. If your current chaotic style of work is to continue as it is, then you better stop charging advance fees from your clients. Also inform your clients plainly that there being too much of a rush of clients we cannot cater to more clients till a certain date. So if clients still insist you may warn them that their readings are likely to get delayed.

Thereupon Manohar (Manu) and Subburatnam, the main Naadi readers at the Tambaram Naadi Centre agreed to maintain a register and appoint more staff for pending-work, with immediate effect. Future clients may feel the difference if any.

However, many more facilities are called-for such as, drinking water, clean toilets, serving snacks to the hungry, tea-coffee, provision of newspapers and Magazines to while away the waiting time etc. All such vital amenities are totally absent. However when it was pointed out that the rooms are dark, covered with spider webs, smoky, lacking sitting arrangements, no wash basin to clean the inked thumb etc. some recent visitors have reported that some improvement has taken place. Taking a cue from my experience, as narrated above, people visit to the Agastya Naadi centre at Tambaram. However, intending visitors may also approach other Naadi-centres, for their Naadi reading, if they so choose.

AGATYAR NAADI OF GINDI

Two residents of Ahmednagar called at Sri. Om Namah Shivay's Agatyar Naadi Centre located in the Gindi area of Chennai. When the Naadi-reader informed them that the fee was Rs. 504/- the clients complaining that the demand was exorbitant, showed him my book which mentions the fee to be Rs. 100/-. Complaining of the fees demanded, the two brothers returned without availing of the Naadi reading. They wrote to me in detail about their infructuous and disappointing trip. I used to revisit Naadi Centres to which I had been earlier, to present them a copy each of my book on Naadi Astrology. On one such visit to the 'Om Namah Shivay's Naadi Centre', I was instructed while outside the gate itself that I should enter only if I had an appointment. Despite that, when I entered, I was kept waiting for some time. The in-charge of the centre was alone. The house appeared to be well-maintained and adequately furnished. A car and other vehicles in the garage were signs of affluence. In one dark-room the Naadi reader was seated with a table infront of him. He appeared to be 30-40 years of age, speaking fluent English. But his tone sounded arrogant. I gave him my book as a present. He kept it aside without even looking at it and remarked that I should have written the book in English. "Who will read it in Marathi?" He exclaimed. That made me wonder about the propriety of my travelling that far.

I reminded him that I had contacted him on phone in response to his advertisement in the daily Hindu, expressing a desire to discuss about Naadi astrology with him and to know more about his Pattis; But since he told me that he had no time to spare for interviews, I could not meet him. Even then, I had included his name and address in the book. "This is that same book." The Naadi reader retorted that I should not have published his name and address. "I do not need such advertisement. Now you may go, people are waiting for me" he curtly said and wanted me to clear out. When I inquired whether the Naadi's with him mention individual-names of the seekers and others, he repeated " Please get out. I have no time." So saying he stood up and threatened me. I continued sitting and said with raised voice, "Gentleman, behave yourself. Sit down. I am not going out. I must get the information. There is nobody outside waiting for you. So don't try to pretend that you have no time." That retort of mine softened him. Then I told him that I wanted to know some details about the Naadi book with him, such as - its script and language, the exact method of locating the specific strip of palm-leaf; whether any names appear therein? If so how do they happen to be mentioned there? What is the secret behind that? How did the Naadi books come to him? Whether he had received any complaints that the forecasts were wrong etc. Thereupon he opened his mouth. He said " Agtyar (i.e. Agastya) Naadi came to him through heredity. How ancient it was he did not know. The predictions have to be searched for by tallying horoscope, with details mentioned in Naadi-readings. The client has to mail him the horoscope. Based on that he looks for the appropriate Patti and if he locates it, the client is invited to a personal visit. He added, "my fees are Rs. 504/-. The fees have to be paid in advance. There is no facility of tape or notebook." I reminded him that when I talked to him on the phone, he had informed me his fees to be Rs. 100/-. He wriggled out of it saying that he did not remember it. I showed him the relevant reference in my book and warned him that he must not disown his earlier statement. By that time, he noticed the names and addresses printed in English in my book, and exclaimed, " Oh! You are the author of this book! Two visitors from Maharashtra had come with this book, and when I told them my fee was Rs. 504/- they went away!" He inquired whether I wanted my future to be read? Thereupon I told him that since I considered my book to be a compilation work, if he agreed to tell me my future free-of-cost, I would hand over to him my horoscope, since I was really not interested in knowing my future. He then changed the topic. He also avoided informing me whether individual names appear in his Naadi? Here I again raised my voice and said, " you are sitting in front of Goddess Durga, with Bhasma on your forehead. So tell me the truth. If you are telling me a lie, then as mentioned in other Naadi books, the Naadi sage will be displeased with you and you will be punished". Thereupon he softened and said, " There is no name in my Naadi. But at times there are some indirect references to individual names. However, I am honest. If I don't find someone's future in the Naadi, I return the amount received as advance. After I talked to you on the phone, I have increased my fees with effect from 1 January 95. He firmly but politely refused to allow me to handle the Naadi Pattis. While conversing with me he feigned ignorance of any other Naadi Pattis and the procedure thereof. When he offered me coffee, I exclaimed that he should have shown me that courtesy at the very beginning. Then I opened my mind. In the ensuing conversation when he heard that people like Ramani Guruji of Kak Bhujandar Naadi have been reading Naadi free of charge and helping people with remedies for years together, he could not resist saying, "Such people reduce the value of forecasts by extending free of cost service, and as a result we lose our business!" He added, "I am rendering useful service through Naadi reading, to those who need it". I suppose, the original author of the Naadi forecasts may have no objection to the custodians earning some money out of them to lead a comfortable life. But, if clients are exploited by demanding money for Shanti- Deeksha, not mentioned in the Naadi, and charging fees as gift (Dandakshina) etc. that is condemnable. Finally, I warned him that I would have to consider whether I should or should not include his name and address in the second edition of my book.

The Irrattai Naadi in Chennai

The Naadi reader, Dr. Om Ulagnathan maintains an air-conditioned office, displaying lots of photographs and visiting-cards indicating his acquaintance with actors and actresses and political leaders. I have narrated in detail my surprising experience, about his Naadi stock in a separate chapter. Ram-nama alias Sri. Ramkrishnan mentioned in that chapter owned a factory near my office. Therefore I have a good acquaintance with him. He praised Om Ulagnathan but with some bitterness, and added, "There is no doubt about the astonishing Naadi he has with him. But this Naadi reader adds his own spice to the Naadi account and he also does not hesitate to exploit people by demanding extra money. That creates a dislike for Naadi astrology". He suggested that I should make a special mention about his charging large amounts for different rituals and gifts to temples etc.

As per the instructions, in Irrattai Naadi, I was a witness to the reading in New Delhi in July 2009. It was for a party from UP. The reading was impressive. However, the party reported that the later repercussions were sore.

❑

My Experiences of Naadi Centres in North India

During November/ December 1994, I left on a tour of Delhi, Meerut, and Hoshiarpur etc to visit Naadi centres in North India. I reached Delhi by an Air Force flight and later travelled by bus or rail to other places. I noticed a lot of difference between people of the North and South; their behaviour, talk and their views about Naadi astrology.

PANDIT JUGAL JOSHI OF ARUN SAMHITA

The late Pandit Haveliram had his Arun Samhita Centre in Daryaganj, Delhi. The late Sri. Shantaram Athawale in his book "Naadi Granth" published in 1965 mentions his address. Pandit Jugal Joshi (son of the late Pandit Haveliram) received the letter I mailed to that address. His reply, mentioning the Arun Samhita, which he possessed, invited me to call on him when in Delhi. On reaching Delhi, I phoned him, introduced myself and asked for his appointment. When he said he was too busy and asked me to phone after two days, I informed him that I had published his name in a book and I wanted to present a copy to him. Thereupon he agreed to receive me at noon the same day. Although I am familiar with Daryaganj fairly well, it took me considerable time to locate his house. Finally I reached a three story building. That was Haveliram's "Haveli" meaning a grand building. There was no board of the Naadi Centre outside.

I went inside. In the central courtyard a baldly man was seen playing cricket with kids. He came forward. When I introduced myself as 'Wing Commander Oak', he said, " please be seated in the reception room. I shall pleasantly meet you."

The hall was well -kept with attractively laid books. Jugalji sat on a strong teak wood chair and said, 'Be brief, some party is expected soon.' He had already ordered tea and biscuits from his kitchen. I gave him my visiting card and a copy of my book. He praised my efforts to locate his postal address and looked over various chapters of my book. He remarked that never before had he come across such a detailed treatise on the topic. He added that he had some information about Naadi Centres in South India but about the method of locating Naadi forecasts from thumb impressions of clients, practised there, he knew nothing. However, he went on debating on the superiority of the Bhrugu, Surya and Arun Samhitas. He also expressed regret that of late these Samhitas had earned a bad name in the North. He was angry with "fake Samhitas". He added, "Anybody comes up and claims on oath that he has the authentic Bhrugu or Ravana Samhita etc. But all that is fake." I agreed with what he said, because I have gone through the large volumes available in the market priced at Rs. 2500 to 3500/-. The sellers of those books do not allow the customer to inspect the book until he has remitted the price. Because even a quick glance through the pages would convince one that they are not of the quality of South Indian Naadi's. That is why dealers do not allow buyers to pull out the volume from its silken shroud and wrapper until they get the full price. Consequently I thought of a stratagem. I told him that I found it inconvenient to browse through the Ravana and Bhrugu Samhita volumes outside on the street, so I showed the dealer my bank credit card (which he doesn't accept) and inspected the volumes (inside the shop), which I had no intention to buy anyway.

Pt. Jugalji explained in detail specialities of the Samhita he had and as to how Pandit Haveli Ram came to possess it. He said, "My father was sitting by the side of a fire, when among heaps of scrap-paper being brought out for burning, a burning piece caught the attention of a Sanskrit Pandit present there. When he examined it they were identified as pages of a Samhita. He taught Pandit Haveliram (who was of 8 or 9 years old then) Sanskrit language and astrology etc. Pandit Haveliram became very popular in Delhi and Mumbai, because he possessed Arun Samhita." Pandit Jugal Joshi honestly confessed to me that he found it difficult at times to grasp the subtle-meaning of passages in the Samhita. When I inquired repeatedly whether the Samhita mentioned specific names of seekers he said, "No". He slightly changed his stand later to assert that at times names are mentioned but the Bhrugu Samhita in Hoshiarpur is fake. " He tried to impress on me again and again that the Naadi Samhitas available in the South must also be fake as he alone had the authentic Samhita! Then I had to tell him firmly that he had no right to condemn other Samhitas as fake. I then asked him whether he had seen Naadi astrology in the south and the Hoshiarpur Samhita himself. He said he did not consider it necessary since he got reports from people that they are fake. "Wait," he said, "I will show you a copy of the page from Hoshiarpur Bhrugu Samhita." He brought out from his drawer a soiled white piece of paper of a size bigger than a post card. It looked like a thick blotting paper. On one side of it was a horoscope, while on its backside there was some writing in Devnagari script, but a bit complicated one. I examined that paper which was 'an authentic' sheet of the Bhrugu Samhita, though according to Jugalji it was a 'fake'! He pointed out to me the names of a girl 'Tripta' and her father 'Ramprakash' written there. I started deciphering some words such as "Kaliyugadi, Uchchpadadi Iti, Bharat Desh, Rajya Bhogo" etc. He appreciated my grasp. Pandit Jugalji then handed me some more pages from his Samhita. The pages were of thick, green old paper. The Sanskrit script on it appeared to be difficult to read. But he allowed me to take a Xerox copy of a page of his Samhita and of the page from the Hoshiarpur Naadi Samhita. That was indeed an important gain for me. When I asked him about his fees he said he charges Rs. 1100/- but added that he increases the fees depending upon the party concerned. According to him he gets rich Marwadi clients from Calcutta. Then he exploits them. (In my recent visit in June, 1999 I came to know that he had shifted to a new residence and has increased his fees to Rs. 5000/-)

I took leave of him but with some bitterness in my mind, because of his attitude. That Samhita is a dialogue between two persons about the client's future, if persons unable grasp the meaning of the contents, naturally the people will denounce the Naadi volumes as something fake etc.

My Experience of The Bhrugu Samhita of Hoshiarpur

I left Delhi to proceed to Hoshiarpur. I alighted at Jallundhar railway station by midday and got into a bus. On the way I recollected, while I was serving at Adhampur Air Force Station in Oct. 1972, my senior officer used to volunteer to accompany important persons to call at the Bhrugu Samhita at Hoshiarpur. He had also asked me to accompany him. Had I not rejected his proposal at that time, I would not have been required now to come all the way from Chennai this time! That indicates how all our movements are destined!

By 2 p.m. in the afternoon I reached the lane of the Bhrugu Samhita Centre in the Railmandi area. I had heard that all the Bhrugu Samhita readers stay in that lane. I had sent Warrant Officer Sadhuram to one Samhita reader-Amrit Anand. Unluckily he was insulted and was driven out of the premises. I have mentioned that in the first edition of my book in Marathi. So I decided to visit the centre myself. When I inquired at the first building in the lane, I was told, "He has gone out". When Sadhuram had called there he too had to hear the same plea and wait. I therefore decided to visit other Naadi readers. I proceeded further to enter a two storeyed building of Satish Janardan Deo. In that well-kept hall, there were already 5 to 6 persons sitting on the sofa. I helped myself with cool water from the cooler there. As I was about to take my seat there, a message was conveyed to all of us waiting outside, again and again, that the reading of a Delhi Party was going on inside and so all other appointments stood cancelled. Among all those sitting outside, was a well-dressed lady doctor who had arrived from Mumbai. She pleaded that having come all the way from Mumbai by appointment; she ought to get her reading that very day anyhow. When her appeal was rejected, she started making angry remarks. I was observing all that. That lady being really very upset, may be in order to win my sympathy, she confided in me that having heard a lot about Bhrugu Samhita predictions she had come there all the way from Mumbai. Thereupon It occurred to me why not I pass on the information of my book and addressees of Naadi centres to such a needy person? So I drew her attention to some addresses mentioned in my book and told her to return to Mumbai and visit the Naadi centres there and in South India. She shook hands with me as she boarded a taxi to proceed to Jallundhar Railway Station to catch a train to Mumbai. Tears welled up in her eyes as she thanked me profusely for the Naadi centre addresses in Mumbai and South India. She added it could be that her Destiny made her to visit Hoshiarpur just to obtain those addresses!

When Naadi Shastri Mrs. Satish Janardan Deo emerged out of the inner Naadi chamber. I requested her for an appointment. She agreed to meet me after 5.30 p.m. Since there was lot of time in between I decided to walk back to the house of Amrit Anandji. The house of another Naadi Pandit Ratish Mohan Shastri was on the way. So I inquired at his residence whether he was at home. I was told that he wasn't there. Being a bit puzzled, I entered the house to ascertain the exact position. In my conversation with the inmates, I gathered that the Naadi reader Ratish Mohan is the son of Pandit Gurudayal Sharma and is related to the 6 sons of Pandit Desraj. Out of the 6 brothers 4 had died. The widows of the expired brothers Janardan Deo and Anand Amrit, namely Srimati Satish and Srimati Sneh are running their respective centres. I was surprised to hear that. The Hindi expression, *"chale gaye"* which I misunderstood to mean 'is out of town' actully meant, 'he had expired!' It was exactly opposite of my earlier experience. At the residence of Babubhai Chhaya Shastry in Mumbai, when his son Harshadbhai informed me that his father 'had gone.' He meant that his father was not at home, though I presumed that he was no more! When a reader of my published book told me that Babubhai was still very much alive I issued a correction. Later on in 1995, Babubhai really expired! That was thus quite a comedy of tragic errors!

Sri. Ratish Mohan was in fact out of town! In his house, I saw a very impressive oil-painting of Bhrugu Maharshi. I felt drawn towards him with profound respect. The atmosphere in that house was very good; clean, white mattresses, multicoloured garlands, cool, comfortable lighting, scented environment etc.

There I was informed that Pandit Desraj possessed Samhita Pattis. Those days, his 6 sons would help matching visitors' horoscopes with those in the large size Bhrugusamhita and when matching ones located the predictions were produced on Post-Card size serially numbered pages.

To avoid disputes among his sons, their deceased father had ruled that all the volumes of the Samhita should form their common library. Yet the brothers living separately charged anything between Rs.150 to Rs. 350 with none of them knowing what the others charged! So when I inquired from one of them as to why that was so, he inquired from me as to what his other brothers were charging! That was a funny imbroglio.

Being informed at the house of Amrut Anand that Mrs. Snehji was out on a group-pilgrimage. I could not meet her. So I returned to the house of Mrs. Satish, where I met a person who was about to leave her centre. I hurriedly got introduced and asked him about his experiences. He said, "I come here quite often. I have a factory elsewhere. My sister, who is in a foreign country being worried about her daughter, I came here to perform Shanti Deeksha for them. A lot of expenditure had to be incurred. Let us await the result." But I forgot to ask him his address.

As fixed earlier at 5-30 p.m., when I presented myself at the residence of Mrs. Satish I was asked to be seated on the other side of a big table facing Mrs. Satish. The lady appeared to be fatty but fair and with a mien of good lineage. She spoke Hindi with a Punjabi accent. She spoke with dignity. Next to her was seated a youth of about 20-22 years. I handed my book to her. She gingerly said, "I take only 2-3 cases a day. I cannot cope with more." I stop working after 5 in the evening. There is an adverse effect on our business because of increasing terrorism. "I informed her that I would like to have a look at the Pattis from a research point of view. She replied that she does not handle the patties after sunset. Yet because of my repeated requests, the lady was impressed by my admiration for Naadi astrology. She went inside to fetch the Pattis. I was offered tea, but the lady did not come out for long. I was finally told that the patties would not be shown to me. I then pulled out a Xerox copy given to me by Jugal Joshi, and inquired whether that was authentic? Her son took it from my hand, looked at it and remarked, "looks authentic", while the lady frowned. She asked me how I had obtained it? I informed her that somebody obtained it from Pandit Desrajaji, from whom I got a xerox copy. She said, " That is improper." "May be" I said, "but please read what is written on it" Her son started reading it. But the lady interrupted saying, " Sorry, we don't work after sunset!" I too had to retort saying, "That is improper." By that time it was about 7-15 p.m. When I was informed that the last bus was at 7-15, she hurried to drop me at the bus stand by their Maruti car. During my bus travel, on my way back my mind was occupied by the happenings during the day. The limited working hours from 10 a.m. to 5 p.m.; differing rates of fees; catering to only three to four clients a day and unnecessary secrecy surrounding Naadi readings. I wondered how and when would all those *"Galat baten"* - improper conventions - would be set right?

Experience of Bhrugu Samhita of Shamacharanji Trivedi, Hoshiarpur

It is a pleasant surprise to meet Panditji, in his Bhrugu dham on Una road. His very informal style and warm demeanour makes very soothing impact on who so ever visits his centre. He had a special leaf called as Akshya Patra. The script changes as the reading goes on. I was the witness to it. In Karnal (Haryana), where Panditji had his other centre, the statues of his father late Jagannathji and Bhrugu Maharishi are very impressive. A detailed reporting is available in my Hindi version of this book.

Pandit Shamacharanji was invited as Chief Guest for a conference on Astrology in the year 2006 in Pune. In that function, he demonstrated the Bhrugu patras to the inquisitive persons.

Experience of Pandit Mahashiv's office in Hoshiarpur

My leaf stated that I was to reach there to get this reading at Chanchalpuri - name of Hoshiarpur in Samhita, on Teej, i.e. thritiya, Thursday, of Chaitra month. That was on 31st March, 1998. It was very crucial date for an Accts Officer. I could not have left office, because of the closing of financial year. Yet in spite of all odds, I attended it by travelling from Srinagar by special Air Force Plane! When I look back the entire episode, it appears as a fairy tale. My family members got equally impressive readings from him before I left Air Force in 2003. However, he tends to give impression of great hurry in his readings with strong Punjabi accent.

Experience of Bhrugu Samhita at Meerut

I left Jallundhar by Frontier Mail and reached Meerut at 5 a.m. I had planned to call on Pandit Shivkumar Dixit at Budhana Gate. It was cold in the morning. I whiled away some time sipping tea till it was broad daylight. At 6-30 a.m. I reached Budhana gate by a cycle rickshaw. There I noticed a Hanuman Temple. I asked an aged person squatting among a group there about the house where Bhrugushastri Dixit lived. But they all pleaded ignorance saying they had not even heard about Naadi literature. One person vaguely said, 'may be near that dilapidated hut.' I immediately proceeded there. There I met another old man who said to me that no Dixit lived there. It is near the Hanuman temple! I came back to the same previous location! There I enquired the address from a sweetmeat shop owner. While he denied any knowledge, I noticed a signboard bearing Shastri's name. It was there in the adjacent building on the first floor. I entered the house climbing up an old staircase. The floor of the room lay scattered, with a lot of things covered with dust rising from some nearby construction work. That was a bedroom - cum - study room. A number of books and notebooks were lying on the table and chairs. Sri. Ramesh Dixit, son of Shivkumar, had just come out of his bed, it appeared. However, I was offered tea. I showed him my book. He too showed me his interview published in the 'Kadambini' magazine. He continued his father's profession while practising law too. So he was very busy. There were heaps of notebooks lying on his table since 1982 awaiting Panditji's attention. When I heard this I pitied them. After a lot of chitchatting, when I asked him to show me the Naadi Pattis, he first showed me some papers with typewritten notes, and then showed me Naadi Pattis. Those were written in ink, in big lettering in a stylish handwriting and were systematically stored. To my question, whether the Naadi mentioned specific names he responded affirmatively. Thereafter Panditji entered an inner room. In the meantime, I glanced over a Naadi Patti there, which bore names such as Madhav, Narayan, resident of Nagpur etc. I asked him to give me a xerox of the same. He wondered how it could be Xeroxed since that would damage the Patti! He told me not to ask for a copy. May be he suspected I might misuse that copy. I tried to reassure him that I had no malafide motive.

I informed him about the Naadi's in south India and how they readily provide their clients tapes and notebooks of those predictions. When informed that they charge only Rs. 100/- he said, "it is a wrong thing." He dubbed Rs. 100/- as a mere pittance because it induced people to underrate a very 'authentic' Naadi collection that he owned. When I asked him as to who gave him the right to denounce those Naadi's as 'fakes,' without studying those Pattis in Tamil language? He argued that since the Pattis he owned were genuine others elsewhere must be fakes! He felt a bit awkward in mentioning his fee as Rs. 1100/- He accepted my horoscope and promised that he would search for my Naadi and communicate to me the prediction, but only after those waiting since 1982 had been attended to. I had no alternative but to wait for a long period.

I was shocked at his attitude of extolling the Pattis he owned as genuine and denouncing those with others as fake. Comparatively speaking, in South India Naadi prediction is handled with reverence, faith and honesty. Photographs of various Naadi Maharishees, and of various religious-symbols are exhibited at those centers. They mention other Naadi's and Naadi readers with due respect. The strict routine of morning ablutions, bath, worship, talking to the clientele with due respect etc. are factors, which foster a sense of affinity and confidence. But for the language problem, the Naadi's in the South and North could have come closer. However, a large number of people have been motivated to consult Naadi predictions because of Surabhi Programme and Japanese Programme on Television channels and my books and articles. This is no mean achievement!

TAMIL NAMES OF ENGLISH AND HINDI MONTHS

Sl. No.	Names of		
	English Months	Hindi Months	Tamil Months
1.	15th January	Pausha	Tai
2.	15th February	Maagha	Maasi
3.	15th March	Phalgun	Pakuni
4 .	15th April to	Chaitra	Cittarai
5.	15th May	Vaishakh	Vaisahi
6.	15th June	Jyeshtha	Aani
7.	15th July	Aashadh	Aadi
8.	15th August	Shravan	Aavani
9.	15th September	Bhadrapad	Purrattasi
10.	15th October	Ashwin	Aepasi
11.	15th November	Kartika	Kartikeyi
12.	15th December	Margashirsha	Marghazhi

❏

The Headquarters of Naadi Astrology Vaideeshvaran Koil

Author's experience is narrated in this chapter about some large Naadi centres in the country for the compilation and preservation of Naadi literature.

Vaideeshvaran Koil is a small village. Its main attraction is the old temple of Vaidishvara (Lord Shiva). In the front yard of that temple, there is an idol of Mangala (Planet Mars). From ancient times, this temple and its surroundings have been an important centre for the compilation and preservation of Naadi literature.

One can still see a number of Naadi centres outside that temple. Those Naadi centres are located in small, ground level rooms as well as flats in high-rise buildings. Long queues are seen at those centres. To visit them one has to take a somewhat circuitous route from Chennai. The route leads via Pondicherry and Chidambaram. It is 18 kilometers away on the road to Mayavaram alias Myladuturai railway station. The railway station too bears the same name. I had been there a number of times. My experience is narrated hereunder:

Sri. Swami Sadashivam of the Agasthya Naadi

Sri. Swami Sadashivam, elder brother of Dorai Subbratnam, chief of the Agastya Naadi centre at Tambaram, runs the above Naadi centre. His well-managed office is located in a beautiful "Ved Bhavan" building. I was introduced to him earlier. He welcomed me with affection. Swami Sadashivam is a very talented and expert Naadi reader. A number of foreigners avail of that centre for their Naadi reading.

Sri. Pusai Mutthoo of the Vasishtha Naadi Centre

A very simple looking Sri. Mutthoo is an erudite scholar. Once when a "question chapter" was being read, it was mentioned therein that Sri. Mutthoo would give information about the history of Naadi-astrology. He answered all my questions. According to him Naadi astrology is more than five thousand years old. Vishwamitra and Vasishtha started writing Naadi predictions much before Parashar and Vyas, who are historical personalities. This Naadi centre is located in a large building and the Naadi reading is conducted in a number of adjoining rooms. There I met Professor K. Natarajan. His command over Tamil and English languages is excellent. This centre has a library of Naadi Pattis. There is always an atmosphere of secrecy in Naadi centres. The room where the Naadi patties are stored is always closed. He agreed with my suggestion about microfilming the Naadi Pattis for their preservation, carrying out a Carbon-14 test to determine the antiquity of Naadi Pattis and also to free Naadi reading from religious dogma. A senior Naadi reader Sri. Mohanan of that Naadi centre is adept at analysing the Dhyan kandam (Knowledge Chapter)

Sri. Jemini Selvraj of the Kak Bhujandar Naadi

Sri. Jemini Selvraj is the chief of this Naadi centre. He very willingly showed me his collection. He even allowed me to handle Naadi Pattis. He read out some portions of a Naadi leaf slowly and explained to me the meaning. He also explained to me about the way names of Naadi-seekers are quoted in the Naadi. He said that his Naadi is in the form of Pattis i.e. strips whereas the Kak Bhujandar Naadi with Sri. Ramani Guruji of Tambaram is of the Jeeva Naadi type. That is to say it is sage Kak Bhujandar who speaks through the medium of Sri. Ramani Guruji!

Sri. Tanikanchalam of the Saptarishi Naadi

Tanikanchalam appeared to be an expert Naadi reader. He allowed me to handle his Naadi Pattis and explained to me the meaning of whatever he read out. He also gave me addresses of his Naadi centres at Erode and at Trichi (Trichanapalli), in Tamilnadu State.

Dr. C. Ravi of the Bohar Naadi:

I could not meet Dr. C. Ravi at that Naadi centre. However, from the crowd of the customers, the centre appeared to be an important one. Recently a Naadi centre opened at Pune is a branch of that centre.

Swami Sachchidanand of the Agastya Naadi

I could not meet Swami Sachchidanand. From the photograph displayed there, it appeared that Film actor Sanjay Dutt had visited that centre. From the number of Naadi readers and the customers there it appeared to be an important centre.

Sri. Sundar Murty of the Kaushik Tulya Naadi

I called at him after 10 O' clock at night. Even then he welcomed me affectionately. He pointed out to me the speciality of his Naadi collection. However, for want of a good translator, there could not be a good discussion. That is a popular centre.

Sri. Venkateshan and Sriniwasan of the Agastya Naadi

There were fewer crowds at that centre. Two young Naadi readers at that centre work fast. Their service is quick. For those who prefer getting fast service, that centre is convenient.

So far I have visited almost all the Naadi centres in the country. During my travels to Naadi centres I sensed that people have a poor opinion of Naadi Centres in the North. My conclusion, however, is that all Naadi records are authentic. But the crucial question is whether the clientele gets the required accurate Naadi reading as applicable to him or her. The Naadi Centres in the south appear simple, friendly and emotional. There appears to be no competition among Naadi readers to bluff clients. The photographs of various Gods, Goddesses and scholars of various religions which include those of Naadi stalwarts as well are reverently hung there and worshipped. I was very happy to note that all workers looked upon their profession with profound respect as a pious, hereditary mission and not as a mere money-spinner.

One thing that impressed me at all Naadi Centres, whether north or south was that they welcomed and helped me review and study their profession. According to them my study of various Naadi Samhitas undertaken by a well-educated, respectable person, with an Air force background, in spite of the lack of knowledge of both Sanskrit and Tamil languages was a unique mission. I am happy to make all that information available to readers through the medium of this book. Nowhere has all that information, about Naadi's in Tamil, spread over many places, been available so far. The Naadi readers at the various centres said, "If we praise the greatness of Naadi treatises, that could be misunderstood as self-praise. So it is good that a third person like you has reviewed Naadi astrology for readers. Go ahead and publish your books on Naadi astrology in various languages. They added, "we shall be looking forward to the publication of your book."

❑

Enthusiastic Anuradha and Naadi Predictions

If a person loses his mental equilibrium because of the good or bad prediction made about his or her future, that person should be deemed to be undeserving to know the future in advance. But inquiring into how the future was divined and how it got recorded is a totally different study. That art could be useful in the betterment of mankind. Naadi recorders have luckily not bothered about such doubters and objectors.

The family of another Wing Commander resided in the quarter opposite mine. His wife Anuradha is known for her liveliness. She is also an expert cook, a beautician, proficient in computer science; who speaks sweet English, Punjabi and Hindi and is very hospitable. Though herself a Punjabi, she married a Keralite defying the opposition of her parents and other elders. Both the families, viz. her father's as well as that of her in-laws are affluent. Her children are intelligent. So she doesn't have to attend to petty household matters such as children's homework, housekeeping etc. They own 2-3 types of vehicles, which she uses for her outings. She is amused when I jokingly address her as the "Lady on wheels!"

I have described Annu, her pet name, in some detail above only to help readers visualize her personality. One day when the topic of Naadi-reading came up for discussion between that Wing Commander's family and mine.

They got interested. They were residents of Chennai for a number of years. Some near relations of their had obtained Naadi-readings when they visited Chennai. Induced by others, who had their readings, Annu was to have her Naadi-reading done. So one day she called at the Naadi Centre. But on her visit to the Naadi Centre she was fed up with having to wait for 2 to 3 hours. Probably her Naadi took time to get located. That not only upset her but she also suspected the authenticity of the whole affair. So she rang up my wife to say that she would be visiting us that evening to inform us that the Naadi talk was all humbug.

My daughter, Neha was worried. She asked me repeatedly, if I was not going to lose in the argument with Annu aunti. My wife also used to be somewhat uncertain. While on the one hand she was confident that I would be able to dispel all of Annu's doubts, on the other, she also felt happy that I was to meet somebody who would bring me back to my senses, since I was too much carried away by Naadi astrology. We met in the evening. With a cup of tea in her hand Annu said to me, "Bhai sahab (dear brother), all this Naadi business appears to be humbug. All those who seek Naadi predictions are mad and all those who stock them are fools"! She thus kept on denouncing the entire Naadi business as a senseless craze.

I took all that denunciation lightly, replying with a smile, " What you say is absolutely right. To seek to know one's future is sheer madness. Those who foretell are there to drive you mad."

Annu retorted, "These days one finds thousands of fortune-tellers sitting at the roadsides, in lanes, at fairs and pilgrimages. Why don't they improve their own lives by peering into their own future by using gem-rings, and other talismans etc.? Why do authors of books like "How to become a Millionaire?" knock the doors of a publisher? After all one has to keep trying, to get results. Can knocking at the doors of astrologers and paying visits to Naadi Centres be of any use? I admit that if one knows one's future in advance one won't suffer any feeling of suspense. If while watching a movie, one is able to anticipate every succeeding scene will not one be bored? Similarly will not life lose all interest if the future course of events is all known in advance? If and when a happy future is predicted people will stop striving.

I replied, "Annu, you don't probably know that I had directed a drama in a competition held by the Brihan Maharashtra Mandal in the year 1983 while I was in Delhi. It was titled "Gulam" (The Slave), its author was the famous dramatist S. N. Naware. I played the main role and also directed the play. The theme of the play was that the hero was keen to know his future in advance. The message of the play was "Don't be a slave to the addiction of depending on the predictions about your future. Do your duty in every given situation and don't bother about the future." The dramatist has on one hand depicted that events do shape as predicted but has on the other hand shown that those who are told their future in advance, become inactive.

Hearing that admission from my own mouth Annu's face lighted up. She retorted, "That is exactly what I say and feel". I then argued that I merely mentioned the theme of the play. What the dramatist had conveyed through his theme was all-correct. But how had the dramatist depicted the exact happenings of the events based on astrology? How were those predictions made? Who was the author of those predictions? What were his credentials and Qualifications? What was the purpose of his writing the future? I have been concentrating on specifically these points.

If a person loses his mental equilibrium because of the good or bad prediction made about his or her future, that person should be deemed to be undeserving to know the future in advance. But inquiring into how the future was divined and how it got recorded is a totally different study. That art could be useful in the betterment of mankind. Naadi recorders have luckily not bothered about such doubters and objectors.

Thereupon Annu changed the topic and remarked, "Alright, leave it at that. Why should not the Naadi Centres at least arrange to provide snacks and tea for those kept waiting? They just don't care and have no consideration for visitors' time. Some of them could even have come leaving a kitty party, only to be left waiting hungry and idle at the Naadi Centre?"

I replied, "Annu, that was your reaction probably because you went there for the first time. Searching for the Naadi Patti of the visitor from his or her thumb impression takes time. In some cases it is easily available but in others it takes a lot of time. And matters don't proceed till one's Patti is located. They have to continue searching till they get it. Searching for the Pattis takes a lot of time, and they can't leave the search of one visitor's Patti because other visitors are waiting. They do have arrangement for serving tea or coffee, but one has to pay for that." I told her.

She added, "Forget about that. What I want to convey is that those people inquire from us a lot of details about our lives and recount them back to us, as though they themselves had discovered them."

I had anticipated that comment of her's because I had heard a lot of people say the same thing. According to them, the Naadi-reader takes one Patti in his hand and says you have three letters in your name. One has only to say yes or no. But inadvertently one replies saying that there are 4 letters, not three in one's name. Is mother living or dead? So he gets the answer to that too. Then he asks if the name of one's father begins with pa, pha, ba, bha, ma, or ya, ra, la, wa, sha? So from such or similar questions he gets the required information about names and other matters and then with a flourish as if they have discovered the details they feign to surprise you by repeating the very names which one has already disclosed to them. They continue to trick you by telling you your future accompanied by some sweet words; you pay the fees with great satisfaction and return with a notebook and a tape.

I told Annu, " It is not from you alone, I have heard a similar opinion expressed by the curator of the Madras Oriental Manuscripts library who is an official caretaker of the Naadi patties recorded by Dhruva, Saptarshi, Dev-Keralam etc., and I was surprised. I would ask you the same question, which I asked him namely, "Have you had your Patti ('Ola'-the Tamil name), read out to you? He hadn't. He believed that it was all-imaginary. The same is your case. You better first verify by obtaining your own (Patti) predictions after ensuring that they don't narrate the very details, which they obtain from you, and then tell me your opinion.

Later Annu obtained her Patti. And conveyed to me her reaction. Her opinion had now totally changed. She now admitted that her experience of her own Naadi-reading was "unbelievably miraculous". She added that when she saw the very names of her father, mother, and husband mentioned in that Patti her earlier doubts became meaningless. It is impossible that they obtained the information from me and recorded it in the Patti. A Tamil-knowing person can even read the names of persons written on the Patti.

A few days later, in the course of our conversation, Annu remarked, "These Naadi-readers are looting people! My mother-in-law, sister-in-law, and others are very religious people. So far they have squandered over Rs. 40,000/= in obtaining their Naadi forecasts.

In the general chapter, they say that you are likely to face some problems and experience some bad developments because of your last birth's sins and the results of the present-day planetary situation. But you need not worry. If you carried out the suggested worship and chanting etc. prescribed in the 13th & 14th which are Shanti and Deeksha chapters, those rituals would ensure a peaceful and happy life for you. With those suggested remedies, who on earth would not get those chapters read? So once again pay the fees for each chapter! Thus, if one has committed a lot of sins in one's past birth, one has to undertake a number of remedies for obtaining Shanti, such as paying homage at temples, arrange Abhishek on one daity or the other. To perform the Abhishek to 3 or 4 different gods or goddesses, feed 9 handicapped persons, light a certain number of holy lamps on such and such a day of the week etc. takes a lot of time and expenditure.

In addition, one has to pay the Naadi-reader, his fee, a dhoti (Lungi), 5 fruits, boxes of sweets etc. Imagine the amount of expenditure involved in travelling to townships where Naadi Centres are located and living there until readings are obtained. Annu remarked, 'Imagine the expenses we would have incurred in travelling by air-conditioned cars with 7-8 persons!'

What Annu said was absolutely true. Giving ones thumb impression and obtaining the tape of the general chapter used to cost Rs, 125/= (at least till August 1994). But undertaking the rituals, spending on the suggested temples rituals and remedies is quite expensive. And for those who want to have all the 12 chapters read out, it is certainly a very heavy expenditure at the prescribed fee per chapter.

It is my guess, that if one has all the chapters read out and carries out recommended remedies etc, one has to shell out about Rs. 7 to 10 thousand. The expenditure incurred on places visited and staying there etc is in addition to that amount.

Take my case for example. I had to worship Rahu in one temple and then proceed yet another recommended Shanti and Deeksha at three or four places and besides feeding nine handicapped persons, as also offering cash Dakshina to 9 priests. The Ganesh Yag- puja etc. all-told, it cost me about 5 thousand rupees.

A number of people asked me, "Dear Mr. Oak, do you also believe in these Puja, Shanti-Deeksha rituals etc?" Since this is an oft-repeated question, I would like to record my opinion about them later in this book.

Readers may not bother about who this Annu is, but I would like to introduce readers from Indian Air Force background about what the Naadi text says about her with her permission.

"She is born in the Vikarinam Samvatsar, in the Masi month according to the Tamil calendar, on the 12th day, which was Wednesday, and the Nakshatra was Uttara Ashadha. She belongs to a good family, and the youngest in the family.

Parents alive (till 1994). One elder sister of hers is married. She herself married into a different caste. She has one daughter and one son both school students. Her husband is an officer in government service. Her name is Anuradha. Her father's name is Yograj; mother's name is Sheela, and her husband's name is Govindan. (All this information recorded in the Patti was accurate) Her husband, Group Captain (then Wing Commander), P.N.R. Govindan was (then) an instructor in FIS, in the Air Force."

TAMIL NAMES OF DAYS AND PLANETS

English Names of		Tamil Names of	
Days	Planets	Days	Planets
Sun	Ravi/Sun	Nyais	Ravi
Mon	Chandra/Moon	Tingal	Chandram
Tue	Mangal/Mars	Savvaya	Savvaya
Wed	Budh/Mercury	Budhan	Budham
Thus	Guru/Jupiter	Guru/(Arsan)	Viyarain
Fri	Shukra/Venus	Waili	Sukiram
Sat	Shani/Saturn	Sani	Sani
-	Rahu	-	Rahum
-	Ketu	-	Ketum

TAMIL NAMES OF ENGLISH AND HINDI BIRTH SIGNS

Sl. No.	Names of Birth Signs			
	English signs	Hindi signs	Tamil signs	Symbols
1.	Aries	Maish	Mesham	Ram
2.	Taurus	Vrishabh	Rishabam	Bull
3.	Gemini	Mithun	Midhunam	Young Couple
4.	Cancer	Karka	Kataham	Crab
5.	Leo	Simha	Simmam	Lion
6.	Virgo	Kanya	Kanni	Virgin
7.	Libra	Tula	Tulam	Pair of scales
8.	Scorpio	Vrischik	Vrischiham	Scorpio
9.	Sagittarios	Dhanu	Dhanusu	Archer
10.	Capricorn	Makara	Makaram	Crocodial
11.	Acquarius	Kumbha	Kumbam	Pitcher on sholder
12.	Pisces	Meen	Meenum	Pair of Fishes

Shanti Deeksha Kandam

One must use one's critical faculty while perusing the Naadi. If one does not accept the remedies mentioned in the Shanti Deeksha, one should not bother about them at all.

The train halted. Some passengers got down. There was quite a rush of those who wanted to get in. In that crowd, one could spot a man carrying his luggage on his head. He got in and the train started. Even after other passengers took their seats, this gentleman appeared from a respectable family continued standing with luggage on his head! He had a black dot on his forehead. He wore a surf -white shirt, coat, and a dhoti.

One elderly lady taking pity on him suggested, "Brother dear, ask the other passengers to move a bit so that you can place your head-load on the floor"

The gentleman did not pay any heed to her suggestion, while other passengers in the compartment kept laughing at the funny sight of a gentleman standing with his luggage on his head!

Everyone inquired from him, one after the other, as to why he wasn't off-loading his head?

"It is a matter of principle with me. Since I have bought a ticket for myself, but not for any luggage-space, so it is proper that I should carry the luggage on my head," the gentleman replied!

"That is alright, but when the railway has no objection how does it matter whether you carry your luggage on your head or place it on the carriage-floor, since ultimately it is the rails which bear the entire weight; so why should you suffer unnecessarily?" Somebody argued. Thereupon that man replied, "Have you had your Naadi prediction read? If not, have it read and then talk to me."

Look Mister, I know just two Naadi's, viz. one that of the short pant which Dada Kondke, the comedian - actor wears and the other of patients i.e. the pulse, which the doctors feel. Now, tell me what is that third Naadi you refer to? The standing passenger replied, "The Naadi I am referring to is the one which records one's future on the basis of one's thumb impression. I had that prediction read recently. Consequently I am proceeding down south to perform the recommended puja etc. in the Shanti and Deeksha Kandams of my Naadi Patti". "Does it mean, you have read the article by one Mr. Oak of the Air Force, and obtained your Naadi prediction too?" "Of course, I am not one of those who would send their thumb-impression and money by post and await the prediction!" "That's OK. but what is the connection between your Shanti Deeksha Kandam prediction and the luggage you're carrying on your head?". He explained, "It is like this: - If we don't know what is going to happen, we leave everything to God and do nothing. However, when you come to know the prediction in the Naadi-reading, one's mind starts brooding. Some have marital problems. Some are worried about being childless. Some don't have jobs. Some do not succeed in any of their undertakings. It is therefore suggested that to get rid of thousands of such problems, one should obtain a reading of the Shanti and Deeksha chapters of the Naadi Patti, and carry out the suggested remedies which include paying obeisance at places of pilgrimage, worshiping certain deities and planets at various places, feeding the indigent, offering food to people, and a number of other measures such as performance of Shanti-Yag under the guidance of professional Brahmin priests etc. "Oh! If such are the remedies suggested along with unfavourable predictions, then of course readings must be deemed helpful" someone remarked!

"What is wrong in it? Do we not undertake pilgrimages? Similarly paying visits to holy places and undertaking the suggested rites to overcome the anticipated difficulties and problems should be welcome," someone observed.

In order to prevent any future misfortunes and ensure a happy, carefree future, one has to go to distant places to carry out the suggested holy rituals. But what about the expenditure involved and other matters such as obtaining leave, buying tickets for the journey, spending on lodgings at the places visited, etc.? "There would also be the language problem!" some one counted the practical difficulties.

"It is very appropriate that one offer food to the needy and obtain their blessings," said another.

A dissenting voice intervened, saying, "It is improper to feed the hungry and indigent thronging the temple out skirts; and earn blessings for oneself. In fact it is the responsibility of the government to feed them." It was a typical suggestion from one of those who blame the government for everything and hold it responsible for all ills.

"Feeding the needy be accepted. But it is sheer folly to carry out Yag (Fire worship), Puja and bowing before and pouring milk on stone idols in temples just to atone for one's sins supposedly committed during one's earlier birth, just because it is stated in the Naadi leaf?" Someone remarked in a socialistic vein!

The person standing with the luggage on his head said, "as long as I did not know my future; it was easy for me to leave everything to God, but now, that I am apprised of my past birth sins, I cannot leave everything to God. Mustn't I strive to take the load away from God?

Once one is apprised of the Naadi prediction, one is inclined to undertake the Shanti-Deeksha. In fact one avails of the Naadi prediction in order to seek remedies to one's misdoing. That is to say one willing to carry out the Shanti-Deeksha rituals is the one who volunteers to bear the burden of his sins. That is exactly what the passenger carrying his own luggage (of sins) as a head-load graphically and literally personified!

All through that journey, the passengers were engrossed in discussing Naadi predictions.

"But if some calamity is to befall somebody in the future, how can Sage Agastya or other Naadi Maharshees prevent it?" asked one passenger posing a genuine problem.

To that another replied, "That's right. When it is raining outside, what do we do? We protect ourselves from rains with an umbrella. One has no power to stop the rains agreed, but we can at least protect ourselves from the shower. Similar is the case about, undertaking divine worship and other propitiatory measures to avoid future calamities or soften their effects".

One must use one's critical faculty while perusing the Naadi. If one does not accept the remedies mentioned in the Shanti Deeksha, one should not bother about them at all. However those in favour of undertaking the suggested remedies should certainly carry them out with deep devotion. If not done in that manner one's expenditure on them will be a total waste. So be cautious!

The head-load traveller added, "If one has faith in divine worship one should certainly offer worship at the indicated shrines and look upon the idols as symbolizing divinity. But one's own skepticism is the real hurdle. One hesitates to bow to and pray to the divine idol. What would people say if they see you are going to the temple? That is the fear lurking in some people's mind. One experiences similar mental constraints while sponsoring fire-worship or other rites etc. at one's own house. One is afraid of the reaction of one's own near and dear ones. Overcoming all such disturbing thoughts, I undertook this holy journey and though a professor by profession I am on this pilgrimage of faith carrying my own luggage on my head" said the standing passenger.

While some passengers kept alighting at their respective destinations. Some others however were in a dilemma whether to avail of Naadi predictions or not?

❑

The Bhrugu Samhita and Me

After reading this chapter it can be said that the future happenings in Bhrugu Samhita are mentioned very briefly. Some positive and some Negative aspects of Bhrugu Samhita is mentioned here under.

From my father and others, I had heard of Babubhai residing at Dr. Bhadkamkar (formerly Lamington) Road in Mumbai. I also recollected having read his name in my younger days in an article written by the late Shantaram Athawale. But I had no opportunity to call on him.

I had met with a road mishap in July 1976, in which my wife died of fatal injuries. So I was at home on long leave. Later, before proceeding to join my duties in Srinagar, I thought of spending a few days at my sister's house in Dombiwali, near Mumbai.

My brother-in-law Sri. Avinash Ranade has also been a resident of my hometown, living in the same lane and enrolled in the same school. So we ware not mere relatives but intimate friends too. Once, while roaming in Mumbai, he had an impulse and said, " Shashi, shall we call on an astrologer?" I nodded assent and we called at the residence of Babubhai. That was 27 November 1976. The time was noon 12 O' clock. When the son of Babubhai Joshi, Harshadbhai opened the door and inquired whether we had an appointment? He added that we could not meet him that day. But I persisted saying that I am from the Air Force and have come all the way from Srinagar in Kashmir and it may not be possible for me to come again soon, so please help us to meet him today itself and now. "Ok! Then come around 2.30 p.m. since he has an appointment later at 3.30' he said. So we called there again at the given time. Those days I used to carry my horoscope in my pocket. I handed it to him. Shastriji placed it in front and then from his tabletop he lifted a bundle of Pattis, and after praying for a while, started reading one of the Pattis.

I had thought that on observing my horoscope, Shastriji would go into his library to fetch out my particular Patti. But even without getting up from his seat, he pulled out the required Pattis! While talking to us, he said he had a premonition about our visit. He then inquired from us as to the language in which he might explain us our future in Hindi, English, Gujarati, or Marathi? I replied that we would prefer Marathi.

Then he started reading. The first few Patties were discarded since those contained the names of his other clients and that of their parents. The details recorded in the next Patti mentioned my father's name as Jagannath. When I said, 'no,' he discarded that Patti. Thus he went on eliminating a number of Pattis. Later the details mentioned in one Patti tallied totally, namely my place of birth-Pune, my Brahmin family, Vashishtha Gotra, Chittapavan group, birth date - 31 July 1949.

Surgery of my throat at the age of 11 years (I had undergone a Tonsils operation in the year 1960)

No brother, two sisters (That was correct)

I joined college at the age of 17-18. My employment began at my age of 22 as a gazetted officer in the defence services, especially in the Air force. (All this was correct)

Will marry with a bride from the same caste. Due to the malefic influence of Mars, her death will occur at the age of 27 years. Her name was - Chhaya. (I was married on 2 March 1975 – with Miss Chhaya Behere but lost her the succeeding year due to a road mishap)

Mother: Mangala, father: Janaradan (alive then),

The client's name is Shashikant. Accompanying him, is another person who has had prediction read out to him.

About the future it said:

"Building castles in the air" is his nature. (Later the Agastya Naadi, in its Chapter No. 11 noted that I would entertain people with imagination–) viz.

A hobby of drafting crossword puzzles in Marathi and Hindi, on general knowledge, Sports, Cinema, TV and Languages.

Possibility of a second marriage at my age of 32 was predicted. It recommended propitiating Mars, so that there would not be any danger later. (In fact in those days I was reluctant to think of a second marriage. Subsequently my father performed the Mars Shanti Puja)

The second wife was predicted to be from the same caste, educated, not very tall, fair, healthy and somewhat of a quick-temper. (All those details proved to be true in later life)

The prediction said whosoever comes in contact with you at your age of 14, 26 and 30 may pass away. (Nobody came into my life at the age of 14. But at the age of 26, my wife expired. My first child was born on 29 July 1978, who is still alive! May be because he was born two days before I completed 29 years of my age!)

In the same reading it was mentioned that I would retire at the age of 55/56, children would get married and my death would ensue at the age of 64 because of heart trouble. (Agastya Naadi seems to be more liberal as regards life as in its 8th chapter it predicts 'long life'!)

I was overwhelmed on hearing the above prediction.

How did I meet with an accident? Why did my wife expire? I was very much eager to know about this. So I paid more money to Shastriji to read additional chapters. The details recorded therein said that my vehicle brushing against a quadruped caused my wife's death. There were actually three different versions of the mishap.

According to one Maharshee, an animal hit the wife, but the husband did not realize it. Wife got up out of fear and again fell down in her hurry to run, got hit on the head and died. The other version stated that an animal trampled over the head of the wife. The third version stated that, the horns of an animal wounded the head of the wife and so she died.

The Bhrugu Maharshee version stated that the vehicle hit the belly of the animal, so the wife lost her balance, fell and died. (I feel that the Bhrugu version is more accurate.)

It so happened that while I was posted at Chandigarh, accompanied by my wife Chhaya, I had desired to see the Pinjore garden. That was on the evening of 11 July 1976. (The Guru Pournima –Full moon day) On the way back, near the gate of the HMT factory, I suddenly got hit on the left-hand side of the handle of my scooter. I lost my balance and fell down. The scooter fell on my thigh. A herd of 4-5 buffaloes being driven by a boy were proceeding in the same direction. The boy lifted the scooter from my legs and made me free. When I was hit, I heard a scream from the rear "Shashi!!!" I was looking for Chhaya in that direction. The light of an approaching vehicle illuminated the spot where she lay. I saw her lying on her back in the middle of the road. As I reached her a passing Ambassador car also stopped. Its kind inmates transported Chhaya by their car to the Chandigarh Military Hospital.

Luckily, that was a standby car of the Home Department of Haryana State, as I could gather from their 'walkie talkie' conversation. Chhaya was moaning while on the way to hospital. I thought she might have fainted. My pant was torn, the scooter handle broke but I had only some scratches on my leg. In the hospital, a Major took charge of her case and I was sent for dressing my wounds. When I returned from the dressing room, a Major came and putting his hand on my shoulder said, "Sorry, young man, your wife is no more!" The medical report said "skull fracture" caused the death. Because of the fierce glare of lights of a vehicle approaching from the opposite direction, a buffalo passing by brushed my scooter from the left. I lost my balance and Chhaya fell off the scooter pillion; Her head hit the road and she died."

In those days, I was also interested in acting in Marathi dramas. Chhaya and myself used to participate in stage-plays organized by the Air Force personnel. I was eager to know what the Naadi had to say about that hobby of mine. It was stated therein that I would get more scope in that hobby after I completed 32, and would give it up after I was 42. (During the years 1981-87, I used to take part in dramatic activities every year. From 1990 onwards, I lost interest in drama.) That proves the veracity of the prediction.

❑

The Bhrugu Samhita and My Relations

However, there was no mention that his son would be an Air Force employee. On the contrary, the prediction stated that I would look after his cloth shop business. There was no mention of a fatal traffic mishap of his daughter-in-law.

My brother-in-law Avinash Ranade has had his Bhrugu Samhita reading at Babubhai's establishment as under:

Avinash Ranade had first obtained his prediction from the Bhrugu Samhita on 11 October 1973. – The names of his parents were accurately mentioned. His birthplace, Mumbai was also right. His love affair with Lata (my sister) meeting with initial opposition from her parents but would later taper off after their marriage and relations with all concerned would be fine if Puja of Saturn and Mars were undertaken, it was stated.

Later some alternatives were mentioned viz. that if he did not marry Lata, chances were that he would marry a beautiful girl with no character or an employed girl at the age of 29. (He was married to Lata in 1974)

A break in his service would occur at his age of 28-29. (He resigned his job, to start his own factory to manufacture Dry battery-cells a year or two earlier). The Bhrugu Samhita did not contain any mention of an independent business. But it said he would progress in his second undertaking.

The prediction that at his age of 34-35, he would be the happy owner of a house, a vehicle etc. had proved correct. His age of 37-39 would be a period of prosperity. (The factory did prosper and he got rid of partnership and from 1987 became the sole owner of "Leo" brand battery-cells at Sangli)

The prediction further stated that he would live for more than 70 years. (However, on 6 May 1989, at the age of 39, he and his friend died in a traffic mishap when a milk tanker collided with the Maruti car in which they were travelling.)

After 1973 (the late) Avinash Ranade had once again sought his prediction in the year 1981. In that too there was no mention of any fatal mishap to him. On the other hand the prediction described happenings between his age of 67 and 73 and death on Vaishakh Ekadashi (11th day of the month of Vaishakh) but all that proved wrong.

My father, (late Janardan Oak) had heard about Babubhai from his friends. He had obtained his own life prediction. My information was limited to that. I never had a chance to discuss with my father his horoscope recordings. He expired in January 1981. While glancing over his papers, I noticed his notebook, which contained the prediction. The notebook had names of mother, father and birthplace all accurately. He was to have a house and a vehicle. He had his house, but he never owned a car. He did suffer from diabetes as predicted. A minor surgical operation at the age of 64-65 was predicted. His heart-trouble and abnormal blood pressure at his age of 66 were foretold. His death was predicted on Paush Shukla Ashtami due to a heart attack. (8th day of the Paush month, the tithe mentioned in Panchang on 10th January 1981 was-Paush shukla shashthi (6th day). That proved to be just two tithes and a year short of the date of his actual death!)

However, there was no mention that his son would be an Air Force employee. On the contrary the prediction stated that

I would look after his cloth shop business. There was no mention of a fatal traffic mishap of his daughter-in-law.

'My father had perused the prediction concerning my sister Lata sometime in 1966 when she was 13 years old.

It stated she would have college-education, but will not obtain a degree (That was correct initially, but later she did complete her graduation)

Her life during her age 14-22 would be full of tension. (She married at the age of 21 (The tension did arise from her parents' disapproval of the match.)

A Son at her age of 28 and later 2 daughters were predicted. (Actually she gave birth to a son at her age of 22. Later she had only one daughter not two as predicted)

A foreign trip predicted for her at the age of 32 proved wrong. She will own a vehicle at her age of 36 (Actually she owned a car from her age of 33)

There is a mention of her husband in different contexts up to her age of 58. There was also no mention of any danger to his life. After his death, herself and her brother-in-law are looking after his business of battery-cell manufacture.

There was no mention of that in the prediction. (However in Agastya Naadi death of her husband, owning of battery-cells factory and finding difficulties to run it, have been most accurately foretold. It is also surprising to note that Naadi notings have exactly described the dry cell batteries as a modern instrument - producing instant electricity!)

From the above it can be said that the future happenings in Bhrugu Samhita are mentioned very briefly. The noting even from Babubhai hardly covers a foolscap sheet of paper. There is no certainty about the happenings predicted in the Bhrugu Samhita. Some happenings find no mention at all, while some did not materialize.

❑

The Experience of Sri Bhope: About the Bhrugu Samhita of Hoshiarpur

Sri Bhope, a retired judge of the Labour Court of Maharashtra State is currently practising in the Mumbai High Court. Besides, Sri. Bhope is a well-known novelist and playwright with the pen name 'Madhuranjan'. He had an occasion to consult Bhrugu Samhita at Hoshiarpur 30 years ago.

It so happened that he was touring North India by car along with his friends. Someone in Delhi had suggested that he visit Hoshiarpur too to consult Bhrugu Samhita. Since his friends evinced no interest in consulting the Bhrugu Samhita Sri. Bhope proceeded all alone to Hoshiarpur and called on Amrut Ananda Brugushastri at his Railway Mandi Lane residence. There one was supposed to carry one's own horoscope and look for an identical one in a volume containing thousands of horoscopes. Once an identical horoscope is found, Brugushastri searches for the visitor's prediction-papers in his stock. Then the located prediction is read out to the caller.

When Sri. Bhope reached there, a number of earlier visitors were already looking for their own horoscope prototypes, in the laid-out charts. Some visitors kept looking for horoscopes tallying with their horoscopes for more than 8 days. When he came to know about that, Sri. Bhope lost his enthusiasm. He thought that it was impossible for him to find a prototype of his horoscope in a day. He expressed his anxiety to Amrut Bhrugushastri. But soon thereafter, Sri. Bhope was able to locate the required horoscope and could get a narration of his future. Some of those notings about him are quoted hereunder with his permission.

The horoscope is of the Raja Yoga (Royal) variety. His name in the present birth is Madhukar and father's name is Ram (Ramachandra).

His name in the previous birth was Vasant Dattatraya having been born in a wealthy Kshatriya family of Bombay. He was a senior officer in Bombay Province. In this birth he was born on Saturday on the 1st day of Shravan Krishna, at Poona. He is on a visit to obtain his Bhrugu Samhita reading at his age of 37, while on a trip, accompanied by his friends.

The wife of a brother of his died in 1978. Another brother had a hard life and met with an accident during 75-76. Sri. Bhope himself is likely to wed a second time because of his Mars and Venus union (all that was correct).

He has one son (already born) and will have a daughter later. (Who was born in the year 1972)

The inquirer is a senior Govt. official working as a judge.

After the age of 45 his fortune will sore and he will attain fame as an author (all correct). Sri. Bhope had earlier got his prediction from Babubhai in Bombay on 13 October 1973. But according to him that was inaccurate and sketchy.

Sri. Bhope narrated an interesting incident in this regard. I quote his own words "Although I had a very good practice as an advocate, only because of my father's insistence I had to shed my black robe and take up the job of a judge. I was unhappy at that change undertaken, because earlier I could earn in single case as much as a judge's monthly salary. Since I was destined to be a judge according to the Bhrugu Samhita, my father's insistence was the medium through which destiny brought about that change. There was no point in my blaming my father. I communicated my feelings to him. I confessed and apologized to him as I realized that he was not to blame since it was my own destiny, which brought about that change. My conscience was then at ease". Unquote.

There was a mention of the word 'Poona' as his birthplace he said. On that I asked him whether it was Poona or Pune? He confirmed that it was Poona and not Pune. Because of that experience in Samhita when there was a public demand to rename the name Bombay as Mumbai he wrote an article quoting the Bhrugu Samhita mention of Pune as Poona and advising the public not to be insistent about Bombay being changed to Mumbai. (However since 1998 Mumbai is the new name given to Bombay and Chennai replaced the name Madras.)

Like Sri. Bhope I also got my misunderstanding cleared.

It happened as under: - I was posted at Srinagar, Kashmir. My wife Alka had gone to her mother's place for delivery. At that time football matches for the Santosh Trophy were on in Srinagar. I enjoyed those matches at times sitting in the stadium and at other times listening to the radio commentary. One Chinmoy Chatterji was a prominent player in the Bengal team. I liked that name Chinmay when I saw him play and also when I heard his name mentioned again and again in the commentary. Moreover I have been an admirer of Swami Chinmayananda. Therefore I had decided to name my son as Chinmay. When I got the telegram of his birth I suggested the same name to my wife and she readily accepted it. That made me feel that it was I who had named my son as Chinmay.

When I got a reading of my son at the Agastya Naadi Centre, it stated the father's name to be Shashikant and mother's name as Alka. It was then that I realised that my gloating over the name I chose for my son was futile. Since it was there in the Naadi-reading already. That convinced me that it is not we who shape our lives, we are mere pawns in the game which destiny plays! ❏

Sri. Satya Sai Baba and Naadi Astrology

Sukra Naadi declares that Sainath is 'Maha Vishnu incarnate'. Incarnating is easy for him. He had 101 previous incarnations so far. One of his incarnations was that of Saint Kabir and recently he was Sai Baba of Shirdi, a very popular figure.

While writing the present book "Naadi Bhavishya", it occurred to me that devotees of Sri. Satya Sai Baba would love to know what the Naadi records have to say about gifted spiritual masters such as Satya Sai Baba.

Naadi Maharshees are ever- ready to record the future of ordinary persons. In fact, they help people to solve their problems, by recommending ritualistic remedies in Deeksha, and Shanti-chapters. So, they would naturally feel thrilled to record the Naadi predictions of godly personalities, I felt.

About Sri. Satya Sai Baba, the 8th chapter of the book titled, **"Living Divinity,"** by Smt. Shakuntala Balu, reproduces the observation as per the Shukra Naadi, as under :-

"Professor Ganjur Narayan Shastri of Bangalore got a number of pages written about Satya Sai Baba in the Sanskrit Naadi "Shukra". The words in single quotation marks are those published in the Sanskrit Naadi.

Shukra Maharshee says: the birth of 'Sainatha' in 'Akshya samvatsara', in the month of 'Kartik', on 'Tuesday' 'Krishna Chaturdashi' (Satya Narayana was born of Aishwariamma on 23rd November 1926. His father's name is Pedda Venkappa Raju. Village name: Puttaparti.) At that time it was the fourth leg of the Ardra Nakshatra. From then his miraculous life started. In his previous life he was in Shirdi. Sainatha completed his school education in the village 'Uravakonda', where previously there was the Lingayat Math.

Sainatha will have 'Sankalp Siddhi' but he will have no attraction for money or riches for himself. Shukra Maharshee further says, 'This child will be always in the 'Nirvikalp Samadhi', will protect religion and give religious discourses. His important mission will be the welfare of people. Sainatha will have a number of disciples. And he will be addressed as 'Satya Sai Baba'.

This great soul will be a bachelor throughout his life. He will treat men and women alike. He is the personification of love. But those who will realize his greatness will see in him the personification of total bliss.

One of his ashrams will be located at a place with a 'Bahu Chakra Vahan' i.e. a vehicle with many wheels - a railway connection. (His White -field Ashram at Bangalore is located by the side of the railway track)

He will raise a number of educational institutions, but their basis will be spiritual.

Sainath will guide people to attain spiritual progress in two ways: one by 'self-meditation' and the other by 'divine glimpses.' For those who would go to him with unstinted loyalty, he will remove their sins, difficulties, and sorrows and instil in them bliss and happiness by showering them with peace and sanctimony. He will appear in person at many places at one and the same time to help his devotees escape difficulties.

The devotees at Shirdi Sai Baba will see Satya Sai in the 'Samadhi' pose. His impact will increase tremendously after 1979. On one occasion by sheer psychic force of resolution ('sankalp'), he will keep an aeroplane flying in the air sans fuel and then land. He will be on friendly terms with devotees, joking, leg pulling etc. Even if he grows in age, he will never be infirm. He will be young forever. His life will be for the welfare of the public and also for holding high the flag of spiritualism. He will end his incarnation at his will. However, for the sake of devotees, he will take their sufferings upon himself. The place of his residence, will become a world-class pilgrimage Centre.

Shukra Naadi declares that Sainath is 'Maha Vishnu incarnate'. Incarnating is easy for him. He had 101 previous incarnations so far. One of his incarnations was that of Saint Kabir and recently he was Sai Baba of Shirdi, a very popular figure.

A number of people will criticize him knowingly or unknowingly. But slowly there will be a transformation in their minds and his followers will increase in number. Because of his "Spiritual Power" and "Personality", India will see good days ahead.

There is still a lot more in the Acharya Shastri's Shukra Naadi that can be mentioned. All that will be included in the book titled, 'Sai Charitramala'. Smt. Shakuntala mentioned that in her book, in 1980. However, that book has not been published so far. Sri. Ganjur Narayana Shastriji is no more. His son is now a Naadi-reader at 'Naadigriha' Chamraj Peth, Bangalore.

❑

9th Chapter of Sri. Agastya Naadi and Me

As a result of your spirituality you are heading towards spiritual enlightenment and self-realization. Therefore, you will meet a spiritual guide very soon. His guidance and blessings will help your spiritual advancement.

A number of days had passed since the general i.e. the 1st Chapter about my destiny, in Agastya Naadi had been perused. Later the other chapters too were read out to me. During that period I had carried out the recommended rituals of Shanti Deeksha. In the May vacation my wife and children had been on a visit to Pune-Mumbai. I couldn't accompany them for want of leave from my office. Being all alone at home, I was utilizing that time to read books on various aspects of spiritualism. Unlike others TV programmes and Newspaper reading didn't interest me. I wanted the 9th chapter to be read out to me but since Rajendran (English translator) was busy with something else the recording could not be done. However one day I decided to go there and get my recording done. Some of the contents are reproduced hereunder.

Until then I had never thought about future developments. There was nothing special I could anticipate in the

4-months period ahead. But what was predicted in the 9ᵗʰ chapter is simply astonishing. The readers would find the description interesting.

Soon after obtaining the reading of Chapter 9, I had an opportunity to visit Pondicherry. I am quoting the prediction hereunder.

Predictions Recorded in Agastya Naadi's 9ᵗʰ Chapter.

Chanting "Om Namo Narayana." The reader bowed low in obeisance to the supreme deity Narayana and saluting Ardha Nari Nateshwar and the Goddess Ishwari, he started reading.

"This prediction is concerning a pious son (punit maidan in Tamil language).

Dhanusu-Lagnam, Kanni- Rashi. The person concerned is a qualified, fortunate and intelligent person. He has a high moral character. The name is Shashikant, father-Janardan, mother-Mangala, first wife-Chhaya, the existing wife is - Alka. This reading is undertaken at his age of 45.

During this period your mind will be preoccupied with very pious and spiritual thoughts. Your mind will be ruminating over the spiritual power governing the Universe. You are a Government servant working in the Defence Dept. Your father is no more. However, you will have a vision of your father. He is your first spiritual guide. His blessings and those of other saints will purify you like rippling oceanic waves. All those great souls are no more. Your life hereafter will be prosperous and happy. You will make spiritual progress. Between the age of 46 and 48 you will attain fame and lead a respectable life.

Because of the directions given to you by your mentors and their blessings, your spiritual progress will be speedy.

As a result of your spirituality you are heading towards spiritual enlightenment and self-realization. Therefore you will meet a spiritual guide very soon. His guidance and blessings will help your spiritual advancement. That spiritual guide is stationed in Tiruvannamalai and you will meet him on a new moon day. A number of other devotees too will be present there. On that occasion a person will accompany you, when he initiates, blesses and guides you. He is named after Rama. (The divine vanquisher of the Lanka ruler Ravana) His blessings will help you acquire spiritual knowledge. (There is indeed a person named Ramsuratkumar at Tiruvannamalai who is also known as the one with a Palm-leaf fan in his hand i.e. 'Visari Sami' or 'Fan Baba', added the Naadi-reader). Thereafter for further spiritual progress you will proceed to the Arvinda ashram in Pondicherry. On a full moon day, go there and look for a suitable location for meditation. Meditate there concentrating on the central point between your two eyebrows, keeping your vision still, with the help of Pranayama you will have subtle knowledge flashed on your mental curtain. (Moun Nilai in Tamil). That will be the spiritual zenith of your life, when a flame of super-knowledge will illumine your soul. That flame is known in Tamil as 'Bimbam'.

Your future thus is very good. One day at the fag end of your life you will have a glimpse of Lord Shiva in the form of a divine flame at twilight i.e. between sunset and moonrise.

❑

An Unprecedented Day–Buddha Paurnima: 25th May 1994

Everybody has some indescribable experiences in life, which could be recorded, for the future guidance or solace of others.

Buddha Paurnima is the day marking Buddha's all the three outstanding events of the his life, viz. His birth, the day of his enlightenment and the day of his death alias Nirvana. I thought to myself, that since that day is just 2 days away, why should I look to any other full-moon day for meditation? Moreover, when I found out in a couple of days whether somebody 'Ramsurat Kumar alias Fan Baba' exists, why should I wait any longer? So I decided and got into the bus for Pondicherry on 24th May at 6-30 p.m. While in the bus, I had a discussion with a Marudai youth, about meditation, guru, etc. We reached Pondicherry by 10:00 p.m. I took a rickshaw and rushed to the Ashram directly. I was told that it would be all-quiet at the Ashram at night, the Samadhis of Arvinda and the Mother and the meditation hall would be closed by 11 p.m. At the Samadhi, I was in two minds whether to sit facing the photos of

Arvinda and Mother, or otherwise, because in the opposite direction there was a bed covered with satin cloth amidst white curtains. I sat with folded legs and straight back for meditation. For some time I concentrated on my breath, concentrated my mind on my inhalation and exhalation and tried to keep my look fixed at the point between my two eyebrows and the tip of the nose. While doing this 2/3 times my head became very heavy. My brows became numb and I felt tense. My eyes were half-closed. For 5-6 minutes I sensed that something was happening. I felt somebody's footsteps behind me. I told him that I knew that I could sit there up to 11 p.m. only. And again concentrated my mind on the tip of my nose. In a short while, I could concentrate my gaze in a straight line towards a dot and felt drawn towards it. There appeared some clouds in the blue colour horizon and also white dot. I also felt that the dot looked bold and later I saw it become faint with cloudy blue -violet shades. I felt that it was a game of hide and seek between those two colours. What was it then? I was perplexed for quite some time. After a few moments, I heard the sound of footsteps behind me. I became conscious. It might have been 2 minutes to 11 O'clock. So whatever I experienced had happened within 12 to 15 minutes only. I was not satisfied. I came out, rushed to a hotel and within 25-30 minutes I squatted on my bed again. I must have been in the same position for about 15 minutes. I recalled Dada (my father). I saw his smiling face, but in a pensive mood. I saw a number of saints one by one. Pradnyanand, the spiritual Guru of my father was caressing my back with his palm, I sensed. Mahadba Maharaj another Guru was applying the bhasma on my forehead with his thumb. I felt as though I was lifting the palanquin (Palkhi) of Ma Anandmayi. I saw the personality of Nrusimha Saraswati as described in Guru Charitra. I saw the photo of Dr.Kakasaheb Upalekar of Phaltan. In fact there were others also, whom I don't recollect now. Subsequently it was all-dark. When I looked at my watch, it was about 10 minutes to 12 midnight. I tried to push aside my thoughts 5 to 7 times and concentrated again on my breath and the tip of the nose. Again the same violet coloured cloud appeared before my vision. When I noticed it again, I was sure that what I saw earlier was no hallucination. The violet colour was a fact. When I was reflecting on that, I noticed the white dot again. It vanished once or twice. Thedn I saw suddenly the statue of the Buddha. I saw a smile on his face and his steady gaze. Again I suspected whether it was a hallucination? When I regained consciousness, it was 2 minutes past 12 midnight. My back had become heavy. I sat with folded hands. I felt as if I touched my mother's feet. Gradually unknowingly I lapsed into deep sleep.

❑

"Your Objective Will Be Achieved"

If it was my objective to see my spiritual guide, it was upto him to give me further guidance. It was me to whom he must have assured in Hindi, that my desire would be fulfilled– "Your objective will be achieved!"

Dated 26th May 1994.

Next day, I arrived at the Pondicherry ashram early morning. On my way there I bought lotus flowers and incense-sticks. I offered them at the Samadhi Sri. Arbindo. I squatted there to meditate at 7-10 a.m. There were a lot of other people around also. The atmosphere was pleasant. I sat through the meditation for the next 20 minutes. I had the same vision of different colours as the day before. But I didn't see the white dot. I felt like getting up at 7-30 am. The next 30-40 minutes I spent observing the surroundings of the ashram. Near the samadhi a number of people were sitting with their head touching the samadhi. I tried to sit there in the same position, but I felt uneasy in my stomach and feet. I bought 2-3 books and boarded the bus to return to 'Tiruvannamalai". It was hot and sultry inside the bus. The bus reached my destination by 12.30 p.m. I got a rickshaw with the help of a police constable. The rickshaw took me to Yogi Ram Surat Kumar's Ashram. The Yogi was scheduled to emerge out to give darshan between 4 and 6 p.m. Prasad - food was available there. I had Sambaram and rice, and waited to see the Yogi. By 4 O'clock, about 50-60 persons gathered there. Swami arrived after 4.00 p.m. Men and women squatted in rows in front of Swamiji. There was a space of 2 feet in between. For quite some time religious songs and bhajan continued. After that Swamiji got up and strode up and down in between the rows of men and women. He used to cast a look at the devotees and proceed further. He would look at the men while pacing from one end to other, and he would repeat looking at women while going back. He was walking briskly. He would cast a momentary glanced at the gathering. I was sitting in front of him. He squatted on his seat and got engrossed in his singing. Again he would get up and walk up and down between the rows. He did not speak to any body. Again he sat on his seat. His disciples drew his attention saying "Swami, look at the hill beyond, it is raining there". He exclaimed "Oh! What a beautiful shower" and again got engrossed in his singing. For about 4 times he got up and walked briskly in between the rows. Next time, I looked at his feet while he was walking. I heard him saying in Hindi," Your objective will be achieved". When I looked up I felt he was addressing the assembled people. He again went back to his seat. I was wondering as to who this entity could be, and to whom his addressed to. Nobody had mentioned about anything to him. Nor had he cast his glance at anyone in particular. And when all the assembled devotees were Tamilians, his remark in Hindi," *Tera kam ho jayega*" appeared strange. At that time the crowd outside had increased. By now over 150 persons had gathered inside. They started to push out people who were sitting near the Yogi for long. I also got up, bowed with folded hands, and walked away before anybody asking me to make room for others. Outside I asked a few questions to the trustees and proceeded to the bus-stand. I had mixed feelings. The appearance of the yogi, his behaviour while I was there and the atmosphere made me a bit uneasy. I was in that mood for quite sometime. It rained heavily in-between. Later then I was at ease. Having regained my composure, I recalled the remark "Your work will be done". Everybody who had come there had some motive. So did I. Did that assurance then apply to everybody's aspiration? I asked myself, If everybody's desire was to be fulfilled, what was my desire? In fact I had come in search of my spiritual guide. I was sure to locate him since Agastya Maharishee had asserted that, If it was my objective to see my spiritual guide, it was upto him to give me further guidance. It was me to whom he must have assured in Hindi, that my desire would be fulfilled - "Your objective will be achieved"!

When I boarded the bus, my despair vanished. The sky too was clear. It was 8 p.m. I saw the full moon from the bus window. While I was peering at the moon I recalled the white dot I had seen the previous night. Similarly when a cloud covered the moon it became lusterless. My mental condition was similar to that of the previous last night. It was then that I understood the meaning of the word "Bimbam" namely- not a flame, but a beam of light glowing peacefully like the Moon's reflection in water, I wondered whether both of my aspirations were fulfilled? Only the future would reveal, who else?

❑

Once Again Yogi Ram Surat Kumar

After the visit of 24 May 1994, I again felt an urge to visit the ashram of Ram Surat Kumar. I suggested to my wife that we go to Pondicherry. She could first do some shopping there. Later would visit the Ashram and stay in a hotel at night.

Next day we would call on the Yogi at Tiruvannamalai and would return the same evening. My wife tried at first to veto my proposal, but later I won her over, and she agreed.

We left on our trip to Pondicherry and thence to Tiruvannamalai. We reached the Yogi's Ashram by 9-30 in the morning. I took with me sweets and fruits as an offering. The Yogi stays away from the Ashram. He arrived in a taxi accompanied by 4-5 ladies constituting a holy choir (Bhajan Mandali). The Yogi squatted on the floor leaning against a wall. The Yogi didn't converse with the congregation. He walked between the rows of squatting visitors and blessed people with gestures, and squatted on his seat. While this happened, the choir had started singing. Devotees are barred from touching the yogi's feet, or narrate to him their woes to receive his blessings. Therefore I couldn't converse with him. So I thought I should pass on a chit to the Yogi, and see what happens. Accordingly I scribbled a note in Hindi on piece of a paper, "I am Shashikant Oak. According to the Agastya Naadi you are my spiritual guide. So I have come here to see you. I await your guidance. Kindly give me your blessing." I placed that chit in an envelope ready to be delivered to the Yogi. When the assembled devotees were instructed to go inside, I too rushed in. As I was approaching the Yogi, the disciples shouted at me "Get back, get back etc". I went ahead, bowed to the Yogi, and placed the envelope in front of him. The Ashram Trustee Sri. Subramaniyam stepped forward seized the envelope, and shouted at me, " Why should you come so close? Does this behove your Air-Force discipline? etc. Then I squatted on the floor. My wife became very nervous. I had no alternative but to hand over the envelope to the Yogi. The trustee noticed that the note was in Hindi, So he handed it to the Yogi, who was apparently noticing all this. It appeared that he read my note carefully. The choir-singing was going on. My mind became peaceful. The yogi rose to pace between our rows. I watched his moving for a few rounds. Then suddenly he coming very close to me, sat down, took my hand in his, and asked me "which state you are from?" My body shivered. My eyes started moistening. I felt that my whole body was energized. In my trembling voice I replied "Maharasthra". He held my hand for quite sometime. Then he left my hand and returned to his seat. Then he backend to me and suggested that I squat in front of his choir. While suggesting to me to come again for darshan between 4 and 6 in the afternoon, he ordered, "This beggar desires that you stay on for the evening darshan". He calls himself "a beggar!" I thought to my self ; what humility!

While returning to me my pen and presenting me a book of poems on him by an American poet, he wrote on that book "Shashikant-Om" by way of his blessings. While he handed it to me he was in a different mood. He looked straight into my eyes, muttering something to himself. Other visitors were surprised to see that he was addressing me again and again and giving me his blessings. Thus ended that meeting.

We had our food of sambar and rice. Then in the afternoon we bowed to him and started on our way back with his blessings. While leaving I informed the trustee, "I am extremely happy today". He took my hands in his and said, "Of course, the Yogi has given you his blessings. You are welcome to call on him whenever you wish."

It was 12 O'clock midnight, when we returned home travelling 160 kms. I handed over the Naadi-reading of my ninth chapter to my wife. Naadi-prediction about me stated that on a New Moon day, accompanied by somebody, I would meet a holyman (the Yogi) who will bless me. Then I ascertained from the Panchang (the astronomical almanac) and mentioned to my wife that 7 Aug 1994 was indeed a New Moon day which proved the accuracy of the Naadi prediction to that minute detail!

❑

Flabbergasting Irrattai Naadi

I had paid 3 to 4 visits to Dr. Om Ulagnathan at Vadpalani, Chennai, to meet him, ascertain from him details about the Irrattai Naadi and also to get readings about my own future, from it.

On my first visit, I met the tantrik and Mantrik Sri. Ravindranath. In my next visit I got introduced to Dr. Ulagnathan's niece, Miss Aradhana. She works in the field of TV and movies at Chennai. She is fair, attractive and smart. She speaks good English. Being desirous of working in Hindi Filmdom, she is keen to learn Hindi. While talking to her, I came to know that a number of politicians come to Dr. Ulaghnathan for their predictions. I asked her to tell me names of some politicians. She asked me whose name should she mention? And asked me if she could tell something about Rajiv Gandhi. She produced a photograph of Rajiv Gandhi with Dr. Ulaghnathan and said, "we were invited about 7 to 8 months before his death, to Delhi to tell his future. Since my uncle has no mastery over Hindi or English, generally he takes me with him, so I accompanied him to Delhi. He was told that there would be re-elections and that he would again come to power. However, he was advised not to proceed south on campaigning, especially in Tamilnadu. But when in the course of elections, we came to know about Rajiv Gandhi visiting Tamilnadu; we tried to convince the local leaders about the danger to Rajiv Gandhi in Chennai. I sounded a warning that if he comes to Chennai these days he will go back in a coffin! So try your best not to bring him here! But everybody knows what happened!

Former Chief Minister of Tamilnadu M.G. Ramachandran who was a cine actor too, was a very popular person. I was eager to know if in his case a Naadi-prediction had been made. She told me about that too. Initially M.G.R did not believe in astrology. But later in his old age, when he lost his power of speech, he was foretold that because of public insistence he would have to be the leader, even if he was weak. He would be required to go abroad for treatment. When the predictions proved true, he also believed in Naadi astrology. He was warned not to visit Meenakshi Temple, since he won't return! That warning was ignored, because some senior central leaders were to visit there on some mission and as Chief Minister out of protocol formalities M.G.R. had to go there, and later on he died"!

"I remember one more incident" she said, "when M.G.R. died". While some Naadi-reading was underway, I was there as a witness. I was told, "Remember dear daughter, one very firm prediction. There will be rains in Tamilnadu the next day causing a flood"! I did not believe that at that time. Because meteorologists had not predicted any rains on the next day. (Since the cyclone hits the eastern shores many a time, there is an alarm system in the region.) The next day also there was no sign of rain. The newspapers carried lengthy accounts of M.G.R.'s death. The state was in mourning, and people were literally crying aloud to express their sorrow. Some people burnt themselves to death as they could not stand the death of MGR. (In Tamilnadu, the common man is very sentimental. So the public knows that there is nothing new in mass shrieks, wails and other modes of expressing sorrow as also immolation). When Naadi-reading commenced I was again asked. " Dear daughter, so? Wasn't there any rain flood? It was not of rains, but of tears shed over the beloved popular leader's demise! Thus the prediction was figurative!"

We had a lot of discussion about such predictions. I told her I had a number of questions about Naadi astrology, like who wrote them, what was the motive behind it? what are the characteristics of the Naadi?, can one know about the future of a nation from the Naadi etc. She said my uncle has no time, so he may not be ready to discuss these things. Moreover, you will have to bring with you a person who can converse in English and Tamil both. I am away many a time for shooting movies, so I don't necessarily be available at the Naadi-Centre.

Later I decided to ring up Dr. Ulaghnathan himself and fix up an appointment so that my visit there may prove useful. But things don't turn out as per one's hopes or wishes! I could not contact Dr. Ulaghnathan on phone too. Whenever I phoned I was told that he had gone to Erode, Bangalore, or Mumbai etc. Those days my sister and my mother were on a visit to Chennai for performing their Shanti Deeksha puja. On the way back by bus accompanied by my sister, after performing the puja at Karumari temple near Chennai, I came to know that the bus route lays via Vadpalani. So suddenly I decided to call at the Naadi-Centre run by Dr. Ulaghnathan. I mentioned this to my sister. She agreed and we arrived at the Centre. I sensed from outside that the air-conditioning was on, so I surmised that Dr. Ulaganthan would be in and today at least I could meet him. I thought it would be nice even if I can just meet him in person, leave aside prediction. On inquiring from the attendant I came to know that somebody's Naadi-reading was in progress in the ante-room and it would finish within half an hour i.e. by 2 O'clock. So my sister (Mrs. Jayashree Ranade) and I went to the near-by-famous hotel 'Saravana' for lunch. Being non-rice eater, we ordered for

Chapaties. But they had no chapaties! So we had South Indian meals and went back to the Centre by 2 O'clock. The earlier reading was still in progress. Arrangements were on for serving lunch, viz. laying banana leaves etc. In the meantime some person who emerged from the A/c room said to me, "Sorry, the Naadi-reading is expected to continue till 8 p.m., so you better come some other day." I heard what he said, but continued to tarry there. After a while, I was again advised not to wait, as Dr. Ulaganathan would not be able to see me. I said OK and yet continued to occupy a chair there, pretending to be watching the TV programme. My sister being restless was urging me to leave the place. It was my guess that Dr. Ulaghnathan was bound to come out for lunch. Another 5 to 7 minutes passed. The door was opened and I was called in.

Dr. Ulaghnathan was seated in a revolving chair behind a large Sunmica table. There were ten others seated on chairs and sofas around him. A short, bald person, with a simple dress and fatigued face, shook hands with me and spoke in broken English, "No Time.., come later.., Please go!" I replied, "Since I was waiting only to contact you I shall take your leave now. Approaching the door, I looked back and said, " I have a desire to watch the method of your Naadi-reading. So if you and these people have no objection, we will sit in a corner and just observe your proceedings. If there are no chairs, we will even stand."

The Naadi-reader after some hurried consultation among the persons present agreed and said, 'Why stand, please be seated.' So saying they fetched two chairs for my sister and me. Dr. Ulaghnathan continued his Naadi-reading. His voice was clear and loud. He was reading in local Tamil. Suddenly the reading was stopped, and all the people began to look at the two of us. Someone said, "There is a mention of both of you in this Naadi." The Naadi rishi's words were, "We were waiting for these two witnesses and they are here. Since yesterday, you were thinking of returning. Rama nama, (the person about whom the reading was being conducted) do you know who these two persons are? He is a government officer who is connected with a vehicle that runs in the air! And he is requesting humbly to be witness to that reading of your Naadi. We were waiting only for them!' We two were to hear the assertion. Later, while the reading was continuing, Dr. Ulaghnathan stopped in between and inquired have you had your lunch? But perhaps you did not get what you desired to eat. In reply we said, "yes, we could not get chapaties". Everyone laughed! Later I was asked again while the reading continued, 'You are not an astrologer, but do you undertake research in astrology?' I said, 'Yes'. He read further, 'you have a lot of questions regarding Naadi but you did not get satisfactory answers. You are always in search of answers. Now you have come here, see if you could get some answers'. (All this Dr.Ulagnathan was saying from his reading of the Patti. So the conversation was between the Naadi rishi and the Jatak, i.e. me. Dr.Ulaghnathan was just reading and explaining it to us. He spoke halting English. Some others were helping him in his English. There was occasional mention of others including us too, which we were not able to make out)

Later there was a mention of my sister, which said, "A close relative of this woman died in a car mishap. It was a sudden death." When my sister confirmed it saying, "Yes, my husband died in a car accident", everyone was amazed. It further said, " Dear lady, we are sorry, we could not prevent the death of your husband. It is now 63 months since your husband expired. And 64th month is running (The readers may count from the date 7 May 89 to 2 October 94)

"He died because his car collided with a heavy vehicle." It was Maharshee Vishwamitra speaking through the Naadi. He continued, "Dear lady, we feel very sad that nobody had ever warned you in advance about that Arishtha Yog (calamity). So you might wonder what is the use of astrology to humanity? It is because of this that people have no confidence in astrology and predictions. Lady, excuse us" That reading included such regrets and apologies three or four times later!

I hoped there would be some mention in the Naadi about my sister's business and her current worries about it. But there was no such mention in the Naadi. In between, I was instructed to gaze at the face of Rama nama i.e. Ramkrishnan) and predict his future! "How could I tell his future by merely peering at his face, since I was no soothsayer! I thought to myself. So I politely declined. Others said, " Please tell us our future, why not? There is nothing wrong in it". Thus they insisted on my predicting the future. Sri. Ramakrishna himself urged me to predict his future because the Naadi said so. I started thinking. I looked at his face and thought what can I say about the face of this person with a grown beard?

Ramanama was in a hurry he said, " Tell me, how am I going to earn money in the future? Whether my business will grow?" I said, "Wait, let me see your face clearly first." Everyone laughed on my remark. Then I went on saying whatever came to my mind. " Business will be okay. But you will have to work very hard. You will always face a shortage of funds." I went on saying like this as the words came to me. In fact I blabbered something. After that the Naadi-reading continued. Again there was a question put to me saying."Hello, man. Since when did you start face reading? Do you know anything about this science? Do you know the art of face-reading?"

I replied, "No! Since you instructed me and others here too insisted I dared to utter whatever came to my mind. Otherwise who am I to do any face reading?". I replied forcefully. Thereupon Maharshee Vishvamitra spoke through the mouth of Dr. Ulagnathan, " Just as you said something like a parrot, we also predict the Naadi. It is not our knowledge. We are just like you. The real prompter, talker who enables us to predict, is different. It is our tongue that reads, predicts because of the blessings of Lord Shiva. Otherwise what power do we or anyone else can have to tell anybody's past, present or future? Do you understand this now? Since you have a research- oriented mind, has our elucidation satisfied you?" I was really shocked to hear that explanation. So the answer to my question was that the great sages who have jotted down the Naadi predictions did so through the wishes and dictates of Divinity itself.

In between someone present there inquired whether I was a Maharashtrian? That was an unexpected query in Marathi! The questioner was Mr. Gopalrao Ekbote, a grocer, originally from Hubli. He was settled in Bangalore for some years. Speaking in Marathi in the Kannada accent he gave us a lot of information about Dr. Ulagnathan of the Irrattai Naadi Centre. He said, " The doctor is an humble person, popularly known as 'Anna'. He often presides at seminars of south Indian astrologers. Influential persons often take him to different cities for predictions. He visits different holy shrines as per the directions in Naadi. In Sept 1994, he had been to Pune to visit Dagadu Sheth Halwai Ganapati, Ubha Ganapati, and other Ganapati temples. On the way he visited the temple at Tuljapur too and received the blessings of the goddess there.

Foreign Governments also invite him to undisclosed destinations to inquire about the future of their nations. The reading is in the form of a conversation between Saptarishis (seven sages) in the Naadi, which he has. It is different from the usual personal predictions. Anna is the 7th child in the family. He himself has 6 daughters and a son. The son will continue the Naadi-reading family tradition in the future. Miss Aradhana is regarded as the niece of Vishwamitra. When she came and sat near her uncle, her name was mentioned in the Naadi. It instructed me to recall my meeting with her earlier. She showed me photographs of Anna with the then President Dr. Shankar Dayal Sharma, Venkatraman, Prime Ministers Indira Gandhi and Rajiv Gandhi etc. and their visiting cards bearing their signatures!

In the course of the reading, there was an interesting reference to the goddess at Tulaja Bhavani. It said, "Oh Ramanama, you went to Bhavani and returned, but never had a darshan of the goddess. The witness next to you (me) has blessings from Bhavani goddess, because in his previous birth he was a devotee of Tulja Bhavani. But he died as a child by drowning into a well. (There is no well in the Tuljapur Temple. But there is one in the surrounding area. I located it when I was on a visit there in December 94!)

By this time, I was introduced to all those present. There was Ramanama, for whom the prediction was being read. Next to him was an old Brahmin. On the other side there was a person named Vinayak, in the corner was a young bespectacled person, seated next to him was a person who spoke in Hindi.

Later the Naadi–reading said, 'Oh Brahmin, you worried about the job of your son. This new visitor (Me) will solve your problem. Request him to help you in getting your son a job.' When I replied, 'I would try'. The Naadi-reading addressing the Brahmin said, 'Now you can go, since you were in a hurry to return home since yesterday.' When the Brahmin continued to tarry there, the reading added, "Why are you not leaving? You must depart since you have been saying so!" Everyone started laughing, because this old person has been saying since yesterday that he would go and was cursing the Naadi! Later the Naadi added 'Now you may have coffee'. This is a speciality of this Naadi. It contains directions to the witnesses to go, come, have coffee, take meals etc!

While having coffee outside, the Brahmin mentioned in the Naadi, Sri. Ardhanari (Retired Head Master of the school at Erode) talked to me. His 19-year-old son had a diploma in automobile-repairs. He was unemployed. So he requested me to see if I could get him some job. I assured him of my help. While writing on the visiting card, 'Your Job will be done' I remembered the prediction of Yogi Ramsurat Kumar, 'Your job will be done.' Actually I cannot ensure employment to anybody in the Air force or elsewhere. So I did not know how I was going to help his son. But somehow I felt confident that I would be able to do something!

After the coffee was served the reading resumed. The Naadi inquired, "Oh Brahmin, is your work over? Did you receive a visiting card duly signed? Then the Naadi addressed me saying 'since you have assured the Brahmin to help his son of get a job you have blessings of this Brahmin and myself (Vishamitra rishi). And these blessings will benefit your sister's son!'

The name of the person mentioned as Rama nama is Ramkrishnan. While he was proceeding in his NE 118 car from Chennai to Bangalore, on the way is a township called Bhavani. There he changed his original plan of proceeding to Bangalore and instead decided to meet Dr. Ulagnathan at Erode. Dr. Ulagnathan brought him to Chennai for his Naadi-reading. Dr. Ulagnathan had his doctorate in astrology. A friend and Sri. Ardhnari also accompanied him. They had started Naadi-reading. But they were abruptly instructed to stop reading midway. 4-5 days passed and yet the Naadi did not contain instructions to resume reading! Persons present there were all waiting with no bath, hardly any sleep and lack of proper food. The Naadi instructions were that they must await the arrival of two other visitors. Those waiting were fed up and they began cursing the Naadi.

At 6 O' clock in the evening, there was a direction in the Naadi that the group may have meals, so food was served on banana leaves, kept ready since 2 O' clock in the afternoon! Sri. Ekbote invited us also, to share some food with other dinners.

So we had *rasam* and *rice*. Later when I met Sri. Ramkrishna he informed me about later developments viz, that the Naadi-reading questioned, "Ramanama, why he sold away 'Anjaneya vahanam' (meaning the Maruti car). Now you sell your other vehicle to a bespectacled person here and until you have a replacement vehicle, use the Maruti van of Miss Aradhana!

I never met Sri. Ardhanari subsequently. May be he already had his son employed as per Naadi-reading. When I asked Sri. Ramkrishna about the expenses for his Naadi-reading, he said that the Naadi -reading charge and the expenses incurred on performing *yadnaya yaaga*, holy offerings etc cost him quite a big amount. According to him the reading in the Naadi predictions are accurate. But persons conveying their experience to others make it more spicey!

On that particular day we were allowed to leave after 5 hours of Naadi-reading. The Naadi allowed me a 'blank cheque' permission to witness anybody's Naadi-reading. I return to my destination. Later I never got an opportunity to attend the Naadi Centre at Chennai, to witness anybody's Naadi-readings!

❏

Saint Dnyaneshwar and Naadi Prediction

While acquainting myself with Naadi-records I always felt that Naadi-readings of outstanding personalities would be a great experience.

The Naadi-reader himself is never reluctant to read the Naadi predictions about ordinary persons too. In fact, they help people solve their problems, by performing the recommended remedies mentioned in the Deeksha Kandam.

A lot of information is recorded in the Shukra Naadi in Sanskrit, possessed by Professor Ganjur Narayana Shastriji of Bangalore, with reference to Sri. Satya Sai Baba. Similarly with the help of a translator, Sri. R. Raghunathan in the Sugar (Shukra) Naadi Centre at Chennai, belonging to Dr. A. Karunakaran, Naadi-readings about Saint Dnyaneshwar were searched for.

Prof. Krishna Gurav is the editor of the Marathi special annual Diwali issue of 'Pailteer' magazine. It was devoted to Saint Dnyaneshwar. So in order to ascertain what the Naadi record said about him, he sent me two horoscopes through his friend Sri. A. B. Karveerkar. At about the same time I got my transfer order and also because of some other assignment, I could not visit that Naadi Centre. Finally, I contacted Mr. Raghunathan and conveyed to him information about Dnyaneshwar on the phone, and earnestly requested him to immediately search for his Naadi. After 2-3 days he rang me back saying that he had located the Naadi and the reading was on. However, it would take some time, as it would be done at intervals. So, I was advised to find time and go there as the reading of that Naadi was meaningful and highly satisfying. Another speciality was that different Maharsheesre very eager to speak about Saint Dnyaneshwar. In one Patti, a number of Maharshees had blessed Saint Dnyneshwar and also me and him, too. That was something special!

The reading was done on 2,4,11and 16 April 1996. Among them, I was present on 4 and 11 April. By that time the photo of the Naadi Patti was also available. In that I underlined the places on the Patti, where the names of Dnyaneshwar, Rukmini (mother), Vitthal (father), and Madi Kant (Madi in Tamil means Moon alias -Shashi) were mentioned! Thereafter due to various reasons, the reading of further stanzas was not possible. May be it stopped because the reading would require other witness for its reading. On the above 4 dates, altogether 31 stanzas were read. The beginning is made by Pullipani (Pulli means tiger or lion and Pani means 'hand'. So together it means: tiger's hand) but Shukra Maharshee stops him and starts to speak. It is a matter of great curiosity to know as to how many are those Maharshrees that would be participating in the reading. These stanzas are full of praise and respect. There is no much of prediction in them, so it is not being reproduced here.

In spite of my persistent requests to Sri. Raghunathan no Naadi-reading could be carried out on 3 April 96. However reading was resumed on Thursday 4 April 96. I was convinced that the reading would have been possible only on Thursday. I tried to make out the translation of the next stanzas somehow before leaving Tambaram. It is as follows Shuk Maharshee says:

" I am describing a great miracle of knowledge of Kali Yuga. In spite of numerous misdeeds of miscreants against you, you pardoned them and accomplished the task for which future generations will revere your name till the end of the world. Your achievements will make them happy and feel satisfied. At this point there was a direction that before further reading you two should pay obeisance to Shiva and Vishnu in their respective temples.

When as per that directive we (myself and Sri. Raghunathan) carried out the command, the reading was resumed on 11-4-96. Therein Agastya rishi says, 'Your devotees worship you like their own parents. Oh great son ! who treats one and all equally, irrespective of age or education, who gives happiness to people. You are currently incarnated as Sai. As Satya Sai you are carrying out day and night your divine duty and uplifting people. He is none else but Dnyaneshwar incarnated.

Further reading was continued on 16-4-96. In that Vashishtha Maharishee says, "All enlightened souls are born as human beings as ordained by Shiva. Repeated perusals of the holy Dnyaneshwari will enable its readers and listeners attain spiritual-bliss and peace, that is the holy versified composition of spiritual discourses by Saint Dnyaneshwar on the epic Geeta.

I request readers of this book and the lovers of Naadi astrology to look for Naadi Pattis of outstanding personalities like Dnyaneshwar. Such persons for instance are Albert Einstein, Shakespeare, Hitler, Christ, Osho, Mahatma Gandhi etc.

Sri. Raghunathan has, on his own, tried to locate Naadi Pattis of Satya Sai Baba, Shirdi Sai Baba, Adi Shankaracharya, Bhagwan Buddha, and Ramkrishna Paramhansa etc. In looking for these Patties, Sri. Karunakaran has not demanded any money from me. He said that a perusal of the Naadi notings pertaining to those great personalities being a reward in itself he didn't wish to charge any fee for that pious task.

How could the Naadi Pattis of dead persons or of great souls such as Dnyaneshwar be located without their thumb impressions? may be a problem for many Naadi lovers. In this context, Dr. Karunakaran explained that they have some Patti bundles, which pertain to dead persons. There is a distinguishing mark on those Pattis. So one has to be cautious in tackling them. I communicated to Sri. Raghunathan by telephone whatever information I received from Prof. Gurav. After completing the daily routine at the Centre, he concentrated on that research. Dr. Karunakaran searched thorough a number of Pattis and brought out a bundle of 18-20 inches length Pattis. He then started perusing them one by one. There he located the Patti concerning Dnyaneshwar. When the names of Dnyaneshwara's parents and other points tallied, a notebook was made. And on the next day i.e. 2-4-96 afternoon again the reading began at 4.25 p.m. Sri. Raghunathan made notings. Wherever the Naadi bade that reading be stopped for the day, the reading would be stopped. Since the Naadi Patti is quite lengthy, I had to take 3 to 4 photographs of the same. Their enlargements could be made available. The Negatives are with Sri. Raghunathan.

The writer and translator of this Patti Sri. Raghunathan introduces himself as follows: -

"I am one of the many devotees of Sai Baba. I am a Vaishnav Brahmin over 60 years of age. I got voluntary retirement after working in the dockyard office in Chennai from 1967 to 1992. I have read a number of Tamil and Hindi books. I am working as translator in English and Hindi in the Naadi Centre of Dr.Karunakaran for the last seven-eight years. In a number of Naadis there is a mention that I was the elder brother of Saibaba of Shirdi."

❏

Astonishing Experience of the Prashna Kandam

QUESTION CHAPTER OF THE NAADI

Thousands of years ago some Maharishees, with their divine vision visualized the future of millions of unborn people and recorded it on Tadpatri in precise words. That record is known as "Naadi Astrology"

In Naadi Astrology, there is a mention of the name of the person concerned, names of mother, father, and husband/wife as also the Tithi of the birthday and the planetary situation at that time. In other forms of predictions names are not mentioned. Therefore to me Naadi astrology is a mind-boggling experience.

If the person whose Naadi-Patti is being read, desires to know specific details about future developments he may ask specific questions to obtain proper guidance from the Question chapter. That is the general nature of the question chapter. I had an opportunity to read the question chapter twice. My mind-boggling experience about that is as under -

I continued to frequently visit Naadi Centres for looking, first for my Naadi, then my wife's, then of my children and of relatives etc. I was obtaining and collecting more and more addresses of Naadi Centres. Since I knew Naadi-reader Sri. Rajendran, who started to work at the Vasishth Naadi Centre, I paid frequent visits to that centre.

Cricketeer Srinath expressed his desire to have his Naadi-reading. One afternoon, I called at the Naadi Centre to look for his Naadi Patti. Readers may wonder as to how I could acquire the cricketeer's thumb impression? It so happened that I had read in one newspaper that, cricketeer Navajyot Siddhu had obtained his Naadi-reading from the Agastya Naadi at Colombo, Sri Lanka during the free time he got when rains interrupted that test match there.

I felt inclined to meet him and know about his experience as also to help other players to obtain their Naadi prediction if they so desired. In October 1994, at the time of the India-West Indies One day Match, I was appointed as the head of gate management at Chepauk Stadium on behalf of the local Air Force station Tambaram. There I could contact the players. I managed to hand over a copy of my Naadi book to Sachin Tendulkar and Ajit Wadekar. Vishwanath already knew about Naadi astrology. Sachin did not seem interested. However, he motivated Atul Bedade and Javagal Srinath to give their thumb impressions. Veankatesh Prasad evinced considerable interest in the Naadi-reading. In a chat in the presence of all his colleagues, Navajyot Siddhu remarked, 'There is no cheating in Naadi-readings. In my case, there is a birth-sign on my back, about which I came to know from the Naadi-reading. Later my mother too confirmed it.' He was told that he would have a daughter, and that proven right. Later, in June 1996 he had a tiff with Azharuddin and others in England and returned to India. I was also curious to know whether the Naadi-reading had predicted the match-fixing rumpus!

After some months, on the occasion of a test match with New Zealand, Srinath inquired about Naadi astrology, revealing his interest in it. I could not locate Srinath's Patti, till I left Tambaram for Srinagar in May 1996.

Vinod Kambli told me that he had to obtain his father's permission for the Naadi-reading, while Azharuddin remarked that he doesn't believe anything other than Allah's blessings. Srinath's Naadi Patti could not be located.

Anyway, that day in that Naadi Centre after I had a cup of coffee. I felt fresh and since I had nothing important on hand I thought why not seek some answers from the Prashna Kandam, i.e. the question chapter. This time I thought I would change the Naadi readers.

I started noting down my questions. It was all a random noting. I wrote some questions in English as they occurred to me and gave them to a Naadi-reader. He recorded the date 22April 1995, time 4.05 p.m. and told me that he would look for the Patti after a few days. Even on that day I could not get the Naadi Patti of Srinath.

On 7th May 95, I called at the Vasishtha Naadi Centre. The afternoon was very hot. Sitting below the fan, after waiting for an hour, I was wondering why I was sitting there in search of answers. How Maharshee was suppose to understand my questions? Questions were in English. Though they were explained in general to Naadi-reader. He had no clue about the answers. How Vasistha Maharshee could have written down the answers at the time, when the questions were not conceived? Leave aside the questions, the person who was to pose those, had not taken birth on the Earth! Exhausted, I fell asleep. When I woke and moved out of the slumber, I noticed Arvinda swami the Naadi-reader coming with a bundle of Prashna Kandam. He then asked me to accompany him.

I was curious to know how answers to questions are located in the Prashna Kandam chapter. The method was to determine the Rashi and Lagnam on the afternoon of 22nd April 95. The day on which the question was conceived. It was Kanya (Virgo) Lagnam. Immediately a bundle was opened and within 10-20

Pattis, the proper Patti was identified. I was surprised. I had not imagined that within 5 minutes I would get answers to all my questions. To convince myself, I asked him, "how do you know that this is the Patti for my questions? He smiled and countered, "'Would you be sure if your name is mentioned in it?" "Of course," I said. He started reading. The second line contained the name of the questioner viz. Shashikant. I took that Patti in my hand. Since by practice I knew how the name is carved on the Patti, it did not take me much time to find my name recorded there, even though it was in archaic Tamil!

When the planetary positions on that tithi (date), in the Panchang at the time when the question was posed that mentioned in the Naadi tallied, the reading started.

Answer No. 1: This Naadi writing commenced during the Dwapar Yuga (Era).

That was in reply to my about the age of the Naadi Astrology Granth.

Answer No. 2: After the war the country of the questioner will rank number 2 in the world and its boundaries will expand.

My question was– 'What will be the position of India after the 3rd World War?'

Answer No. 5: The vastu (i.e. the building known as the Tajmahal) is the temple of Shiva since the ancient Treta Yuga (Era), and after some period it will again function as a Shiva Temple. (Though for the last few centuries it has been misunderstood to be a Muslim mausoleum)

The above answer pertained to my question as to when will the Tajmahal resume its role as a Shiva Temple?

Answer No. 4: After your sister's Shanti Deeksha and Jupiter's entry into Sagittarius (i.e. Dhanu Rashi) her business will prosper.

The question was - When would (my sister) Lata's business prosper?

The question regarding where would my next posting be? Remained un-answered.

It is proper that I convey to the readers the context of those questions, which I had posed so they may not be puzzled.

While dealing with Naadi astrology, I had always wondered that since the Naadi-reading mentions the exact age of the person seeking Naadi prediction, I would like to know the exact age of the Naadi itself.

"Ille Swami" (No, Sir) they would reply and stop, and if I insisted further they would say the answer would be available in the Prashna Kandam. That is why I had asked that question.

Now some readers may think that the Dwapar Yuga (era) is too vast and vague a period to which the compilation of the Naadi texts is attributed, since it is asserted that one day of Brahma (the creator) encompasses 432 crore human years!

According to me, it is accepted that the Kali Yuga started after the Mahabharat war. Accordingly the current Yugabda (Kali Era) Year is 5100. The Era Period prior to that was the Dwapar Yuga. So it may be safely assumed that Naadi Astrology compilation began 8 to 10 thousand years ago.

Why was there a vague answer to my question? This needs to be ascertained. The answer lies in my question itself. I had inquired about the age of Naadi and not about the date on which a particular jotting commenced. Naadi-writing was carried out by different rishis in different periods. Therefore a specific date cannot be given.

To my question No 2 the answer was not 'India ' but 'the native's country of the questioner'.

It is possible that what is currently known as India may have borne some other name in the past. So also there is no guarantee that the name of the country will be the same in future. I had posed a number of questions seeking clarifications on many such points, such as when would there be a third world war? Whether India would be involved in it? Whether India would come out of it successfully or get destroyed? What will be the future of India? What would be the status of India in the post war world? etc.

From the answers obtained it is clear that there will be a third world war. India will immerge from it successfully. And

India will be a No. 2 power in the world. Which means that compared to its present status India will become a big power and a respectable country in the world. The answer also adds that the boundaries of the country will expand.

The background of question No 5 is as follows: - The building currently known as the Tajmahal is famous as an example of outstanding architecture of the past. It is famous for its aesthetic excellence. It is believed to contain two cenotaphs in the name of his wife Arjumand banu and Shahajahan himself, and of other harem-women in annexes around. According to current history, it is believed that Shahajahan commissioned the Tajmahal. However, historians Sri. P. N. Oak, Sri. V.S. Godbole and others claim that the edifice existed centuries before Shahajahan. In order to use this construction for the purpose of his wife's memory he got it from Raja Jai Singh. Shahjahan plundered all the costly fixtures in the edifice and patched some Koranic extracts around the doorframes.

As per the discovery by Sri. P. N. Oak the term Tajmahal is a current malpronounciation of the ancient Sanskrit term Tejomahalaya connoting a Shiva Temple. It had fabulous fixtures such as silver doors on all its seven stories, a gold pitcher dripping water on the Shivalinga, a gem studded gold-railing around it and gems stuffed in the spacious octagonal lattice surrounding the gold railing. Raja Jai Singh the Maharaja of Jaipur (who was a vassal of the Mogul monarches) owned that fabulous-building located in the Mogul capital Agra. Emperor Shahjahan coveted that fabulous wealth. He therefore made the death of his wife Mumtaz as a pretext to grab the building, transport all its wealth to his treasury and bury her corpse in the central chamber, incongruously raising two cenotaphs for one corpse, to cover up the two Shivalingas consecrated in those two storyes.

Will that building continue to be mistaken as a fabulous mausoleum raised by Shahjahan for his wife Mumtaz or will the truth be established, that wonder monument was built as a Shiva Temple? I posed that question to seek an answer from the Naadi text.

The answer is that the shrine has existed there since very ancient times i.e. the Treta Yuga. That is altogether some new information we got from the Naadi. The word Ishwar in the Naadi refers to Shiva alias Shankar and not to Divinity in general. That was discussed among the Naadi-readers.

There was no answer to my question about my next posting. Members of my family were disappointed. However, as I interpret it, it is not that the Naadi makers did not know the answer but that the time had not yet come for me to know the answer.

Why do I rate the Prashna Kandam as a mind-boggling matter? Because it is natural for anyone to answer a question when asked. But here in the case of the Naadi the answer is already recorded. How could anyone imagine as to what questions would be asked after a thousand years? Moreover, I posed the questions in English. The Naadi-readers tried to grasp my questions in their Tamil language. They had no means or technique to communicate to the Naadi Maharshees the exact question in my mind. And yet the answers are ready in such a way that as soon as a question is asked the Naadi-reader reads out the answer within 5-7 minutes!

It is the experience of every inquirer that Naadi recorders had total omniscience of the past, present and future. In addition they could pre-conceive the questions that myriads of people would raise in the future, and therefore, their answers have been noted in the Naadi records!

I had one more occasion to read Prashna Kandam earlier at the Tambaram Naadi Centre. There was a difference of one year between the birth date of my wife and the one, which was noted in the Naadi. I inquired from her father and also at the hospital where she was born, and with that confirmation, when I asked the Naadi-reader why there was a difference of one year the answer given to me was that it was simply a mistake and was accepted.

However, it is also clarified that it was not a mistake of the Naadi author but a clerical mistake of the reader. Whenever the husband of the concerned person will ask such a question the Patti with that answer is ready. The Patti mentioning the actual birth date of his wife is also ready separately and will be read out at the proper time.

Accordingly on 7.1.95 I found my wife's correct birth-date and year noted in the Kaushik Naadi at the Tambaram Centre. The photograph of that Naadi and detailed description is reproduced in Chapter No.24

With regard to the Prashna Kandam the curious thing was that there were actually three Pattis dealing with my wife's birth date but those were located on three different occasions, only when the relevant questions about them arose. Had the Naadi Patti located on 7-1-95 been discovered earlier there wouldn't have been any confusion. But the patties are located only as ordained by Divinity. The Naadi authors aware of a mistake in the matter of a particular detail accept it sportingly. Moreover they also foresee that it is the husband who will come for a particular Patti, and not the concerned person herself! Therefore one more Patti is ready for the occasion when the wife arrives looking for it!

Now is that not very mind boggling?

❏

Naadi Astrology Defeats Blind Faith Eradication Committee !

The article quotes the opinions of respectable astrologers on, whether it is possible to cast a horoscope from the thumb impression and forecast the future. As for me however, after an in-depth study of Naadi Patties.

I have authored a small book in Marathi titled "Mind Boggling Experience - Naadi Astrology". Later my articles on the same topic were also published in the Hindi newspaper 'Rashtriya Sahara' (New Delhi), in the English magazine 'Star Teller' (Chennai) and in Gujrathi daily in 'Janmabhumi' (Mumbai). My booklet titled 'Naadi Jyotidum' was also published in Tamil in the year 1996.

Dr. Narendra Dabholkar who heads an organization, Superstition or Blind faith Eradication Committee, which pledged to eradicate superstition of people in Maharashtra, had his article published, criticizing Naadi astrology. He challenged me by name that he would pay Rs. 5 lakhs if the validity of Naadi astrology was proved to his satisfaction. In another magazine article, he dubbed my faith in Naadi texts as baseless, hoping that I would accept his challenge.

Readily accepting his challenge, I wrote a personal letter to him saying, "As per my experience Naadi astrology are miraculous written records of all future events. But your Blind Faith Eradication Committee has been denouncing my experience as unwarranted on the plea that no written documentary proof was ever presented to them. However, the written record of Naadi astrology Pattis can be produced even in a court of law. Therefore, the Blind Faith Eradication Committee's assertion is based only on its irrational assumption that the future can never be foretold; a view based only on faulty and far-fetched logic and bland adamance." It is because of their communication-skills, social status, and contacts with the newspaper world, that their articles and assertions are readily published under bold headings, while the articles or statements, which challenge their lies, get totally ignored and suppressed. As a result, in spite of the statements issued by the of Blind Faith Eradication Committee being totally false, readers believe in them and their body is considered respectable and prestigeous!

I don't claim to be a reader of Naadi astrology myself, since I don't know Tamil language. Yet as a kind of public service, I consider it to be my duty to inform the public of the unique compilation which foretells the names and roles of all humans anywhere and everywhere, and dispel the general impression of the uninformed that Naadi literature was a fraud. They should know on what grounds Dr. Dabholkar challenges me to prove the authenticity of Naadi assertions. It is for him to prove me wrong. Initially, I too carried the impression that Naadi literature was a fraud. However after visiting the Naadi centers time and again, and after closely examining all its aspects, I was convinced that it is a fact that detailed information about every human being's future is available in Naadi records and that it is something beyond the human imagination. Therefore, I have been suggesting through my correspondence with Dr. Narendra Dabholkar, Dr. Jayant Naralikar, (Internationally acclaimed astrophysicist) and others of the Blind Faith Eradication Committee that they should themselves come forward to ascertain the veracity of Naadi-readings. However it has been their habit to keep denouncing Naadi predictive records as a fraud avoiding personal verification.

In one of their articles they offered to send me 10 thumb impressions, which I should refer to the Naadi-readers, and convey their predictions. Thereafter they would publicly investigate those predictions and then if convinced the Blind Faith Eradication Committee would accept the claim of Naadi Astrology, even if 90 % of Naadi predictions were found to be correct. They would then wind up their movement in Maharashtra. That is a totally wrong approach. They are basically challenging me and at the same time they want me to look for Naadi-readings of their horoscopes. This is a snare, which would enable them to accuse me of conspiring to jot down the details about their lives as known to me and passing them on as Naadi predictions.

When they failed to entrap me that way, Dr. Dabholkar himself organized a press conference on 27 Sept. 1995 in Pune and got the news published in almost all the newspapers under the heading as 'Credibility of Bhrugu Samhita will be tested'! That news item stated that he; the organiser of the Blind Faith Eradication Committee, obtained the photographs of the Naadi Pattis from the Naadi Centre! (That was a total lie! In fact those photographs of Naadi Pattis concerning me were obtained and forwarded to Dr. Jayant Naralikar and Dr. Dabholkar by me!) The newspaper-item added, "Some Wing Commander Oak from Madras claims that the language of the Naadi Patti is Tamil." To prove that claim the B.F.E.C. had appealed to all the local Tamil-speaking people to attend the meeting to be held at Apte Prashala, in Pune City on 30.9.1995."

If the Tamilians among the audience assert that the language of the Patti is not Tamil then even without proceeding to Chennai for verification, Naadi astrology would be proved to be bogus. By sheer chance, I happened to be in Pune on that day, so I attended that meeting.

About 80 to 100 persons, including 3 or 4 news-reporters, a video cameraman of a local cable network 'Pune Varta' and some local workers and representatives of the Blind Faith Eradication Committee attended the meeting. However Dr. Dabholkar who had thrown the great challenge at the earlier news conference was himself absent! By chance three Tamil-speaking people attended the meeting because of the news they read in the local newspapers. At that meeting, they saw the photo and confirmed orally as well as in writing that the language in the Naadi Patti photo was indeed Tamil! However since it was an old and obscure Tamil they were not able to read it or explain its meaning. Thus that attempt of the Blind Faith Eradication Committee of denouncing the Naadi Pattis as fakes failed miserably and yet not a single newspaper carried any news of what transpired at the meeting! I personally conveyed the report of the meeting to 11 newspapers in Pune, but the news was conveniently suppressed. Although the appeal made was in Marathi, three Tamilians were present and they vouched that the language in the Naadi photo was Tamil. It was impossible for Dr. Dabholkar to denounce fallacy of the Naadi Pattis. However, blissfully unaware of my presence at that meeting, Dr. Dabholkar in his letter dated 14 Oct 95 made a totally false statement that, "not a single Tamilian could confirm the language in the photo to be Tamil!"

The Tamil language in the Naadi Patti being ancient, even Tamilians from Chennai are unable to decipher it. So it is no wonder that the Tamilians in Pune were also unable to do so. However if in the future they claim that I was behind the meeting as also in inviting the Tamilians I will not be surprised! Therefore I leave it to the public whether to believe Dr. Dabholkar or me!

A subsequent attempt by some supporters of B.F.E.C. in Satara on the eve of annual Astrological conference, to publicly burn horoscopes and almanacs (Panchang) to denounce the science of Astrology in general, as also Naadi Astrology in particular, proved a failure. Contrarily; a procession was organized, parading a donkey, labelled as Dabholkar and denouncing his opposition.

Prof. Adwayanand Galatge and I pursued the matter. We addressed many letters to Dr. Dabholkar. He got cheesed off of our persuasion. As a result Sri. Srikant Shah of Satara was deputed by him to Naadi Centers in Chennai to verify the predictions concerning the ten thumb impressions on behalf of the B.F.E.C.! But Shah himself was not interested in that investigation. He sought his own prediction. Therefore he did not bother about the Naadi Pattis concerning the Ten thumb impressions entrusted to him. He just handed over the packet of thumb impressions to the Naadi Centre and left. He happened to call on me, at my residence later. When I met him, he said that Naadi astrology is not something bogus as ascertained by him from the experience of the Naadi Patti of Sri. Ashok Akolkar of Mumbai who had accompanied him. I warned him that I would quote his appreciation in my future articles about the Naadi predictions that he had believed it to be a miracle. However, when Shah returned to Satara, he changed his mind and denied having made any statement in favour of Naadi! Thereupon, Dr. Dabholkar wrote to me that I should apologize to Shah and take up the work, which was left out by Shah! I wrote to him saying that I was not at all surprised at Shah proving a turncoat! Albeit on Dabholkar's loud boast that he would reward me with Rs. 5 lakhs, if I could prove, to his satisfaction, the veracity of Naadi astrology. I asked Dr. Dabholkar to arrive at Chennai with a demand draft of Rs. five Lakhs, Intending also to test the B.F.E.C.'s financial standing. Being involved in the service of public trust, I also requested him to confirm whether his B.F.E.C. was a registered Public Trust? If yes, then to send me registration number of his Committee, the bank a/c. number and the latest audited Balance Sheet so that the public may come to know whether the B.F.E.C. really possesses funds of that order with them? I also added that I had the moral right to get those necessary details. I also demanded that he send me the audited Balance Sheets for the last 3 to 4 years along with the statements of amounts received and payments made for the challenges he had thrown to other persons earlier. To avoid admitting his ignominious defeat in the matter of Naadi Predictions, he failed to furnish me the required details. He has even discontinued all correspondence then on as if he has nothing to do with the Naadi astrology controversy started by him! One Sri. A. B. Karveerkar from Kolhapur also threw a similar challenge through his article published in the Marathi daily Pudhari ,but none of the B.F.E.C. following responded. Readers of this book are requested to demand an explanation from Dabholkar and his associates and communicate to me their response if and when received.

On 18.2.96, I went to Dabholkar's dispensary as well as his house in Satara to try to persuade him to come to verify Naadi astrology. However I could not meet him and he too did not bother to write to me.

However his organization continues to campaign against Naadi Predictions. They posed one more challenge to me through one Sri. M. S. Risbud. He had a grouse against me, because I had refused to oblige him in tracing the Naadi Pattis for some of his relations. It has been my standard practice not to accept anybody's request to furnish him his or her Naadi Predictions. More so in his case because he was trying to challenge the Naadi Predictions. I told him that I should not be involved in the process of tracing his Naadi Patti leaf. However, I must be present to oversee that he does not play foul with the Naadi-readers! Yet, without verifying, he came out with some mathematical calculations concluding that if a certain number of people have read their Naadi Pattis in 2000 years, the total time required for writing of Naadi Patties would be multi-million days; therefore as per common sense Naadi Pattis are bogus. According to him those who go to visit Naadi-centres to have their future read are fools. He has also got his letter to the editor published in the Pune Marathi-Daily Sakal, questioning the dependability of Naadi Predictation. Sakal however played a partisan role in not publishing my rejoinder. Since Naadi is a subject much beyond the scope of mathematics and logic, the mathematical formula presented in the letter is not applicable to Naadi astrology at all. His other objection was to the fact that as soon as the Naadi patties are read, why are they tied up in a bundle and kept away in the cupboard, instead of handing them over to the respective seeker? However, since this was a matter for Naadi Shastris to answer I asked him to get the needful explanation from a Naadi Shastri. My suggestion that he better personally test the dependability of Naadi astrology, he avoided on the pretext of ill health!

The same Sri. Risbud in another letter denounced, a staunch rationalist and non-believer Sri. B. Premanand for his article on his experience of Naadi Predictions in India Skeptic Jan 1996 issue. Sri. Risbud wondered that in spite of playing foul i.e. changing of names of the persons, how did he accept that the past Naadi Predictions came true? And if so, why Sri. B. Premanand kept silence about that!

A scholar of English and Philosophy, Dr N.R.Varhadpande of Nagpur, in his bitter reaction to my communication wrote, "I did not read the material you mailed to me fully nor do I wish to peruse it even in the future It does not deserve any serious consideration". He added, 'Prima facie' it was all lunatic nonsensical talk and therefore a sheer waste of time and money, which lacks merit enough even to put it to any scientific test!" On reading that reply, I quoted an observation by Saint Ramdasa, the Guru of Shivaji Maharaja that a person who expresses an opinion without considering all pros and cons is a damn idiot. Moreover what authority has he to sit in judgment and decide the case of Naadi astrology as something to be totally condemned? Now it is for the readers to decide whether to accept the opinion of those who have personally verified the veracity of Naadi Predictions or of those who condemn Naadi predictions as baseless nonsense without any verification.

Sometime later, in Pune I addressed the Rotary Club of Parvati on 'Naadi Astrology: Some misunderstanding'.

Thereafter, one Sri. Omkar Patil of Satara was deputed by the scoffers to visit the Naadi center at Tambaram. He happened to see me talking to some Marathi-speaking persons there. Yet he had no courage to introduce himself and no guts to discuss the matter with me. Later I came to know that the real reason for the same was that he did not want to divulge his reaction to me! He feared that I might test his anti- Naadi conclusion in the Naadi Centre itself and he would have no evidence to prove the B.F.E.C.'s point of view. Thus he conveniently avoided talking to me so that he could write something contrary to the favourable experience of many people. Imagine the honesty of an organization which had thrown a Rs. 5 lakh challenge at me and yet their representative not caring or daring to talk to me!

In the 13July 96 issue of Saptahik Sakal, a Marathi weekly, carried an article headed *'Naadi Bhavishya-yet another cheating Business'*! Dr. Dabholkar had also earlier contribeteded another article titled *'The fraud business of Vastu Shastra Experts'* condemning the principles of Vastu Shastra as humbug.

My reaction to that other article published in the Sakal issue dated August 3, 1996 read as under: -

"NAADI ASTROLOGY NEEDS TO BE RESEARCHED"

As the author of the book titled *"Naadi Bhavishya"*, I am enclosing herewith my rejoinder to the article headed *'Naadi Bhavishya-Yet Another cheating Business'* published in your 13 July 96 issue.

1. Although the article heading dubs Naadi Predictions as a cheating business, no concrete accusations or allegations have been made in the article to prove it. Sri. Omkar Patil had earlier paid a visit to the Naadi Centre, however he did not prove anything except vaguely mentioning that the possibility of cheating cannot be totally ruled out. That is an unjustified observation.

2. The article quotes the opinions of respectable astrologers on, whether it is possible to cast a horoscope from the thumb

impression and forecast the future. As for me however, after an in-depth study of Naadi Patties, I can confidently say that the Naadi Prediction is not based on the thumb impressions or the horoscopes made out from them. The thumb impression only helps locate the relevant Naadi Patti. It is useful to carry one's horoscope to tally with the one cast from the thumb impressions.

3. Although Dr. Narendra Dabholkar, organizer of the Blind Faith Eradication Committee alleges that I am lauding Naadi Astrology without testing it scientifically, why is he conveniently ignoring my appeal made in person as also through letters, from time to time, asking him to visit Chennai and test a Naadi Patti from 7 different angles? Why is he making an irrelevant and unscientific demand that I should find out the predictions for ten thumb impressions even when they stake a challenge of Rs. 5,00,000/-? I have already ascertained the veracity and accuracy over numerous thumb-impressions. It is upto them now to satisfy themselves.

4. Sri. Omkar Patil is the only person from my opponents' camp who has expressed his opinion after personally visiting the Naadi Centre. However, he has not categorically clarified whether he verified from the Naadi Patti the names of his own, his parents and wife carved in the Patti? Dr. Dabholkar also does not clarify whether his Blind Faith Eradication Committee had done it.

5. Scientifically tested the Naadi Pattis based on ten thumb impressions, or whether the Naadi Pattis were at least sought, obtained and read out?

6. A librarian by profession Sri. V.L.Manjul has hastily concluded that the script and the language of the Naadi Patti 'appear to be English'! He has quoted a statement to that effect from a book by one Sri. Oza. It would have been more appropriate for him to get the script read out by those knowing ancient Tamil or inquire from Sri. Oza whether he could read the contents.

7. Anybody who cheats takes utmost care to ensure that no proof, which will expose him, is left behind for the customers. On the contrary, the matter in the Naadi Pattis is transcribed in simple Tamil in a notebook as also a tape recording is handed over to the customer as permanent proof. Moreover, one may also take a photograph of the desired Naadi Patti. If making money is the alleged motive, then what about the Kak Bhujandar Naadi Centre of Ramani Guruji and the Shuka Markandeya Naadi Centre of Sri. Kumar, where predictions are offered free of charge besides a dispensary run by them providing free medicines to the ailing needy!

The B.F.E.C. has been merely beating about the bush all these years, instead of actually seeking and testing the veracity of Naadi predictions in a positive manner rather than negating. "Upto now the B.E.Committee has been merely denouncing Naadi forecasts asserting, 'what it is not'. But now the time has come to find out 'what it is'. That is not my observation but those of the editorial written by Dr. Pradip Patkar in the March-April 1995 issue of the newsletter of the Blind Faith Eradication Committee itself. So, when is the committee going to act on that suggestion ? Is it not possible for Dr. Dabholkar to take Dr. Naralikar with him and visit the Naadi Centres at Tambaram and elsewhere to find out 'what Naadi prediction actually is' to satisfy themselves? Retired Principal Adwayanand Galatge, a rationalist by approach wrote five letters to Dr. Jayant Naralikar suggesting he take the lead to ascertain the truth about Naadi astrology. He or Dr. Dabholkar and their supporters never came forward for scientific tests of Naadi records! Thus in a way they have accepted defeat at the hands of Naadi Maharshees!

It is upto the readers of this book to accept my statement or that of the Blind faith Eradication Committee. All those who tend to condemn Naadi Astrology as something bogus are requested to test it themselves before coming to any conclusion. ❑

Naadi Astrology– a Hoax? Naadi Astrology & Dr. Jayant Naralikar

I have full confidence that readers will give due recognition to my translation and transliteration efforts as an unbiased and inquisitive seeker of the truth.

My Marathi book titled "Mind Boggling Miracle – Naadi Bhavishya" got overwhelming response from all parts of Maharashtra. In that I mentioned that I was desperately trying to understand the basis of Naadi recordings. How thousands of years back, in most primitive conditions the Maharshees, whose names we read only in story books could foresee the life spans of the millions of people, who ware yet to be born? How many Naadis are available? Where? A person from armed forces background who had no connection or basic knowledge of astrology began to seek answers from all possible places.

Many others who had visited Naadi Centres had sincerely narrated their mind-boggling experience of their own Naadi Predictions. Many thanked me for expounding the topic, which generally is not discussed in public. One curious reader Sri. Sonya Bapu Kumbhojkar suggested that in Maharashtra there ware many personalities of repute such as Dr. Jayant Naralikar who did not believe in astrology and other predictive methods. They strongly condemned it as a hoax. Since we regard them as authorities in certain subjects we, the general public, get confused about whom to believe! Why don't you meet Naralikar and convince him about Naadi astrology, some people advised me.

So in Dec 1994, on Sri. Kumbojkar's suggestion, I managed to hand over a copy of the book to Dr. Jayant Naralikar. In a soft voice he agreed to read it and convey his opinion on the subject.

After a month, I received a letter (Please refer Letter No.1 on page 165) stating that, he being a non-believer in any predictive methods he does not believe in the Naadi predictions. However, as a true scientist he suggested that a thousand or two thousand cases of Naadi records be examined for scientific research. In response, I requested him to come forward for scientific research so that the findings would receive requisite importance and recognition in the scientific world and in addition would get the backing of expert human resources and finance available at your disposal. To arouse his curiosity, I mailed two photographs of Naadi leaves pertaining to my name so that he could locate my name "Shashikant" from it, through his Tamil-knowing friends. In the end, I requested him to send his thumb-impression if he so desired to locate his leaf with notebook, tape etc, as a special case. But it was not to be. Dr. Jayant Naralikar returned the photographs with a covering letter (Please refer letter No.2 on Page 140) stating that he could neither locate the word "Shashikant" nor could confirm the script as Tamil on the leaf by any of his Tamil-knowing friends. Therefore he considered it to be a hoax and left it to be relied on by the believers.

Now it was incumbent on my part as a responsible author of this book to establish from the photograph of the leaf what Dr. Naralikar had certified as a hoax, to prove beyond doubt that it was not so. Therefore I got the entire photograph read line by line from the Tamilian experts who could read the coded script and got it translated in English with its Tamil pronunciation in Roman script. (Please refer matter shown below and for photograph see page no. 17)

ENLARGED PHOTOGRAPH OF NAADI LEAF
with Tamil & English line by line translation

Line No.	Tamil writing in roman script	Line No.	English meaning
1.	kantan (KE SHASHI KANTHA PETATHA) kum	1.	husband's name shashikant
2.	yo (KAM MEL ENNA) vannam	2.	Fortune more, unexpected way
3.	kal (UYARAYUL PELAPE) rumal	3.	long life name and fame
4.	se (IGHI YADHA THA) dai	4.	Actions deeds hurdles
5.	seikau (KKUS AWASTHAI PI) ni	5.	Children problem disease
6.	perthil (LA VANAKAL PO) kka	6.	Perform remedial measures
7.	saithidamel (KARI VANAKKMA A) wani	7.	Pray to (Lord) Sani
8.	ve (THREE MIGHUM YO) ghan	8.	Success increase chance
9.	Kan(THANUKKU THELIVU THO) ndu	9.	husband strong clear job

Note:- The Capital letters in the bracket are clearly seen in the photograph. The letters out side the bracket are for reference. The English translation is given for every word. Hence broken meaning can be derived. Tamil knowing persons may not be able to read the script but it is expected that with the help of the pronunciations provided, they will be able to understand general meaning and exactly locate my name.

Here I request readers to kindly get the same verified from their Tamil knowing friends. Let me caution the readers, as I did Dr. Naralikar, that many times even a good Tamil speaking person finds it difficult to read or locate my name in the photograph (It is on the first line between two marked dots). Many may not even understand which way to hold the photograph! But with the help of the meaning and the pronunciation produced side by side many Tamilians would be able to locate my name and grasp some letters or lines.

I have full confidence that readers will give due recognition to my translation and transliteration efforts as an unbiased and inquisitive seeker of the truth.

Now it has been ascertained that the script of Naadi records is in cryptic Tamil code-words etched without lifting the nail like sharp instrument. However many readers who have yet to undergo the amazing experience may suspect that the Naadi-reader may be extracting the required information from the seekers and somehow putting it in the leaf to read out the same, as if it was noted on the leaf. But that is not possible, since the leaf-packets are interlined with a string passing through a hole in every leaf and are opened infront of the seeker. It is not possible to fill any details in some blank spaces and cheat the customers as propagated by Dr. Abraham Kovoor. Of course, those who had some acquaintance with Naadi predication will understand the futility of that argument, which is generally put forth by so called rationalists.

Those who have yet to undergo the amazing experience will have to personally verify it to believe in it.

Whom will you believe?

Dr. Naralikar who considers astrology to be a hoax, without visiting any Naadi Centre and getting his own life read in the Naadi records. He is unfamiliar with the Tamil script and has to depend on some Tamilians who were unable to decode the script? Or he who has got the photos interpreted by the experts and presented to the readers in public? I leave the readers to judge.

One of the persons with whom I got introduced as the author of the Naadi book was a retired principal "Adwayanand Galatge" from Bhoj (Belgaum) Karnataka. He was an experimenting rationalist. He has written books on physics, parapsychology and on occult sciences. He regards those Naadi predictions as products of the divine power of ancient Maharshees. He felt that the response to Naadi records from Dr. Naralikar and the treatment given to Naadi records by Dr. Naralikar was quite lukewarm and non-committal. He therefore entered into correspondence with Dr. Naralikar, and addressed five letters. Dr. Naralikar responded to his first letter in a short and curt manner stating that he disagrees with Galatge on what science stands for. In spite of repeated efforts by Sri. Galatge to enthuse, Dr. Naralikar to come forward for a scientific test of Naadi records the latter preferred to keep silent! After waiting for a long time Sri. Galatge and myself requested even Dr. Narendra Dabholkar of B.F.E.C. to accompany us to Naadi centers in Chennai in Dec 98 to which he never responded. The Naadi leaf of Galatge was located. It contained his name and those of his parents and wife, with other accurate details. What surprised him the most was that Naadi Maharshee, Saint Agastya had stated that Galatge had come to verify the scientific basis of the predictions, accompanied by a person called 'Shashikant'! Let us hope that the rationalist organizations and the individuals who look down upon the Naadi as a hoax will come forward to undertake scientific research and also explore the possibility of divining those predictions about the future of mankind, by the present-day man with advanced technology and modern machines at their disposal.

Reproduced herewith is the correspondence with Dr. Jayant Naralikar which will throw more light on the subject.

Letter No. 1

From: Dr. Jayant Naralikar To Wing Commander Shashikant Oak stating his views on the book Naadi Bhavishya.

Dear Wing Commander Shashikant Oak,

Thanks for providing me a copy of your booklet on Naadi predictions. The book narrates your personal experience. I have never experienced the Naadi predictions. However, due to the following reasons my standpoint is of a non-believer:

1. Till now, I have never come across a single case of predictions, which proved to be exactly true. Even your own experience and of others' instances quoted in your book also point to the same conclusion.

2. Much talked about predictions by Nostradamus, clothed in esoteric phraseology, are usually wishfully twisted and interpreted as uncanny forecasts of certain subsequent happenings. They appear to have been inferred as the truth when the actual happening are compared with the uttering of Nostradamus. The same is the case with Naadi predictions.

3. It is impossible to imagine that Naadi records on palm leaves are already available for all human beings born or unborn. Even if it is presumed that those forecasts are true, then in that case based on the number of Naadi leaves one should be able to foretell the population of India in year 2000, 2010, 2050 etc.

4. If it is presumed that some body's predictions have been recorded in advance, then why is one asked to propitiate the gods to ward off evil predictions? Here it constitutes a head-on collision of two superstitions.

5. If the scientific veracity of predictions on palm leaves is to be established it cannot be based on testing merely on my sample of past and future alone. A thousand or two thousand samples of Naddi readings will have to be possibly investigated, based on objective parameters before arriving at any conclusion.

Yours truly,
(Jayant Naralikar)

Letter No. 2

Reply from Wing Commander Oak to Dr. Jayant Naralikar

Date: 2nd Feb 1995.

Dear Dr. Jayant Naralikar,

Received your letter dated 16 Jan 1995, commenting on my book "Naadi Bhavishya, and revealing that you hold a view of disbeliever about fortune telling in general.

I agree that it is impossible to predict the exact happenings of anybody's entire life, be it by any type of predictive-methods, such as Palmistry, Astrology, Ramal and Numerology. Limitations of human intellect will never enable accurate prediction of every event in every person's life. That is why before being introduced to Naadi predictions, I also held a similar opinion and therefore was not keen to consult them. Later when I happened to encounter Naadi Prediction accidentally, with its most accurate personal details such as names of parents, wife, and myself, Date, Month, Year of Birth and my horoscope etched on palm leaves, my opinion changed. That experience made me look upon Naadi as a miracle! Whether Naadi Predictions prove true or not, is not important to me. But the incessant quest to trace the secrets behind the miracle of Naadi records, is what interests me.

Based on available information, I concluded that Naadi recording had no relation with the predictive methods of astrology. It is not based on the principles of compilations of data, experience and assumptions, etc. It is based on every Maharshee's meditative powers, which could visualise the future of all human beings. Therefore Naadi predictions are beyond the grasp and scope of human intellect and logic.

Predictions by Nostradamus are in cryptic and mysterious language. When an incident takes place, its befitting description with some stanzas amuses the reader. But Naadi predictions, on the contrary mention the precise name of the seeker, the date, day, month and year of birth and other details etched out on palm leaves. So they do not just amuse a seeker but pose a challenge to his rationale. Thus it is superior to the much-talked about predictions of Nostradamus.

You are absolutely right that it is impossible to record predictions about every person's past, present and future. But may be that the records are meant only for those who have been destined to seek them. There may be many persons available at all times who due to want of time, money, disbelief or other reasons may not be keen to seek them. Maharshee's might have omitted those! However, my experience is that whosoever goes to seek Naadi predictions does get his or her leaf sooner or later.

I am very keen to know through the Naadi records the future of regions, nations and of the human race. In some Naadi-notings I have been told that in due course of time I will be able to get answers. What must have been the underlying divine purpose to undertake such a painstaking manual effort of such a gigantic magnitude of millions of inconsequential individuals? May be that the welfare of human kind might have been the driving motive behind those divine writings. But then what is the reason for omitting the future of communities and nations? May be that those Maharshee's thought that it will not be prudent or helpful for the progress of mankind?

As rightly pointed out by you, notings on palm leaves need to be examined on a scientific basis. It is beyond the scope of my intelligence and prudence. A person of your stature and international repute as an astrophysicist should undertake the research concerning Naadi records, so that the research may get due recognition, status and financial and other support.

I will be ever-ready to extend my full co-operation and support to such research. Especially till such time as I am posted in Tambaram (Chennai) I will be able to take part in the research. Enclosed herewith is a photograph of a Naadi leaf and another enlarged picture of the same containing the name 'Shashikant' etched on the leaf. You could get it read by Tamil- knowing persons. Kindly return both photographs at the earliest. I earnestly desire to seek your Naadi leaf. Due to your busy schedule if you are unable to spare time please send your thumb impression and other relevant details. I will search out your leaves and send the predictions with notebook, cassette and photographs pertaining to your Naadi leaf.

In spite your busy schedule, you have been kind enough to communicate to me your views about my book, I am extremely thankful for the same.

Yours sincerely,
(Shashikant Oak)

Letter No. 3

First letter from Prin. Adwayanand Galatge to Dr. Jayant Naralikar

Date: 26ᵗʰ June 1995

Dear Sir,

This letter is occasioned by Wing Commander (Madras) Sri. Shashikant Oak's handing over to me, in person, his book on Naadi (in Marathi) along with the correspondence he has carried on with you and with Dr. Dabholkar of Satara. I am writing this letter to you, because I hold you in high esteem and above all, as a serious scientist and not merely as an internationally reputed astrophysicist. Also I admire your bold and unconventional views on the origin of the universe. I think progress in science more often results from rebelling against the views of the establishment, which in no way are sacrosanct. This same rebellious spirit is to be recommended in all fields of science both academic and non-academic, in pursuit of truth. I need not stress that science harbours and promotes the spirit of free inquiry. It is open to all sorts of investigations. It loses its raison d'etre as science, the moment it loses this open-ness and this spirit of free inquiry. I am saying this, because your two letters written to Sri. Oak (Dated. 16ᵗʰ Jan. & 21ˢᵗ Mar. 95) are sadly disappointing in this respect. Your letters create the impression that you hold Sri. Oak as a highly gullible person, on whom a big hoax has been perpetrated.

But consider the following facts: Sri. Oak is not an ordinary 'run-of-the-mill' person, but holds a highly responsible Govt. post in our country's defence services. Besides, he is highly educated and a cultured person. He has no natural inclination for astrology; but his curiosity about it was roused by his accidentally stumbling upon a fact, which prima facie defies all logic and common-sense, - a fact for whose verification he has not hesitated to approach an internationally famed scientist like you. These facts clearly speak of his honesty and his serious intent and purpose. Besides, he had produced hard evidence for science to examine and on its basis, to determine the worth of the claims he has made. Those claims cannot be easily dismissed as meriting no scrutiny, if science is to be taken as a serious and disinterested pursuit of truth. Clearly Sri. Oak has not been given a fair trail, which he rightly deserves.

I, therefore, make an earnest appeal to you -

1. To invite, through the columns of major local English Newspapers as many Tamil-knowing people, to come forwards for reading the Naadi text of Sri. Oak. (As many as possible because Sri. Oak says that he himself has found some Tamil-knowing persons, who were unable to read the text. This is natural, considering that the texts are very old. At present the copy of Oak's text is with Dr. Dabholkar.)

2. This reading of the Naadi text should be done on an appointed date and time and at a pre-selected place, publicly. i.e. the session after due publicity through newspapers, should be thrown open to all those who are interested. (The members of the Andh.(ashraddha) Nirm.(ulan) Sam.(iti) may attend it, but not participate in it; nor will their prize of Rs. 5 lakhs be made a precondition of the investigation or its result, with a view to pre-empt the issue being unnecessarily emotionally overcharged. Let only the disinterested spirit of science prevail.

3. If the results are negative, the matter will rest there. But if the results are positive, an appeal should be made through

major science journals to come forward for further scientific investigation by other scientists of the country, of the Naadi phenomenon, whose over-all supervision and conduct will be, done by you and you alone.

This is how science works, and should work. Science is public. Let the Naadi phenomena be proved publicly a hoax, if it a hoax. And if the claims of Sri. Oak are ultimately substantiated, let science in its mission as a truth-seeker freely accept the results and incorporate them in its menagerie for their eventual 'taming' and 'naturalisation'. The truth of Naadi phenomenon cannot be regarded as repudiation of all orthodox science any more, the Einstein theory of photoelectric effect can be regarded as repudiation of Thomas Young's Wave theory of light. I earnestly hope my appeal to you does not fall on deaf ears, and give room for history to repeat itself. I need not remind you how the rationalists of Galileo's time with their own pre-conceived theory of the universe, refused to look into his telescope, for fear of being confronted with "brute and stubborn facts" as is amply demonstrated by Galileo in his "Dialogues on the Two Systems of the worlds".

Awaiting and thanking you in anticipation of, a line in reply.

Sincerely yours

(Adwayanand Galatge)

Copy to: 1 Sri. Shashikant Oak, Tambaram (Madras)
2 Dr. Narendra Dabholkar, 118, Sadashiv Peth, Satara. Pin 415 001.
3 Sri. Kumbhojkar, Sangli

Post Script:
1. Your comments that a thousand or two thousand samples of Naadi-readings will have to be investigated for establishing scientifically its veracity is not only a counsel of despair but a highly questionable proposition. How can you forget that only one sample of test on total solar eclipse in 1919 was considered as sufficient evidence in support

of Einstein's General Theory of Relativity? (Let verification of Naadi be regarded as a test of Hindu "Theory of Space, Time as Thought-constructs"). We cannot forget that all scientific revolutions have been historically wrought by a single (one sample) experiment (or tests) like Galileo's expt. of two falling bodies, Young's double-slight expt. on light, Michelson Morleys' expt. on ether's existence, Mendel's cross-breeding expt. on garden peas etc. etc.

2. Your assertion that propitiation of gods to ward off evil predictions constitutes head-on collision of two superstitions, is also uncalled-for in fact, that it is exactly what is to be investigated and proved by a scientific method (namely, that they are superstitions)

Letter No. 4

Dr. Naralikar's terse reply to Prin. Galatge

Ref. : JVN/95-96/   Date: July 3rd,
1995

Prin. Adwayanand Galatge (Retd.)
Bhoj., Belgaum–591263. Karnataka

Dear Principal Galatge,

Thank you for your letter of June 26, 1995. It seems from your letter that there is a considerable gap between our relevant perceptions of what science stands for and what the scientific outlook is all about. My own views on the matter raised by Wing Commander Oak have been quite explicit and I do not wish to elaborate them further here.

Yours Sincerely,
(J. V. Naralikar)

Letter No. 5

Principal Galatge's 2nd request letter to Dr. Naralikar

Date : 10th July 1995

Prof. Jayant Naralikar,
Director, IUCAA, Pune – 7
Dear Sir

Thank you for your kind letter of 3rd July 95 in which you have said that, "There is a considerable gap between our relevant perceptions of what science stands for". It must, however, be pointed out that the issue raised by Wing Commander Oak's 'Naadi' evidence, does not at all hinge on any fine perception of what science stands for. **Consider the following three questions, which must be answered irrespective of the niceties about what science stands for:**

1. Does not the finding of the name of a 20th Century person, with correct information about many of his personal details, inscribed on the ancient palm leaf of 'Naadi' constitute a grave challenge to the belief system of Western science, unless a big fraud is involved here?

2. In the latter case don't you consider it your bounden duty and responsibility as a reputed scientist to expose this fraud **publicly,** for the health of western science, unless you wish to renege that science altogether?

3. Is it your case that any facts that threaten to undermine the foundation of Western science should be conveniently disregarded as simply not existing?

This Challenge of Naadi phenomenon is too serious, Sir, to be brushed aside by having recourse to the niceties about what science stands for. Any failure on your part to meet this challenge boldly and courageously will be tantamount to accepting defeat in the face of what Galileo has called, "Irreducible and stubborn facts", that thus lapsing into the untenable position of his rationalist adversaries, who stand refuted by the history of science. This is a prospect, which no serious scientist will contemplate.

What is even worse, avoiding meeting the challenge by some subterfuge will create the impression that, being already convinced about the truth of 'Naadi' phenomenon, you are searching for some pretext to avoid public denigration of Western science. This fear of denigration, however, is misplaced, as is simply made clear by the strange and irrational ways of Quantum Mechanics.

I, therefore, still hope to receive a positive response from you.

Thanking you,

Sincerely yours,
(Adwayanand Galatge)

Copy to Wing Commander Shashikant Oak, Tambaram (Madras)

Letter No. 6
Prin. Galatge's third letter to Dr. Jayant Naralikar

Date: 21ˢᵗ Oct. 1995

Dear Sir,

In continuation of my previous letter on the subject of Naadi, I write to inform you that the suggestion made by you in that letter (viz. The 'Superstition Eradication Committee' on 30th Sep. has unwittingly carried out the public verification of the Naadi text) in the city of Pune itself. On that date, in pursuance of the public call given by Dr. Dabholkar through Newspapers, people in large numbers gathered at Apte High School at 7 p.m. to satisfy their curiosity about the Naadi text. Strangely enough, Dr. Dabholkar the central figure, himself was found to be conspicuously absent on that occasion. However three Tamil speaking persons fortunately presented themselves at the venue after reading in newspapers about the public exhibition of the Naadi text. Although, for obvious reasons, they could not read the name 'Shashikant' in the enlarged photocopy of the Naadi text, they at least could vouch for the script as being explicitly Tamil, (A copy of their testimony to that effect under their signatures with their addresses is enclosed herewith)

Now that at least three persons from Pune itself, could publicly recognize the script as Tamil, as against your contention to the contrary, you will, I hope, admit that there are possibly some persons in Madras and elsewhere, who have the necessary expertise and skill to read that old Tamil clearly and meet the scientific criteria of proper verification of the Naadi text. In a true scientific spirit, therefore, you will, I still hope, initiate appropriate steps to further explore the subject with an open mind and without any prejudice, to scientifically establish the truth or otherwise of the Naadi phenomenon. At least, there is now no reason, apart from that of your unwillingness, to wash your hands off the subject as a scientist.

Pending your initiation and execution of an appropriate plan for further scientific investigation of the Naadi phenomenon, it will not be unfair, in the light of the proven genuineness of the Naadi text, to expect you to withdraw your earlier charge against the Naadi text as hoax by means of a proper press release. This is the minimum obligation that true allegiance to science requires.

Thanking you,

Sincerely yours,
(Adwayanand Galatge)

Copy to: 1. Dr. Narendra Dabholkar, Satara.

2. Sri. Shashikant Oak, Tambaram, Madras.

Post script: Sri. Oak himself was present at the said exhibition and he again made a public appeal at the exhibition to all concerned to come to Madras for the scientific investigation of the Naadi, by offering to extend, all kind of help and co-operation. If his appeal is still not headed, all those who make wild and baseless charges against the Naadi as was done, for example by Dabholkar in his press release on 29th Aug. stand condemned and exposed (He alleged, without any proof, that the Naadi poses a danger to society).

Letter No. 7
Prin. Galatge's fourth letter to Dr. Jayant Naralikar
Date: 12th Nov. 1995

Dear Sir,

I am writing this letter to seek a clarification from you of a point raised by Sri. Dabholkar's letter of 14th Oct. 95, addressed to Sri. Oak. In para no. 5 of this letter (written in Marathi) he says that your insistence on a very large number of samples (viz. One or two thousand individuals) for the scientific verification of the Naadi text is prompted by your desire to obviate fraud. (Copy of his letter is enclosed herewith in confirmation of this). If this is the reason why you insist on a very large number of samples, I would like to know from you how fraud is obviated by having a large number of samples, since fraud is, in principle, possible in any number of samples, considering that the same time-gap may be involved in each individual case of locating and reading the Naadi text, and Dabholkar is avowedly willing to allow any number of days for the completion of the Naadi-reading of the concerned individuals of those samples (vide his letter)

If you do not agree with Dabholkar's view of your reason for insisting on a very large number of samples, I will be expecting you to write a letter to him, endorsing a copy thereof to me, withdrawing your reliance on him for exposing the Naadi 'hoax' scientifically, in view of the fact that he has no clear or proper understanding of the scientific procedure of the investigating of the Naadi text. Moreover, he does not explain why he relies on 10 or 100 samples, which in his own view, facilitates fraud, whereas, according to you, one or two thousand samples are required. **He also does not explain why he relies on Sri. Oak, avowedly a partisan of Naadi Bhavishya, for the scientific investigation of the Naadi texts.** Sri. Dabholkar is thus, the most unfit person for carrying out the scientific investigation of the Naadi phenomenon. May I hope you will either repudiate him for carrying out this job or persuade him to personally undertake the investigation strictly on scientific lines?

Thanking You,

Yours Sincerely
(Adwayanand Galatge)

Copy to: 1. Sri. Shashikant Oak, Tambaram, Madras
2. Sri. Narendra Dabholkar, Satara.

Letter No. 8

Prin. Adwayanand Galatge's fifth letter to Dr. Jayant Naralikar.
Bhoj (Belgaum) 591 263, Karnataka   Date: 28th
Nov 1995

To,
Sri. Jayant Naralikar,
Director, IUCAA, Pune–411 007
Dear Sir,

Despite my sincere appeal to you through my four previous letters to undertake a scientific investigation of the Naadi phenomenon, first brought to your notice personally by Wing Commander Sri. Shashikant Oak. I have not received any response from you till today except the terse reply letter of 3rd July 95, stating that there is a considerable, gap between our relevant perceptions of what science stands for. If this alleged difference of perception of science between us were the sole reason for your not responding, then at least my letter of 10th July 95 appealing to you to undertake the investigation from the very stand-point of Western perception of science which you espoused, should have evoked a positive response from you. The non-response even to that letter forces me to conclude that Western Science does not care a hoot for such a phenomenon as Naadi. If it cares anything at all, it cares to expose the hoax that it presumes Naadi to be. Your endorsement to Sri. Dabholkar, the Chief of Andhashraddha Nirmulan Samiti, the copy of the letter of 21st March 95 addressed to Sri. Oak, in which you have chosen to call Naadi a hoax, confirms this conclusion.

Now, presuming Naadi to be a hoax, and also presuming that your endorsement of the said letter to Sri. Dabholkar's is intended to throw on him the responsibility of exposing this hoax, one cannot but suppose that you rely on his, (or his Samiti's) scientific credentials and competence for the task of exposing this hoax, or if they lack these, you guide them to do the job on strictly scientific lines. This is exactly what I have requested you to do in my last (fourth) letter of 12th Nov. 95. But even that letter has remained unresponded, which forces me to conclude that you have endorsed the said letter to Sri. Dabholkar only for forms sake and did not seriously intend that he undertake the task of exposing the Naadi hoax in a scientific manner. This conclusion however does not show you in a good light as a scientist, inasmuch as it shows that you call Naadi a hoax without seriously intending to expose it as a hoax or to prove it as such. Perhaps you do not seriously intend to expose the Naadi as a hoax, because you have no means to do it. This is made abundantly clear from the fact that you insist on testing one or two thousand individual samples for the purpose. This is patently an impossibility in practice. This impracticable suggestion of yours, therefore, does not admit of any interpretation other than that you, in effect, purport either to accuse that Naadi- text owners of crass deception without caring to prove it, or to assert that there is no element of scientific truth in Naadi Bhavishya without caring to substantiate your assertion in a scientific manner. This is quite in keeping with the practice of Andhashraddha Nirmulan Samiti, but not with the practice of a professional Scientist that you are taken to be.

Under the circumstance, there is no other alternative for you as a scientist than to depute forthwith a person, whom you trust fully and who has the Scientific acumen and the necessary investigative skill, to undertake the task of testing the Naadi text with Scientific objectivity, if you are not to lay yourself open to the charge that you are avoiding the test of the Naadi text by putting forth insurmountable difficulties on theoretical ground for fear of facing the Naadi's truth. The onus of proving the charge to be misplaced clearly rests with you. Supposing you undertake the test and supposing the results of the first test turn out positive, you are, free to follow it up with additional tests until you are satisfied to be entitled to draw the conclusion that the odds against the results turning out positive are too heavy to be due to chance, after, of course, fraud is completely ruled out. The next step in the investigation would be to find out the cause that produced these results.

I think this is a historical task that any scientist is called upon to undertake, as it would either knock the bottom from under the much-touted Naadi claims, or, if its claims are sustained, add a new dimension to the phenomena that Science has to study in its efforts to understand nature and her laws.

Either way it is an achievement of no small consequence for science, if its objective is not to be defined too narrowly or too academically.

I may add here that, I would like to accompany your deputy to Madras as a neutral observer (or witness) at my own cost if you decide to dispatch him by the end of January next or early February, as my doctor, under whose treatment I am at present, has advised me against undertaking long journeys till then. If, you decide to send the deputy and want me to accompany him but think, it necessary to have a prior discussion with me on the subject, I am prepared to come to Pune and meet you at your place on any mutually convenient day.

Lastly, I beg you, Sir, to pardon me if my letters including this one, have proved a nuisance to you I assure you solemnly not to trouble you with any letter henceforth, even if you choose not to respond this letter also. Which, however, I earnestly hope you will not do.

Thanking You,

Yours sincerely
(Adwayanand Galatge)

Copy to: 1. Sri. Shashikant Oak, Tambaram, Madras
2. Sri. Narendra Dabholkar, Satara

❑

Lodging and Transport Facilities in Chennai

From the foregoing details, readers must have realized that it is most important for them to personally go for their Naadi-reading and get the exciting experience. The simplest way is to send a postcard and seek an appointment for Naadi-reading. Those who get leave travel concession may visit Naadi Centres and undertake pilgrimages on account of Shanti-Deeksha! They may also carry thumb-impressions of other persons with them. If their Naadi-readings are also obtained, they may share your travel expenses.

For going to recommend places for Deeksha and Shanti, by road, buses from Chennai are clean, fast, frequent and cheap. Besides, the state transport network, there are other private buses too. With the help of a map you can decide the route and the timings.

You are advised to reach a temple before 8 O' clock in the morning. You have to have a bath before going to the temple. Buy pooja-material from the shops outside. While handing it over to the priest, **you have to tell him -lagna, rashi, gotra and your name.** The priest returns the coconut, other pooja-material with kumkum and the sweet-prasad. Some temples are closed for darshan between 12 and 4 afternoon. If you want to save your day, *it is better not to waste your time anywhere else.*

There are many hotels suiting the pockets of everyone, in the Egmore area, near Chennai Central Railway

Station, and also at Tambaram. There are also cheap lodging & boarding hotels at all other places. The cheap accommodation costs approximately Rs. 50-80 per bed. However, as far as food is concerned you get plenty of rice!

I would like to suggest on my own that if you feel satisfied or get better results after doing a Shanti-Deeksha or while doing it, you might present a gift to the Naadi Centre, according to your desire and financial capacity.

From Mumbai- Pune there are three trains going to Chennai via, Solapur and Reniguntha. Two trains reach Chennai at night so that it is possible to go to the Naadi Centre early next morning.

There are three fast trains from New Delhi-via Nagpur and three from Calcutta via Vishakhapattnam. The city buses in Chennai with route numbers, 18-K, 51-K, 21-K etc. are convenient to reach Tambaram. T-nagar (Mambalam) is centrally located. If you go by local train, Tambaram is the last station. To go to the Ramani Tambaram is the last station. To go to the Ramani Guruji's Ashram you have to get down at the East side to Tambaram and proceed 6 Kms by Rickshaw opposite the Bharat Engineering College. For going to Agastya Naadi Nilayam one has to alight at West Side of Tambaram and proceed to the back side of philips Hospital.

Vaideeshwaran Koil Railway Station has been closed for gauge conversion. One can also travel from Bengaluru (BG) at night and reach Tanjavour, Trichy, Kumbh konam, Mayiladuturai. (15 Km away from V'koil) early in the morning.

❑

Here is the Proof of Miracle of Naadi Predictions!

It has been talked and discussed about the veracity of the written matter on the palm leaves. Many believers and non-believers, especially those ignorant of Tamil language and its old script, feel that at least the names of individuals etched out on the palm leaf are decoded and presented to them. Therefore, it should be a quesion of life and death for those organizations who all the time, refute about those tests conducted by others.

(A) Written Proof

On many occasions we read or hear about the happening of miracles. Mere claims are futile, unless they are investigated based on the proofs and the truth is established about miraculous occurrences. However, all these investigations have got to be done by the independent and unbiased investigating body, so that no further controversies linger around.

It has been talked and discussed about the veracity of the written matter on the palm leaves. Many believers and non-believers, especially those ignorant of Tamil language amd its old script, feel that at least the names of individuals etched out on the palm leaf are decoded and presented to them. Therefore, it should be a question of life and death for those organizations who all the time, refute about those tests conducted by others.

Here is conclusive proof to ascertain and read the name of the author "Shashikant" found in two different Naadi leaves written for some other persons, with the gap of at least 5 years in between them. Tamil knowing people will be able to satisfy the authenticity of the script by themselves. For the benefit of those curious and investigative type of people who do not know the Tamil language can also vouch for themselves with keen and minute observation of the script shown in the photograph and the other languages script.

Considering the freedom of handwriting, the connectivity of each of the word, the readers are requested to verify the word 'Shashikant'.

It is expected here that the readers should observe two dots on the top of the word 'Shashikant' from the photogaphs and table showing letters in Devnagari Roman and modern Tamil script and cryptic Tamil letters. It appears that Maharshees have taken efforts while writing the proper names of the persons so that any Tamil knowing person would be able to read the name.

(B) The proof of Carbon 14 test conducted in Germany proves the age of Naadi leaf as at least 350 to 400 years old

Recently, my German friend mailed English version of a German book on Naadi prediction named *The Secret of Indian Palm Leaf Libraries* written by Thomas Ritter.

In that book on page 81 to 85 Mr. Thomas Ritter describes his experiences of many Naadi centres he visited in India and the result of Carbon 14 test conducted in the famous "Institute of Ion Radiation of Physics Department" placed in Nuclear Research Centre, Rossendorph, Saxen, Germany. This institute has been responsible to decide the age of ancient paintings and other documents of national importance in Germany. Thomas Ritter contacted expert C-14 scientists - Prof. Fradrik and Dr. Hanse of the institute. He also confirmed from the experts on the Tamil language in Germany that the matter is in fact Tamil language script. It is about predictions and not some religious matter.

On preliminary checking the scientist said that the matter written on the leaf has been etched out and some graphite-like substance has been used so that the matter could be seen more clearly. Clearing the black substance from the leaf took some months. By then Thomas Ritter became increasingly anxious about the result.

Some time in March 1995, he got the much-awaited result, which clearly indicated that the age of that particular leaf was at least 350 years old. Considering the deviation factor allowance generally given for this type of tests the report said the age could be between 350 to 400 years.

Maharashtra Superstition Eradication Committee has been debunking Naadi predictions as a hoax. It has been harping on conduting the Carbon 14 test as scientific proof against Naadi Granths. However, instead of conducting the tests on its own, it wanted me to provide the sample to it. It further stated that if the results indicate that the age of the leaf happens to be only in the range of 100 or 500 years old then the tall claim of Naadi records being very ancient will be proved to be bunkum instantly.

Now the age of Naadi has been proved beyond doubt by C - 14 test conducted by very famous laboratory in Germany. I was aware that had I been involved with SEC in providing the sample of Naadi leaf for C-14 test in India, the same organization would have found me for doing some sort of mischief with the sample and results. If SEC threatens me with a challenge of 5 lakh rupees, why is it shy of collecting the sample by itself and conducting the test independently?

Let us examine SEC's statement that if Naadi leaf is found to be only 100 or 500 years old then the entire Naadi prediction becomes bunkum instantaneously. It is the gimmick of the words. Because if the matter on the leaf about the person at any time without he/she telling it, then at what point of time the matter has been written in the past becomes irrelevant. It may be 100 years or 200, 350, 500, or even 5000 years. It can not be treated as cheating or hoax; on the contrary it proves as an established miracle!

It is quite relevant to state that all Naadi readers tell that the matter on the leaf is very ancient but the leaf on which it has been rewritten on many occasions or periods, last known period being Maratha king Maharaj Sarfoji II Raje of Tanjavur kingdom (A. D. 1798 to 1832).

If person from Germany can undertake the Carbon 14 test why can't SEC here in India undertake the test without depending on me, on its own?

❏

Introduction to Some Strong Naadi Lovers

Some of the new Naadi lovers who are actively participating the research work in their own way.

Most prompt and devoted Naadi lover Wg. Cdr. Rakesh Nanda

One of the front runners of Naadi lovers is Wing Commander Rakesh Nanda serving in IAF. Some 3 years back while he was admitted in Military Hospital in Pune, he got introduced to Naadi predictions. Slowly he developed interest in Naadi astrology. Meanwhile in Dec 2003 he was posted to Chennai.

In very short time, he not only visited all Naadi centres of Tamil Nadu but all over India. His efforts fetched more addresses of Naadi centers and some new name of Naadi Granth Maharshees such as Siddha Naadi, Sadanand Naadi, Jemini Naadi, Dhanwantrari Naadi, Atri Naadi etc.

Along with me he visited all centres of Bhurgu Samhita in Hoshiarpur in Punjab. He got stunned when he read his and my name written in Devnagari script on one leaf of Bhrugu Samhita. Later on in Nov 2004 he got elaborate Bhrugu Phal (prediction) appeared with vibhuti (holy ash) in Sri Shamacharanji's centre. Predictions divined to him by all Naadies are turning out to be true. On his 44th birthday i.e. on 30 April 2005, Rakesh was particularly very fortunate to seek the blessings of Goddess Gayatri. Prof. A.N. K. Swami himself performed *Hawan* and recited *Meenaxi mantras* for hours. More than 175 persons of different Naadi centres and others attended the Hawan. They blessed him and his family members. It was said that next chapter of his life has begun predominantly for holy deeds and *Daan-Dharam*.

Rakeshji does not believe the Naadi Granths blindly. Yet Rakeshji's dedication and commitment towards Naadi Granths is so strong that whosoever contacts him, he is ever ready to render help to any and every person who seeks his help. For that purpose he is equipped with 3 Mobile numbers, so that any person in distress residing in any part of India could contact him with any hassles. To listen to his sweet tongue and non-stop experiences on shanti and diksha rituals is feast to ears!

He likes to visit all Naadi centres. Because of near vicinity from his office, many of affectionate and prompt chief Naadi readers of Chennai respectfully accommodate him. According to him nearly 90% of leaves are found out there.

In Vaideeshwaran koil his contacts are all over. Once while returning, he happened to stop at one of the centres. Till then leaf for his son Hrishabh was not searched, due to his tender (below 13 years) age. All of a sudden Rakesh felt to test this centre, with his son's case. The leaf was found in a short time. While reading Maharashees said the father of this boy has casually tried to test us at this centre. Not only now but also in future on many occasions he will be fortunate to get our messages. He will perform relentless service of our literature in time to come. The words of Maharshees have come absolutely true, because by now hundreds of persons of different varieties have got their leaf searched in many centres and performed pujas in the presence of Rakeshji.

Generally, it is seen that out of husband and wife if one is fond of Naadi the other starts disliking for nothng! But in Rakeshji's case his wife and children are equally devoted to Naadi predictions.

Sometimes even in the services like IAF surprisingly blemishes do take place. One very senior officers of IAF went on retirement. yet with the Supreme Courts' orders he got reinstated in the active service, with the promotion of the rank of Air Marshal! Maharshees' prediction proved true cent per cent in this case! It was Rakesh Nanda's initiative to obtain predictions, which nobody including the Air Marshal himself could believe in the beginning. Later on as the events unfolded even non-believers rushed to Nanda to seek their leaf.

There is another example equally astonishing regarding his own. He felt that delay in his promotion was an act of destiny, as told by many great Maharshees in Naadi Granths, so that he could go to Chennai for Naadi's cause. After the specific period got over, he was promoted! Had he got the promotion in time he could not have got the occasion to serve at Chennai, he thought.

I feel greatly honoured that before leaving the service of Indian Air Force, in Rakesh Nanda I found an able and totally dedicated and pious senior officer devoted to many Maharshees Naadi Granths.

New Experience of Naadi Lover Wg Cdr Rakesh Nanda

I had wonderful experiences with many Naadi centres. I am fully satisfied with it. I have been to at least 200 different Naadi centres over the past 7 years. I must have personally taken 500 persons from different parts of India to the Naadi centres. 90% of them used to get the leaves. They were totally convinced about the results. Many in the beginning used to disbelieve Naadi as some sort of superstition. They used to shun from seeing the Naadi leaf, but later on used to get the predictions, seeing the amazing results of others.

A few wonderful incidence of my father :

My father is a non-believer and advocate by profession. It was in 2002 at Koregoan park, Pune Naadi centre. I took out the leaf for my father, he was 65 years of age. At that time, Naadi mentioned that when he enters 70 years of his age, he will go abroad to visit foreign countries. When I told my father, he said sarcastically that he has never been abroad and at the age of 70, it is just not possible. Friends, you may be surprised to know that when he completed 69 and entered 70th year, with in a month he went to Singapore and Malaysia and then subsequently to Canada and America. As if this is not enough, now he had been to seven different countries including Italy, Switzerland, Germany on an invitation as legal professional! Is it not mind boggling?

Now take the case of my sister:

She was told while seeing Naadi leaf, that she is presently having a job of teacher but will leave the job within a month. At that time, it was impossible to believe. But it so happened that she left the job of teacher suddenly and now for last 6 years she has not picked any job.

Like this, there are hundreds of wonderful experiences of different back grounds, from Ordinary Army jawans to Generals, Air Marshals. I, myself underwent changes in life which I could not have imagined! I was selected for fighter pilot job, but landed as Logistics officer in Indian Air Force. After some years, I got the wing as navigator. From a typical Punjabi career minded officer, fully committed to profession, chicken loving buddy, to now a trained astrologer and twice visitor of Vipassana Camps in Igatpuri of Sri. Goenkaji, its really amazing journey. It's all true Sir.

I will be really glad, if I could be of and help to anyone, from India or abroad. For more information and guidance on Naadi Predictions any one can contact me on my cell Nos: 09986447895, 09823623144 or 09763276806.

Naadi Lover Family: Uday and Pritie Mehta

Mehta family had finally settled in Pune. Before that they

had very distinguished career in world famous institutes like World Bank and UNO abroad. He was highly impressed with Naadi readings, which goes beyond any nation, religion, language or cast. He propounded the theory of karma based on his personal experience of his son, which he believes is the basis of Naadi Astrology. He established website <naadiguruonweb.org> especially for those residing far off places with internet facilities.

Dr. Vijay Bhatkar lighting deepam from right - Shashikant Oak, Uday Mehta; in the background - Rakesh Nanda, Murlidharan, Eashwaran, MP Bala.,

Nine times heart attacks and brain haemorrhage yet hail and hearty Shri Subhash Havare

Subhashji's case was most intriguing. Initially, he saw his predictions in 2000 in Pune. He was advised to take care of his health. Remembering this in March 2002, when he felt uneasy, he rushed to hospital. On admission, he survived 9 heart attacks. Later a brain haemorrhage occured. Only 12% of his heart was functioning. Doctors wondered how had he survived heart attacks! Soon he was transferred to famous Ruby Hall. Under the supervision of well-known Dr. Hiremath, further treatment began. In the meanwhile his another leaf was found! In that it was stated 'since you had performed Shanti-deeksha partially, you got the glimpse of the death. If you wish to survive, perfrom *"Ayushya Hoam"* life saving ritual.' Physically and financially drained out Subhash could not perform hoam imediately.

In May 2003 as per new instructions he lit deepam weekly for Guru Grah (Jupiter planet). After 3rd week of lighting of lamp he earned huge sum of money. He immediately went to Thirukadayur to perform the Ayushya Hoam with Shri Rajan and Meenakshee Vaidya. After that his health improved tremendously. Later he stood first in diploma exams of Pune University, for Modi (old Marathi) script writing. In the meanwhile, he laid hands on some 100 year old Modi literature found in the possession of Shri Rajan Vaidya. Based on that he started practising Ayurvedic treatment. Presently, he has forgotten that he suffered heart attacks in the recent past!

Firoze Mistry : The name for tatal dedication

It is rare to find persons of Firoze's nature who are dedicated to core for the works of Maharshees. He and his son Nausherwan took upon themselves to undertake productions of documentary on the Naadi Granths held in high esteem in village Vaideeshwaran Koil for Australian TV Channel. I am proud that I could take part in that production.

When Firoze and his family got their leaf read, he was totally zapped by the predictions. Some funny things happened while performing the puja. Though *Parsi* by birth, he was asked to visit a temple called Harihareshwar on the west coast of India. Firoze promptly went there and returned happily thinking he had done *puja* as advised by Maharshees. Least realizing that though the temple was the same but the idol was else in the same temple. Luckily, on realization he did go again to the temple and performed the ritual without fail on specified idol. His children got the deserving breaks for their future commitments. While shooting for the documentary in one Naadi centre we were asked to visit a place called Sadur giri, about 100 kms south of Madurai in Tamil Nadu. Firoze with his brother and myself climbed the heigh of about 4 to 5 thousand feet to reach the temple called Santan Maha Lingam. While performing the chanting, Firoze felt that he had seen exactly the same place in his dream a few weeks back which he happened to mention to his wife.

Later on not only his house problem got over but also his long bothering sinus problem got cured. He has been guiding many personalities of film world. He helped many for doing *Shanti-deeksha* in time. He always advises all Naadi seekers that they should not forget to perform the rituals in the same sequence and at the earliest.

Devotee of Lord Shiva Shri Vishnu Kumar Natani of Jaipur

A young man visits south India, seeks Naadi predictions, becomes involved in the construction of Shiva temple in Jaipur. Ardent believer of Sanatan Dharma this young man is none other than Shri Vishnu kumar Natani. He is advocate by profession. But with his single-minded devotion he has fulfilled the dream of many followers of Lord Shiva in Jaipur. This unique temple named as Sadashiv Temple has 12 faces of Shiva, famous as 'Jyotirlingas'. The land acquistition, construction and other formalities were completed as per instruction of Lord Shiva as told in one of the Prashna Kandam of Naadi leaf. He became an active member of South Indian temple trust. Now Naadi centres are running in Jaipur. This is a solid example that even if predictions are divined one has to put in all the efforts to make happen.

Eminent computer wizard and Naadi lover Dr. Vijay Bhatkar

These days it has become fashion to criticize the predictive methods in total and predictions based on planetary positions in particular. The scientists of rationalist and atheistic beliefs got ready-made opportunity to debunk the future prediction being tough in university level courses. On this background Dr. Vijay Bhatkar ascended to fame for his great contribution for making Param Super Computer for India indigenously. He was rewarded with 'Padmashree' for the same.

He has been actively involved in research work by getting Naadi reading for eminent personalities. He likes to co-chair with any other scientist to test veracity of Naadi leaf scripts. In his vision the modern sciences will get much inspiration from the Naadi Maharshees who were the scientists of their era.

❏

Report on Successful conduct of honouring of Naadi Maharishis in Naadi Palm Leaf Conference in Pune

Wing Commander Shashikant Oak
Addressing in Naadi conference.

Introduction

A conference on Naadi Palm Leaf Astrology was conducted on 14 th Oct, 2007 in Pune at Udyan Prasad Karyalaya, from 1300hrs to 1830hrs.

The Beginning

Wing Commander Oak welcomed the Naadi Centre owners and staff from Pune and many cities of Maharashtra.

Shri. Chandrakant Shewale, Chief Organiser of the conference lit the lamps along with Mrs. Alka Oak, Prof Adwayanand Galtage. Chanting of mantras from the Vedas and Upanishads was conducted by Dr. Nityanand Deshmukh and Party.

The second edition of book titled *"Vidgyan Aani Buddhiwaad"* (The Science and Rationalism) was released by the present on the stage. Staff like Naadi readers, translators and Table Managers and helpers except owners of Naadi centres were honoured with a special trophy, a Uparna (Scarf), Flower and Gaurav Patra (Letter of Honour).

Book's Fare

Book shops were doing brisk business to sell worth thousands of rupees on Naadi predictions by Wing Commander Oak in Marathi, Hindi and English and also of other authors.

Unique Experiences

The personalities mentioned in my book having strange and unique instances spoke with authority. Participants were Wing Commander Rakesh Nanda, Pheroze Misty, Rajan Vaidya, and Subhash Havre. Some of them were given chances to speak include Kaustubh Butala, Vijay Sabnis, and magician Vijay Kumar.

Wing Commander Rakesh Nanda spoke how he used to help people from any part of the country when called over on his Mobile Nos. From Air Martial to even Havildars, how he had served without any personal gains but as a service to the Maharshees. Pheroze narrated how he mistook his Puja in one of Shiva Temples. He had to go again to perform it with some reverence and faith. Now he alongwith his family members was rewarded with many opportunities. He had gone on unique pilgrimage to Sadurgiri, 150 kms south of Madurai along with Wg Cdr Oak.

Subhash Havre stated how he is still fighting fit after nine (9) heart attacks and admission in famous Ruby Hospital in Pune. How he learnt the Modi Lipi (cryptic Script in Marathi) and stood first in Pune University. How he was guided to administer siddha medicines as per predictions from Leaves. He also distributed more than 100 laminated pictures of Agasthya Maharshi. Vijay Sabnis narrated his experiences and of others whom he took to Atri Jeeva Naadi in Chinchwad Centre.

Magician enthralled with his trick to produce a note out of nothing but he said that his trick is nothing in front of divining of exact details by great Maharshees of ancient past.

The session was to cut short to allow Wing Commander Oak to speak about the suggestions he had put forth for implementation by the Naadi Centres. The points were read out in Marathi. The same with English version were asked to put up in Naadi Centres along with Trophy presented to them at the prominent Place

Dr. Vijay Bhatkar, Padmashree award winner, Computer wizard and Naadi lover could not attend the function due to his preoccupation with other invitation.

The Chief Naadi astrologers were honoured with

1. Trophy *Gaurav Chinha* as 'Boat'. Concept behind the symbolic boat and Naadi palm leaf predictions- "The time is an everlasting flow of events like copious river. Shores of which none could comprehend. The life of a person is like a boat with two oars. An individual steers the course with one oar of *'Dnyana'*, worldly knowledge, intelligence and reasoning. The other oar is of *'Karma'* – personal efforts and valour. Presuming that I am the sole decider of my destiny. The boat oscillates of its own. With flag mast of *'Shraddha'* (belief), hope and aspiration guided by *'Param Shiv Tatva* - Ultimate universal power - Sky high. The boat rolls on the sails on which great Maharishis have encoded prophesies of countless souls."

2. Bouquet of flowers

3. *Gaurav Patra* - Letter of honour indicating the service they have rendered and expected to be rendered with honesty and devotion to the God almighty - *'Param Shiv Tatva'* and

4. *Uparna*

5. Photo of Agasthya Maharishi. Some of them who could not make it due to various reasons were given the trophy later.

On the occasion Dr .G John Samuels, Director, Institute of Asian Studies from Chennai and Ms Jaya Lakshmi, Senior Researcher on Tamil palm leaf manuscripts, spoke about their contributions in making of sample dictionary in which an extended meaning of some 100 Naadi words were presented in a booklet form. He was surprised to see the tremendous response for the Tamil manuscripts. He stated that even though he had some collection of esoteric topics like Black Magic etc. in many libraries including his own institute does not possess a single leaf of Naadi Palm leaf.

Regarding the material of palm leaves by Naadi centres, he said, his expert staff would get exposure to the cryptic script and in later times could be able to decipher the words and meanings more easily.

Sum up

The greetings from many Naadi lovers came in time. Some were late. The financial support given by willing Naadi lovers was overwhelming. The Naadi Maharshees will provide insight on the next happening of this type of event in future.

❏

How extremely incredible is it to find the Naadi Palm Leaf!

Just imagine that you are standing on the bridge to enjoy the thrilling excitement of the inundated river in the Monsoon season!

Just imagine that you are standing on the bridge to enjoy the thrilling excitement of the inundated river in the Monsoon season!

For fun's sake you take out match stick from the matchbox and throw it in the gushing water of the river. Then draw out another matchstick and throw in the water. Soon those matchsticks will disappear in the course of river. Now, start thinking, 'Will these two matchsticks ever be able to meet again in future?'

Generally the answer will be 'Never'! However, mathematicians may come with intricate calculations and say, 'Yes, it is very rare but not impossible'.

Now think ahead of this. 'Will these two matchsticks, due to some unknown reasons, even after very long time, ever be able to come back in the match box from where they were picked for throw?

Now every one including mathematicians will agree to the answer, 'Most Impossible'!

Why? There are many reasons for that. The circumstances might have changed, the river might have no water in it, you may not be available, the matchsticks might have got broken etc.

In spite of it, if some one says that 'this is possible', every one will condemn him as an insane person.' The logicians will not admit the very notion. Intellectuals will outrightly reject the idea as most ridiculous.

How can it be possible?

Now, presume that the copious river means nothing but very enormous flow of events of Time. The great Naadi Maharshees wrote the palm leaf of a person, sitting in their hermitage at some time, somewhere and set in the leaf on the journey as one matchstick in the river water. Time lapsed for unknown period.

At a specific time, in some unknown place, a person takes birth, as a second matchstick coming out of matchbox and falling in the river of time in the above example. After certain period that person desires to have an experience of the Naadi palm leaf' astrological predictions. Till such time that palm leaf patiently awaited amongst the packets of thousands of leaves gathering dust and decay as if that leaf were well aware that some where, at some time, someone would come to pick up and get the message meant for him. Even though that person may be ignorant of language, may not be keen to know but destined to get it by chance! He may not be in the state of mind to believe that someone, some time back, had taken great pains to write about him. Expecting that person should get the leaf read by the knowledgeable expert, Naadi reader and know what Maharshi thought desirable for him. How that person should overcome the difficult times by performing the Shanti Deeksha rituals?

The time difference between throwing of two matchsticks in the first instance from the bridge in the gushing river water might have been of only few seconds. Whereas in the latter case of writing of Naadi leaf and taking of birth of the person would take centuries!

Now what do you think? Is it possible that the two matchsticks could meet?

The makers of these Predictions have not desired for any material gains in return. Nor have they cursed for not following their advice. Is this not a selfless service? What is called as 'Nishkam Karma'?

Whenever we visit Naadi centres to know our future and get our leaf, do remember that opportunity is preciously unique. That it can happen only once out of million times. Do have a sense of gratitude and reverence to the service rendered by the Maharshees. Try to grasp as much as you can. Enjoy and accept the predictions with happiness. It is up to you to condemn the Naadi predictions as trash or hoax. What can one say for these types of learned fools?

❏

Suggestions to improve the Standards of Naadi Palm Leaf Astrology Centres.

Wing Commander Shashikant Oak, while addressing the Conference made some suggestions to improve the standards of Naadi reading profession. After some deliberations with some Chief Naadi Astrologers, they agreed to implement most of them as far as possible in near future. Let us hope this conference puts them in right frame of mind for the rest of the suggestions.

Wing Commander Shashikant Oak, while addressing the Conference made some suggestions to improve the standards of Naadi reading profession. After some deliberations with some Chief Naadi Astrologers, they agreed to implement most of them as far as possible in near future. Let us hope this conference puts them in right frame of mind for the rest of the suggestions.

{IT IS REQUESTED THAT ANY ONE WISHES TO IMPROVE THESE SUGGESTIONS FURTHER AND / OR TRANSLATE IN TAMIL OR LOCAL LANGUAGE OF HIS/ HER AREA, YOU ARE WELCOME. PLEASE PUT UP ON THE WEBGROUP AND HAND OVER TO THE CENTRES FOR

IMPLEMENTATION UNDER INTIMATION TO THE AUTHOR}

There are many challenges before present Naadi Centres. The younger generation Naadi readers will have to cope up with the requirements of the present day customers. While respecting the old traditions fully, they will have to give way to present day conditions. New paths will have to be build up for the betterment of the divine profession of the ancient past.

Gone are the days when no one was bothered about proper running of any business. Now Consumer Courts, Rationalist pressure groups, Non-believers and Government regulations are out to watch wrong doings at any time and at any place.

Persons without proper ethics and high morale standards are spoiling the reputation of Great Maharishis and their gigantic work of Naadi Palm leaf Astrology. Children of present Chief Naadi readers are not at all keen to learn the cryptic Tamil language. They see pathetic condition of the fellow readers. Disregarding the rituals they are expected to undertake before starting the day's proceedings of Divine reading. Not so good activities in the non-working hours are discouraged. Some code of conduct will have to be observed by all Naadi astrologers.

Few suggestions in this direction are listed below for the benefit of all Naadi lovers to observe minutely, while they visit the centres of their areas. The purpose here is not to criticise any person or any Naadi centre in particular but to understand the reality of profession and suggest ways for the betterment of it.

1. **Regularity of opening of centres:** Open centres by 8:30 a.m. sharp (depending upon climatic conditions and transport facility).

   The centre should remain open to accommodate the last customer. If needed, it works in shift basis.

2. **Cleanliness:** Chief Astrologer's Office, Puja room and other business rooms including toilets and kitchens should be cleaned every day. There should be no cobwebs, black walls due to Aarti and oil lamps. If required, get them white washed at the interval of few months.

3. **Chappals and News Papers Stand:** Provide proper place to keep footwear outside centres. News papers and periodicals must be placed in at proper stand. (Naadi lover Shri Babuji Bhagwat of Pune had provided free stands to some centres in Mumbai and Pune)

4. **Use of TV:** Avoid seeing Tamil programmes, especially when non-Tamil knowing clients are present in the centre.

5. **Morning prayers and Sadhana: -** The chief Naadi astrologers should set up an example by getting ready for Morning Prayer by 07:00 every day. All other readers should perform Japams and Sadhana /Meditation. The clients present should be permitted to participate in the prayers and Prasad conducted before the day's proceedings.

6. **Table attendants:** They must be available at given timings. Avoid taking any thumb print by some other person, unless the person carrying is blood relation and alive.

7. **Visitor's Book:** Visitor's book should be kept ready with table attendants for the clients to write their experiences of Naadi readings. It will be evidence to see by the other to know what were the experiences of others clients who have seen Naadi leaves previously. The names and addresses will help centres to locate persons, if required on later date

8. **Photographic Albums:** Avoid display of Photo frames of celebrities in open. Please make post card size Photo album of the visitors. Also add the photos while giving charity to the needy and the poor from the gifts given to the centres like saris to women, ready made shirts or T shirts and pants; Lungi etc, School stationary or text books to the children. Avoid giving cloth pieces because it will burden them to spend money on stitching charges.

9. **Centre's Opening Celebrations:** Every year celebrate some functions like Pongal, Diwali, or centre's opening day. Invite nearby persons, society residents, celebrities and

distribute sweets and flowers so that friendly atmosphere is created.

10. **Legal Advice and Police Protection:** Please arrange for advocate in advance. He may be from your clients. Meet in charge of area Police Station. Invite him and his staff to centre so that the police are aware what type of activities are conducted. Especially for Non-Tamil speaking area centres Police protection is a must.

11. **Facilities to Staff Workers:** Following aspects may be kept in mind .
    - Proper food, stay and transport facilities should be provided where staff workers reside in the centre premises.
    - Medical and emergency help is to be given without fail. Family members are contacted fast.
    - The staff should be encouraged to bring family members to reside with nearby areas. This will avoid frequent visits to home towns and loss of working hands and days.
    - The staff should be encouraged to celebrate Pongal, Diwali etc. locally. So that the centre remains open without long break.
    - Remittance of money to the family members in home town is to be monitored by the chief Naadi Astrologers regularly.
    - Every staff should be given Name plate to be displayed on chest for easy recognition. Wearing of Name plates should be made compulsory. It is easy to remember names of the reader by clients that way.
    - Staff should not consume hard drinks and create disturbance to co-workers.
    - The staff should be honest to their spouses.

12. **Learning of languages:** Spoken English classes may be conducted for the staff, so that translation and searching of leaf becomes easy. The staff working in outside Tamilnadu in non-Tamil speaking areas should be encouraged to learn local languages.

13. **Employment Opportunities:** A lot of centres have opened up in all parts of India. At present, many boys sent out by parents as useless are joining the Naadi reading job. It is harming the reputation of Naadi readings. If job guarantee is given, many new faces with talent and intelligence will join the profession.

14. **Certificate of grading**: It could be given to the young readers. It will help to know the standard of readers.

15. Naadi astrologers from Vaideeshwaran Koil should provide some financial support and way of regular supply of Naadi leaves to encourage centres run properly. They should get daily feedback from the centres about number of clients served, and other activities of the day.

16. The chief Naadi astrologers should encourage the staff to open new centre. The new centre should not create competition in the same locality of big cities or nearby towns.

❑

Court case verdict on Naadi Centre in Vaideeshwaran Koil

There was a news item on March 4, 2007, in the leading newspapers of all parts of India in various languages stating, "Court summons Naadi reader from V.Koil in cheating case."

There was a news item on March 4, 2007, in the leading newspapers of all parts of India in various languages stating, " Court summons Naadi reader from V.Koil in cheating case."

Now on 29th July 2009, **Hon Judge: Thiru M. Rajendran, BA, BL**

Judicial Officer, Seerkazhi Court, disposed that case "not found guilty of any offence under Sections 417 and 465. The extract of relevant portions of the Tamil verdict has been produced below. (Translated by Advt. Amit Latkar from Pune)

The Author sent following strong rejoinder on 6th March, 2007 to all the news papers by email without any avail.

NOTHING BUT VICIOUS PROPAGANDA AGAINST NAADI PALM LEAF PREDICTIONS - ANCIENT POSSESSIONS OF PRIDE

To,

The Editor,

It is very surprising to note that sundry news items of one Gopalkrishnan from some town gets the front page place in almost all print and electronic media? Just because it is maligning the Naadi Jyotisham! No news paper had ever bothered to print an article on Naadi Grantham. Unless some strong lobby is acting behind this news this much prompt and strong reporting is not possible.

Regarding the news, the court will find the truth behind the case in its usual manner. However the point at issue is who cheated whom? A person producing the thumb print of dead man or a person who has read out the predictions to the person who had all along confirmed the correctness of the leaf? The Naadi reader's job is to read the leaf and inform the matter written in the palm leaf to the person concerned. In usual manner, the person (in this case, Gopalkrishnan) should not have agreed to the portion of statements of the person being alive. In that case the Naadi reader would have discarded that leaf and the search would have continued till the stock in the center of that particular thumb configuration is exhausted.

Therefore, the person (in this case Gopalkrishnan) deliberately kept on saying 'Yes' to all and cheated Naadi reader, knowing fully well that the leaf is not pertaining to the dead man referred. **Few years back similar type of dishonesty was displayed by one of the leading rationalists Sri. B. Premanad.** While he deliberately exchanged the horoscopes' information with some lady doctor accompanied him to test the Naadi palm leaves in Salem in Tamilnadu. Surprisingly, he admitted in his article that the predictions were 100% correct in spite of his hand trick. Not only that one Sri. MS Risbud from Pune had questioned Sri. B Premanad how come a staunch rationalist like him should openly accept the issue of Naadi reading as 100% correct in that case.

A rejoinder was written by Sri.Eshwaran, one of the owners

of Naadi centers from Pune clearing the position of Naadi centers and readers especially of those working out side Tamilnadu. He in that rejoinder had emphatically refuted the charges made by Sri B. Premanad. As usual no one had taken the cognizance of the article including Sri. B. Premanad. **The entire article is on display on** Naadiastrology@ yahoogroups.com Unlike in other methods of predictions; Naadi reader does not foretell or divine the predictions from his wisdom or based on studies of astrology. It is possible that the leaf may be of any other person who is not yet dead but with many similarities with dead person. This entire episode was a facade to trap the Naadi Reader and in turn to malign the Maharshees of Hindu lineage functioning silently for centuries. It is not a case in isolation, in past these types of police cases have been registered only to extract the money from the Naadi Centers just because they have inadequate knowledge of local language and proper connections with strong seats of power.

With this case, the opportunity has come to the Naadi centers especially of Vaideeshwaran Koil to unite and defend the case as an attack on the Naadi Maharsees' dedicated work of hundreds of years. It is not a case against Naadi center of Sivasamy. Thus it will help the Naadi center owners to produce the palm leaves in question to the scrutiny of the Court as evidence. They should not waste away opportunity to get the evidence of palm leaf tested by the present courts.

Then the counter case could be filed for cheating the Naadi Maharshees to protect the lost dignity of the ancient deposit of knowledge.

If this rejoinder is not given due importance by the news papers and news channels, this fact should be brought to the notice of Hon'ble Court, how biased our reporting media is about anything connected with 'Hindu' Tag on it.

At last, it is pertinent to note that the predictions are not restricted to any Hindu community or persons of Indian origin. Irrespective of any religion, nationality or any barriers the unparallel service of Hindu Maharshees is being rendered for unknown period time. Even if one does not believe in knowing the future, why not to understand what Maharshees such as Agasthya, Kak- Bhujander, Vasistha, Sugar, Pullipani and many others have to say in palm leaf letter? If one does not like it, forget it. But one can offer respect for the efforts the Maharshees have taken in ancient difficult times.

Appreciate that much.

With regards,

Wing Commander (Retd) Shashikant Oak,

Pune. Email: shashioak@gmail.com

Before the Judicial Officer, Seerkazhi Court, Judge: Thiru M. Rajendran, BA, BL

Date: July 29th, 2009 (Thiruvalluvar Year 2040, Virodhi Varsha, Monday 13th Shravan)

Case No. 38/2007

Pandharinathan Kumaran Gopala Krishnan

Complainant

Vs

Arumuga Sivasamy

Respondent

Adv. Thiru S. Somanathan for Complainant

Adv. Thiru N. K. Krishna Moorthy for Respondents

Case:

1. The complainant had been to the respondent's Agasthiya Vaakiya Nadi Jothida Nilaiyam placed at Vaitheeswaran Koil on 19.12.2006 with intention to know the future predictions for him. For the sake of finding out the Naadi Patti, complainants' right thumb impression was taken and using the found out Naadi Patti, the future was told to him.

The complainant was surprised to listen to his Naadi predictions. He was told by the respondent that he was married while in fact he was not married. His mother was alive, but he was told that she was not alive. He had studied till 10th standard, but he was told that he was a graduate. In this way he was told the things which were not true.

The complainant complains that with a fraudulent and dishonest view to deceive him, the 'General Kandam' was told to him by the respondent and that for the said General Kandam readings, he was charged Rs. 500/- which was unreasonable in view of the untrue readings.

With a view to ascertain whether the respondents are 'genuine' the complainant went to the respondents carrying an old thumb impression of a dead person. The complainant complains that (a Naadi patti was found out using the said thumb impression and) it was predicted that he will live long. The complainant was shocked to hear the prediction because the thumb impression he carried actually belonged to dead man.

On the earlier occasion the respondent had already asked for Rs. 1500/- from the complainant saying that a Parihaar Pooja was required to be performed to avoid all the misfortunes. The complainant, having his whole belief in the Naadi Patti (Olai Suvadi) readings had also paid off thinking that everything that was being told to him was correct and accurate.

But now (after the dead man's predictions) he suspected that the respondent had created the false documents having ill-intentions of cheating him and had told him the 'created' future prediction and that for doing all this, he charged money. For these allegations the respondent was charged under IPC 417 and 465.

2. The respondent denied the charges.

3. The complainant, to support his claims produced the evidence in form of the handwritten notebook and the audio cassette. In addition to that, 3 persons were examined before this court and the summary of the examinations read as follows ....
....''

4. The examinations were over. Upon asking whether everything that was told by the persons above in the examinations was true, the respondents replied in negative.

5. In these circumstances, whether the complainant proves all his claims or not remains the query for this court to solve and decide.

6. The court has observed that in the written application and oral submissions of the complainant, there are contradictions regarding the date when the naadi finding and reading happened. In addition, there are contradictions regarding who did the naadi finding and reading. The complainant in his complaint writes that Respondent Mr Sivasamy found the naadi and predicted his future, whereas in the examination he submitted that the disciples of Mr Sivasamy did it. Therefore, this court comes to the conclusion that the statements of the complainants are not admissible owing to the said contradictions.

7. The court further observes another contradiction in the statements of the complainants as follows: The complainant in his written application submits that he, the respondent had created the false documents having ill-intentions of cheating him and had told him the 'created' future predictions. In the examinations, the complainant said that the respondent found out the naadi patti and was merely reading it believing whatever he was reading to be true and also the complainant made the respondent to believe that the contents of the said naadi patti were true.

8. Sec 417 IPC has to be read with Sec 415 IPC for the purpose of punishing a person. In the present case, the complainant fails to prove the trueness of the claims that he maintains, due to his own contradictory statements.

9. The complainant totally fails to prove the fraudulent or dishonest behavior on part of the respondent. (Sec 417)

10. The complainant also fails to prove the alleged forgery on part of the respondents. (Sec 465)

11. Therefore, this court comes to the judgment that the respondents are not found guilty of the charges explained in the sections 417 and 465.

12. Therefore, the court orders to set the respondents free of charges.

Signed

Judge.
29/07/2009

❏

Naadi Centre Owner responds to Rationalist of High Repute.

Here is a sample of Questions and answers typically describing how the rationalist persons of high repute write and speak about Naadi predictions {From Indian Skeptic Issue- Nov. 1996}

One of the owners of Naadi Centers in Pune, happen to read the article recently and requested Wg Cdr Oak to pen down his comments to satisfy Naadi lovers who also get carried away by the propaganda created by these organizations in print and Electronic Media.

From : G Eshwaran, Translator and owner of Naadi centers in Pune and Mumbai.

Dear readers,

Recently, I came to know that one Naadi Lovers group is operating on Internet forum for the benefit of all Naadi Grantha lovers, I would like to contribute information available with me.

Let me introduce myself. Since 1999, I am in a unique position of running two Naadi Centers in Pune and one in Ambarnath, a suburb of greater

Mumbai, dedicated to Agasthya, Kaushik, Vashishtha, Mahashiv and many other Maharshees. In addition, for the last 7 years, I possess the most revered Jeeva (live) Naadi of Atri Maharshees read and interpreted by me and highly dedicated and studied Naadi reader - Shri. Vaidhyanathan Guruji.

Before getting involved with Naadi prediction, I was running a business as fashion Designer. Seven-eight years back, I got introduced to this prediction method by chance. As per the predictions, I was told that you are destined to get involved with this system as a profession. Soon, though reluctantly, I began to translate and record readings for the benefit of some Non-Tamilian persons on friendly basis. Later I found interesting to work as full time job. I worked as a translator in many Naadi centers in Mumbai and Pune.

My other brother named Krupanand is also in the same profession and is presently running a center in Dombivali East. Being brought up in Mumbai, I speak good deal of Marathi and Hindi. Thus I am a good link between Naadi center readers and their patrons in Tamilnadu.

I have known Wing Commander Shashikant Oak for last 12/13 years as a staunch Naadi lover. Through his publications in Marathi, English, Tamil and Hindi, he has been introducing the treasure of knowledge of many great Maharshees such as Agasthya, Vashishtha, Shuk, Mahashiv, Kaushik, Kak Bhujander, Bhrugu and many others.

Recently, I came to know from Wg Cdr Shashikant Oak that some information has been put up on Internet by a rationalist publication called 'Indian Skeptic' by Sri Basav Premanand. Shri. B Premanand, leading non-believer, stands respected as a staunch rationalist of national and international repute.

The style of the article published in November 1996 by Shri B. Premanand is in question and answer form. Shri B Premanand answered the Questions to satisfy Shri M. S. Risbud from Pune, who is rationalist and studied astrology in great details to debunk it. Shri. Risbud contributed couple of articles in the book written and edited by Shri, B. Premanand himself - "Astrology – Science or Ego trip?" In spite of this background, he had some doubts to get clarified by Shri. B. Premanand.

It appears that Shri. Risbud is not all that happy about the explanations given by Shri. B. Premanand.

Referring to that article, after a gap of some 13-14 years, since I came to know of it only now, wish to contribute a rejoinder by way of "my comments" to some questions raised, which are as follows: -. (For easy and coherent understanding, I have taken the liberty of combining the questions and answers from the article and also some comments by me are bracketed in bold letters)

Q. by Shri. Risbud: 'The intriguing question is that how the names of the person appear on the strips? ... '

Answer by Shri B. Premanand: After asking a few questions and getting my answers, he (Naadi reader) went inside and brought a palm leaf and read from it my past life which was 100% correct, but the reading was made on a wrong horoscope of a lady doctor, who accompanied him.**(Shri B. Premanand in the article stated that he and the lady doctor played a trick of exchanging the horoscopes to confuse Naadi reader.)** Later it was found that their names and parents' names were there in the horoscope and the other details were collected through subtle questioning. The fact is that at the time of subtle questioning by the astrologers or by their stooges, who also sit amongst you as persons who have come to read their horoscopes the palm leaves are prepared. There is no need for astonishment in this as it is a simple trick, which is practised by all astrologers to collect information and tell it as if they have found it by reading the horoscope.

My comments:

1) **In this type of article where the myth of Naadi is presumed to have been exposed, the exact details are important. In the whole of the article, date and the name of Naadi Center and reader is not found mentioned except 'Salem' as place.**

2) In the South Indian system of Naadi reading from the leaf is found out person's thumb impression obtained at the center at the time of reporting. The horoscope is needed only if person wishes to compare with the one in hand with the other written in the leaf. In the whole article, nothing has been mentioned about obtaining of his or her thumb impressions, which is most important.

3) His observations about debunking Naadi predictions in general is based only on this single experience that too from unmentioned Naadi center which can not be treated as final proof about the validity of the writing in the leaf or otherwise.

Q: 'When (lady doctor's) name and her telling profession mentioned by him were correct, to me it makes no material difference if he had described her as a paediatrician instead of a gynec.'

Ans: It makes lots of difference, as it was the prediction about her based on my horoscope, which has proved that his predictions are not based on stars or planetary positions. We had exchanged our horoscopes deleting our names and our parents' name. We could not suppress our laughter as he was making predictions on my horoscope.

My comments:

4) Shri. B. Premanand is making too much fuss of his trickery. By exchanging the horoscopes nothing has changed so far as Naadi reader is concerned. Because on occasions many persons carry thumb impressions of their near ones. While giving reading that does not mean that the predictions are made about the person presenting the impressions. When the leaf is found out it does not make difference to the Naadi reader whether he is diving for the person producing the thumb impression or the one who is not present.

5) Here in the answer he mentions that the names on their respective horoscopes were deleted. Whereas in

earlier answer he states that the names were picked from the horoscopes. Read the underlined sentence.

Q: 'Instead of laughing at the astrologer, I would have astonished by his skills of fathoming these facts. Further on, you have mentioned that you snatched the palm leaf from the hands of astrologer and you did not find mention about the person who entered with sandals and desanctified the room. This means you were able to read the script and the language of the palm strip. If you were to decipher the contents of the palm leaves, then I will arrange to send you the photocopy of such strip which Mr. Oka **(Shri. Risbud is in habit of deliberately mentioning Wg Cdr 'Oak' as 'Oka' just to belittle him)** had sent to Dr. Jayant Narlikar, **(An Astrophysist decorated with Padma Vibhushna Award in 2004)** and which was displayed by Dr. Dabholkar **(Chairman of Superstition Eradication Committee, better known as Andhashradha Nirmoolan Samiti, in Marathi operating in Maharashtra for last 20 years)** in Pune, inviting Tamil knowing persons to read it.

Ans: If I get good photocopies of the palm leaf inscriptions, I can let you know what they contain. If I get the palm leaf, I could also check up their leaf by carbon dating to know its age. But you have no cared to send them.

My comments

6) Shri. B. Premanand has shied from the stating whether he could read the script in the leaf by himself or not. Obviously not because had he the required expertise he could have realized that the divining is based on the matter stated in the leaf and not based on the information extracted from the clients. On some odd occasions, mentions are found about happening at the time of reading. The person entering in the room wearing sandals may be one of such occasions.

7) Shri. Risbud ignored to send a copy of the photograph. He also deliberately avoided to respond about the outcome of the same "photographs show" conducted

in Pune, on 29 Sep 1995, in front of a crowd of more than hundred persons mainly members of Dr. Dabholkar's Superstition Eradication Committee and three Tamil speaking persons who happen to attend the meeting by accidentally reading in local newspapers about this show of photographs. This show was specially organized by Dr. Narendra Dabholkar to openly declare that the script in the palm leaf, purported to be a Naadi leaf obtained by them from Dorai Subburathinam's Naadi center in Tambaram, is not at all TAMIL. More than 100 persons, mostly strong supporters of Dr. Dabholkar, attended the meeting. In presence of video cameras of media, everyone witnessed that three Tamil speaking persons gave in writing and in front of video camera that the script is indeed Tamil and being ancient it is difficult to read ordinarily.

8) No Naadi center will like to provide the sample of leaf to these types of organizations who are hell bend on proving the existence of Naadi leaves predictions as HOAX at any cost. However, persons of high integrity and sincere in their approach like Wg Cdr Shashikant Oak are given the permission by many centers to take the photographs of the leaves pertaining to their own for the sake of examination and verification of truth of Naadi written by Maharshees in olden times.

9) It is surprising that person like Shri. B. Premanand whose life mission is to debunk the horoscopic or other wise predictive methods has to wait to provide the leaf in his lap. He then would like to the age of the leaf checked by the institute of his favour. What is preventing him or like-minded persons or organizations then? Let them come to centers with reverence towards the Maharshees' work. They will not be sent back empty handed.

Q: The age of any originals of the palm leaves cannot be more than 1700 years at the most. This is certain because Rishies are mentioned in the contents. Rishies came into being in our astrology after Shaka year 300 or so.

Ans: There are no originals of the palm leaves. It is prepared when a new customer comes, but it would look old through chemical treatment. But the age can be known by carbon dating.... That would help to prove the falsity of their claims.

My comments

10) It is not impertinent to mention that a person named Thomas Ritter from Germany had already done the carbon 14 test in one of the most sophisticated laboratories in Germany. He has also got the script decoded by expert available in his country. The findings are that the leaf when tested was at least 350 to 400 years old. The foreign Tamil expert had explained that the matter is indeed divination. In Tamil, it is not some thing otherwise religious scripture. If a foreigner could obtain the results, what is preventing the Indians?

11) It is always stated by the Naadi center owners that the matter on the leaf has been last rewritten in the times of Maratha King Sarfouji Maharaja of Tanjavaur some 300 years back. Thus the leaves may be of recent origin but the written matter is of ancient times. The same argument is confirmed by the Carbon 14 test conducted in Germany.

Q: I wish to know this thing from you: You have mentioned that the Naadi astrologer told your past 100% correct. What explanation can you give for this? How did that fellow get all the information about you? In your article I did not find any answer.

Ans: The fact is that you have not cared to read the article minutely. **(Shri B Premanand has scolded Shri Risbud at places for not having read his article minutely. Here is one such mention.)**

They are:

1. Later it was found that their names and their parents' names were in the horoscope and other details were collected through subtle questioning.

2. After asking a few questions and getting answers, he went inside and brought a palm leaf **(meaning unconnected by string in bundle)** and read from it my past life, which was 100% correct.

3. The fact is that at the time of subtle questioning by the astrologers or by their stooges who also sit amongst you as person who has come to read their horoscopes and the palm leaves are prepared and read. If you give wrong answer the reading will also be wrong. If you give another's horoscope as yours the reading will be on you and not on the horoscope if they have collected information about you. Except the names and your profession, most of the things they tell about you will not be on the palm leaf and what they read would be common predictions, which will be true to every one.

My comments

13. **As said earlier the leaf of any person is found out based on the thumb impression (For gents, Right Hand and for ladies, Left hand thumb impression) of the person and not on the horoscope. Shri. B Premanand has not even made any mention about it. How come? In fact as a rationalist he should have done a lot of drum beating about futility of the thumb impression in exacting the packet containing the leaf of his thumb impression configuration.**

14. **His statement that the Naadi reader went in side and brought (presumably one single) a palm leaf and read from it past life 100% correct. This cannot happen because all the leaves are interwoven with a string through all leaves and packed in two wooden plates.**

15. **It is Shri. B. Premanand's wild imagination that the leaf gets prepared, (meaning, made to order) by**

writers from center sitting inside their so called 'secret Room' and writing from the information they could extract by subtle questioning and through stooges planted has no base. He has not provided any proof to substantiate this statement. On the contrary, as a custodian of all Naadi leaves in the center let me tell you, even though no person is permitted to peep though the secret room of Naadi center, Shri. B. Premanand could have at least found out traces of cut outs of huge heaps of leaves out side the center and some unwanted waste parts of leaves in odd corners. Some half prepared leaves, waiting for some sort of chemical treatment. (Here let me make it very clear, as a owner of the centers and who knows what goes inside the secret room that neither the work of writing of leaf takes place nor any sort of preparation of leaves cutting, from branches, sorting making of holes, various types of sharp needle like stylus pens a getting sharpened for writing on blank parts of leaves. etc.)

16. There is no secret in the so-called "Secret room" except the bundles are stacked in neat manner. Sometimes Naadi readers sit or mostly stand to reach out to the correct bundle pertaining to the required thumb configuration. The Naadi centers, in places like Pune or Mumbai where the packets are in limited number, they are kept in suitcases too. Let me vouch authentically on behalf of Naadi centers that no preparation of new leaves takes place.

17. It is brought to the notice that the present Naadi readers are capable of only reading the matter on the leaves but cannot write the leaves.

18. The theory of sending the stooges in the crowd of visitors is highly impossible outside Tamilnadu. For getting the information with subtle questioning one

will need extraordinary command over Tamil language. If at all, it may be possible inside Tamilnadu to some extent but outside Tamilnadu throughout India, language is the main barrier. Here the problem is other way round, the workers of Naadi center do not know the language of the local visitors. They are so shy of talking to the visitors naturally; it often creates misunderstanding due to the problem of non-communication. Even if some of them try to be chummy with the crowd, they could get easily spotted out as typical Tamilian.

19. Always remember that the visitors are not fools and gullible to discuss the personal information with strangers. In fact, every person seeking the predictions for the first time is suspicious and very cautious to speak to any body from center or other visitors. In addition, we from Naadi center, while taking their thumb impression also caution to all visitors not to say anything other than 'Yes' or 'No' when the search of leaf begins.

20. The present time problem outside Tamil speaking areas, we the Naadi center proprietors face is that there is no proper person who could speak to the waiting customers. There is general dissatisfaction about the quality of translation. The centers these days function in crowded cities in one-bed room flats where there is no place for them to hide the secret writing work to be undertaken along with getting the stakes of palm leaves from far off places. The suspicious neighbours will instantly catch Naadi readers if they see them bringing some fresh branches of palm trees to get more leaves for writing purposes.

21. These types of imaginary actions of writing of leaves, planting of stooges do not happen because there is no need to do all that. All the Naadi readers do is to

read what is readily available in the leaf. But persons like Shri B. Premanand Dr. Narendra Dabholkar, Dr. Jayant Narlikar will never accept the reality. Therefore, they are forced to defend themselves on far-fetched imaginations. Thus the fictitious and queer theory of writing the new leaves inside the center for new customers is valid only for argument sake by the rationalists. In fact, not that they do not know the futility of their arguments, but they cannot accept the miraculous reality of Naadi predictions because it goes totally against their pre-decided negative scientific principles. Even if they wish to accept the truth of the Naadi prediction leaves, they have no face to show to the public. Thus the rationalists have already lost the case, but they will never accept defeat in public to avoid the denigration and ignominy of getting their rationalist organizations closed.

22. Here let me make clear in writing that if any serious verification is to be conducted, I am open to such investigation. However, it should be headed by the team of expert scientists and not by the persons or organizations who had already declared the Jyotish Shastra as bunkum in general and Naadi predictions as fraud and deception in particular.

(As told by Shri. G Eshwaran to Wg Cdr Shashikant Oak)

[Owner of Two Naadi centers in Pune and one in Ambarnath - Suburban outside Mumbai]

The comments and rejoinders are welcome.

❏

Just imagine you write Naadi Predictions!

Recently on 14th October 2007, a conference on Naadi Prediction was conducted in Pune. While addressing the Naadi lovers, Wing Commander Shashikant Oak, narrated a case wherein the matter of the future predictions going wrong from the date of seeing the Naadi leaves was narrated.

Recently on 14th October 2007, a conference on Naadi Prediction was conducted in Pune. While addressing the Naadi lovers, Wing Commander Shashikant Oak, narrated a case wherein the matter of the future predictions going wrong from the date of seeing the Naadi leaves was narrated. He opened the topic saying that every one in the gathering expected to know his views on why the Naadi Predictions go wrong! How? Hot and lively discussion was expected because many had similar experiences. He said that it is impossible to satisfy each and every one on the issue. Therefore, he devised innovative solution. He asked the audience to try to write the predictions presuming that they themselves are the Naadi Maharshees! Live case details of a person were given by him.

He said, "I would like to narrate a live experience of my very dear friend from Indian Air Force. In the year 2002, I was posted at Air Force Station

Halwara near Ludhiana in Punjab. I got introduced to one young **Flying Officer Dhananjay Mote**. He happened to be from my hometown Madhavnagar, suburb of Sangli. That made our bond with extra warmth. He was best all rounder in real sense of the word! He stood first in all tests. He had excellent command over English, being very ardent devotee of Shirdi Saibaba. His morning routine used to begin by Dhyan and prayers. He developed hobbies of drawing, Painting, Guitar playing. He excelled in Boxing, Out-door games and Gymnasium. He used to be the centre of attraction in parties and get-togethers.

He bought brand new Indica car to take his mother and three younger sisters to many places of their liking. He desired to see his Naadi Prediction with me in Pune on our vacation. He drove new car all alone from Punjab to Sangli. While in Pune we went to take out his Naadi leaf. When it was found he was very pleased with the details narrated therein. Very bright careered, promotions to high posts, children, long life etc. were the details. In the Seventh chapter, Maharshi narrated details of his future wife, one staying at a place of scenic beauty, with modern name, engagement due very soon but marriage to take place only the next year of his age.

In those days, he got engaged with 'Sarangaa', the person exactly matching with Naadi description; staying in hill station – Panhala, with dry pond opposite her bungalow etc. Even though Dhananjay was keen to get married in the same leave period, he however agreed to wait for the joint marriage along with her elder sister. We, along with family members attended his marriage which was conducted soon after his next birthday, exactly as predicted.

Later, I joined back the duties. He enjoyed honeymoon. Within 15 days, he was on the way to take back his wife from his in-law's house. On the way to Kolhapur, after crossing Jayasingpur, a truck dashed his car on the railway over-bridge. He expired almost instantaneously, leaving everyone in a state of shock. I attended the funeral on behalf of Air force Station with tears in my eyes.

What is this Mr Oak? How come? Could you explain this? What do you have to say? Many persons, many questions! Some openly, some with mute faces! He keeps on yapping Naadi, Naadi. Good! At least now, he and followers of Naadi lovers will keep mum! What Naadi? All bunkum. Many got chance to express their genuine annoyance. Every one had his own opinion. I was guessing what must have happened? One could not take shelter of blaming the translators or Naadi readers. Since they had no role to play!

The writings of Prin. Adwayanand Galatge were echoing in my mind. From the point of view of the seeker, what his 'past' is, from point of view of the sages (at the time of writing these Naadi predictions) was 'future'. The seekers cannot deny that their 'past' came absolutely true, was based on the correct predictions. Because for Maharshees, seekers 'past' was also 'future' only. Therefore to say that the predictions go wrong is incorrect statement. However, if the predictions go wrong from the date of seeking, then, there must be some definite reason behind it. That is to say, the Maharshees do not see them wrong but narrate them wrong. Predictions are deliberately stated wrong or incorrect. The main purpose of Naadi is not to divine the predictions, but to facilitate the law of Karma to take its natural course of action smoothly and effectively. Apparently it is absurd statement! Let us examine in light of Flying Office Dhananjay Mote's example. Now I request all the readers to assume the role of the great sage. That means, since you know the relevant facts about Dhananjay, you presume as if you were the sage with divine vision to see, and record on palm leaf many, many years ago.

Now you will realise that if the fate of Dhananjay's wife was to become widow within 15 days of her marriage, she had to get married to a person like Dhananjay who is destined to die within a very short span of time. Now Maharshi that is presently you, have two options for Dhananjay 1) Not to write predictions (Simply telling, 'Leaf is not found or available') as his lifespan is very short. Also telling him the 'truth' about his sudden death may make him terribly mentally upset. 2) To write palm leaf in such a forceful way that Dhananjay has no option but to get urgently married. It has to be with the same girl who is fated to be widow in 2 weeks time.

Now if you have opted for the second option, then you will have to keep his palm leaf ready for him to seek the predictions. To make sure about his future plans of marriage you would have kept Seventh chapter also handy with all precise details so that he has no other option but to accept the proposal of the hilltop girl. Now Dhananjay will get married only if his future is depicted as very prosperous and bright. Long life, bright children, smart and beautiful wife are some of the highlights you will state to attract him to get married. Could you dare to write, "My dear fellow, your life is just of few months. Get ready before that, to marry and spoil your wife by making her widow with no fault of hers". You could say, "I am omniscient sage, I see exactly what is going to happen, and therefore, I will write only the 'Truth', however bitter it may be?"

No. You will have to depict a dreamy picture of his married life. You will say, 'I would state all the details of that girl so that not only he but his family members also would get convinced about her, so he will have no other option but to get hooked to her alone.

While climbing the heights of Panhala and witnessing the dry pond before getting down from Indica car at the residence Dhananjay's sisters said, 'Dada, she is going to be our Bhabhi, as stated in Naadi leaf'!

You, mean Naadi Maharishi, could have avoided making his leaf ready and easily prevented the allegations of false writings, deliberately misleading the person, by giving false hope and making one person widow unnecessarily. Why did you write the palm leaf? Why did you become target to tarnish the image of Naadi palm leaf astrology? Why? May be you were not bothered about your reputation as omniscient sage. You were more concerned that the law of Karma should not remain unenforced in the cycle of the events. You were supporting the cause of helping the past karmas getting enforced so that Dhananjay was to be free for the next turn of his enactment on the stage of the 'universal play'. Thus, it appears that your main aim was not to divine predictions to impress the believers and be a target of non believers, but be a catalyst in the smooth and precise flow of events as per Karma Theory. While all along you will have to take care that your writings do adhere to the norms of lyric writings, in the most perfect manner. The last word of the previous stanza and first word of current stanza should have the same word to ensure continuity and rhythm of poetic style. The whole matter without any clerical and encoding mistakes or errors were to be transcribed on the palm leave, kept ready with chemical treatment. The arrangements were also made to keep these packets of leaves ready at the convenience of the seeker with the facility to understand it in the language in which the seeker is most comfortable. WILL YOU NOT DO ALL THIS, IF YOU WERE TO BE A GREAT SAGE OF ANCIENT TIMES?

Now the critics may realise what troubles we take to undergo the process of Naadi writing. Without any monetary gains, we patiently serve the humanity. Yet we are blamed for many shortfalls, wrong or incorrect predictions!

In addition to what has been stated, there seems to be one more solid reason why writing of Dhananjay's leaf was a must. In due course of time, when many will start criticising the Naadi for its incorrect future predictions, Shashikant Oak, his dear friend would use his palm leaf as a classic example to explain the Law of Karma. Is it not your duty as Naadi Maharishi to provide conclusive proof to defend the purpose of writing of your great records?

Like in the past, had you not kept three leaves ready for Mrs. Oak? Just to attract her husband, Shashikant Oak to this work more closely and provide the required evidence by way of photographs of her leaf for scrutiny by the experts? Dhananjay's leaf would also be used for clearing the doubts about our difficult predicament and most complicated prediction making process!

Many times people get upset over our incorrect sayings, for example:- when we say the seeker will get 'son' but it turns out to be 'daughter'. Please understand that in Tamil script there is very subtle difference between two letters in script writing. Marriages do not occur as stated. Because they are actually supposed to be delayed due to past Karmas. In that case, we had no other option but to send them to make visits to holy places so that the interim period passes away.

Therefore, please understand Naadi Maharishis before you start criticising and condemning Naadi predictions.

❑

How come the future Predictions go wrong in Naadi Predictions?

The 10ᵗʰ Chapter of the above mentioned book titled, 'Naadi Grantha Bhavishya : The Nemesis of Rationalists', throws the light on the reasons why the Naadi predictions about the future events of the individual after he consults it are found to go wrong.

Princ. **Adwayanand Galatge** has written a Marathi book titled **"Vidgyan ani Andhashraddha –Nirmulan (The Science and Blind Faith Eradication)"**, from which relevant portions are culled and reproduced in this chapter. The 10ᵗʰ Chapter of the above mentioned book titled, '**Naadi Grantha Bhavishya : The Nemesis of Rationalists'**, throws the light on the reasons why the Naadi predictions about the future events of the individual after he consults it are found to go wrong. The cases mentioned in that Chapter are culled from Naadi Granth: A Study - By Late Shri. Shantaram Athavle (He was famous for his contribution to Marathi Film Industry in Sixties, as a Director, Lyricist and Script writer and admirer of Naadi astrology). Both of these books deserve a close study by the students of Naadi astrology.

The critics of Naadi Predictions say that statements made by the Naadi about the individual's past are found to be correct but those about his future are found to be wrong. This criticism is misleading. In as much as the terms 'past' and 'future' are relative and the 'past' about which the critics speak, was in fact 'future' when the sages (Maharshees) wrote the Naadi Books. So if the past of the individual is correct, it means that the 'future' predictions made by the sages about him, when they wrote them are correct. Now, if future events predicted in the Naadi are found to go wrong after the individual consults it, then there must certainly be some reason for it. Apart from what the reason is, it must be emphasized that the 'Future' as predicted by Naadi does not invariably go wrong as alleged by the critics. At any rate, no body has proved this by undertaking an extensive survey of Naadi Predictions. {One Investigator, nicknamed, 'Giriraj' undertook the study of Naadi Predictions and found that the predictions about 21 persons were found to be completely wrong, those of 3 persons were 80% correct and those of 2 persons were 100% correct.}[1]

There are many cases where all the predictions about the future events are found to be 100% correct. In this context it is relevant to ask: How can the sages, who make 100% correct predictions about the individual's 'past', including his name, his birth date, day, month, year etc. and planetary positions at the time of his birth and many other small details - like the date when he is consulting Naadi, the names of the persons present at the time, of his consulting etc, make wrong predictions about the future events of the individual only after he consults his Naadi? One can not but conclude that it is not the sage should be held responsible the ostensible wrong predictions, but the individual who has failed to interpret them. One is at least justified in maintaining that no judgment on these so called

---

1. Comments by Wg Cdr Shashikant Oak, 'Giriraj' does not mention where and when were his observations conducted, in which Naadi Centres, of which Naadi Maharshi etc. Therefore, these figures should be taken as mere presumptions.

wrong predictions should be passed by any one before through investigation of them is undertaken. Such an investigation has been conducted by a retired Judge late R.S. Vaze of Pune, in late sixties. Even before Shri Shantaram Athavle, the celebrated author of above mentioned book, after a laborious and through study of many Naadis. It pays to survey his conclusions....

The sages do not see future wrong but predict it incorrect. (From page 134) ...

As stated previously, in one case of a person, who took birth along with millions in some part of India, Maharshi Bhrugu in his Samhita could pin-point a petty error being committed while repeating daily mantra-jap as a part of religious ritual. Is it not utter surprise that for an insignificant individual, the sages by their omniscience could envision such minutest details in distant future, can not visualize an event in a life of an individual after he/she consults his/her Naadi Samhita correctly? Yet it is true that the events predicted by the sages after he/ she consult his/ her Naadi Samhita are often found not to be corroborated. They are found to be completely wrong. The obvious inference is that the sages whose ability to see past, present and future - omniscience- is beyond doubt do see the future events correctly even after he/ she consults his/her Naadi but they predict it wrongly. Therefore, one has to conclude that there has to be some definite purpose behind these wrong predictions. Many instances have been cited to strengthen these assumptions. From those incorrect predictions, the sages reveal the intrinsic intention – objective - of writing of those predictions comes to light. The sages want each individual to depend upon his own efforts and not be a fatalist. In other words, the dictates of the individual past *Karma* which in effect means that the individual is left free to reap fruits of his past *Karmas* remain unhindered, by keeping him in ignorance about the future events, while at the same time leaving enough room for his own efforts and initiative for his future progress.

This means that the sages do not expect any individual to consult the Naadi books unless individual finds in dire situation where all avenues of future course of actions appear to be very bleak. It may sound paradoxical to suggest that the sages who have purportedly written the Naadi books to predict an individual's future do not want that individual to know his /her future unless constrained to do so. But this, in fact, is true. It can be substantiated by concrete examples.

Case of Shri.Talekar

It was found in the Naadi of Shri. Vasantrao Talekar, the friend of Shri. Ajgaonkar, that all the details predicted about his life were correct, but the latter part proved wrong. Shri. Ajgaonkar described his friend's life predictions by the Maharshi in the following words :- "Shri. Talekar found his bronchianal problem intractable; it resisted all kinds of current medications. So he consulted Kaushik Naadi by paying a special fee of Rs.75.

The Kaushik Naadi's (Aushadh) Health Kandam correctly mentioned the names of Talekar's father and mother. The names of his wife and four children were also correctly mentioned. One daughter formerly named as Jayashree but name was changed to Sandhya after three years. This small detail was also correctly noted by the Naadi.

The native was suffering from asthma and the reason for this was traced to a former life. The Naadi Samhita had suggested an Aurvedic remedy for it; a list of medicines was given. The Samhita had also given the address of an Aurvedic doctor residing in the south. That doctor gave the medicines and Talekar was completely cured.

" Thereafter Shri. Talekar went to Washington (America) to occupy a high salary post as predicted by the Kaushik Naadi. His life there was very prosperous for 5-6 years. The Naadi also predicted that he would have two houses, that he would retire at the age of 58 and that he would live a life of 67 years."

"Shri. Talekar came to his office and sat in his chair on 10-3-1954. He died there suddenly as a result of heart attack. Some of the events predicted by the Naadi proved correct in every details but he passed away from the world before the event predicted by the Naadi. For the latter part of his life could take place." (Page 158)

Now the question is : Can it be believed that the sage who knew the nature of Talekar's disease, even the address of the doctor where the remedial medicine could be found, could not or did not know the time of his death? Suppose that the sage had written that Talekar was going to die in America during the period of his active service; would Talekar have gone to America? Would anybody take the trouble in order that the prediction of Naadi may prove correct? It is but human nature to avoid death – that too premature death, by any means. It therefore, seems, logical to conclude that the sage Kaushik made wrong prediction of Talekar's death. (And correct prediction of his foreign service)just to mislead him. This conclusion is supported by other Samhitas too. Take example of Bhrugu Samhita.

"Once a millionaire came to Dixit[2] (Bhrugu Shastri) to consult about his future. After verification of his birth chart, the relevant page was opened. It was said in that his future should not be read. The Shastri could not help disappointing the millionaire. It was later learnt that the millionaire had died soon afterwards." (Page 89)

This example clearly shows Bhrugu's intention of not allowing the millionaire to know that he was going to die soon. Otherwise, millionaire would not have committed the acts which he actually committed or would have committed other acts which the sage Bhrugu did not want . Where the Naadi reading is of future cannot be helped, the death itself is wrongly predicted. This is applied to other predictions too. Which ordinary people are not expected to understand and which the omniscient sages alone know through their super sensuous power? Ordinary persons can only see that predictions are wrong, but not why they are wrong. The sage's intention in making Naadi predictions is to give free

---

2. Shri, Shiv Kumar Dixit of Meerut. Presently his grandson Shri Vinit Kumar Dixit divines the Samhita. From House No. 418, Budhana Gate, Meerut (69 Kms from New Delhi, UP, India).

play to the actions of the person and not to keep him hamstrung by them. They do not want him to always depend on Naadi Predictions (or astrology) but to make use of them when absolutely necessary and where the predictions are useful they always prove correct. For example, Talekar's disease was cured only by the Naadi predictions. Where it is not useful, the sages intentionally make wrong predictions. They expect the person to take initiative there. By making wrong prediction about Talekar's death, he was induced to take initiative in a foreign country to achieve success and lead a life of prosperity for 5-6 years. It was within his power to do so. And part of his efforts. However, his asthma problem had proved intractable to current medicine and so the sages gave him proper direction for its cure. There Talekar's efforts had come to a dead end and hence he had turned to Naadi as a last resort and Naadi did not fail him.

The fact that the sages expect man not to know his future and that even if he knows it, he should know it wrong and that he should know his past correctly, suggests that they want man not to be an astrology dependent but be dependent upon his efforts and do his duty (Practice Karma Yoga Of Geeta) and also that he should understand the truth that the nature (or God for those who believe in Him) has so planned the things of the universe that the future should always remain unknown to him. This conclusion is borne out by the study of the Naadi predictions of 25 persons by 'Giriraj' himself referred to above. (See footnote 1) Even though the sample is meager for statistical treatment, the fact that he found the predictions of more than 80% of the persons wrong, is significant, since it confirms the above conclusion. This conclusion gets another confirmation by the example of an extraordinary case cited by 'Giriraj' himself of his own Naadi experience. This extraordinary case of his own Naadi experience is given in his own words.

"One of my friends had committed a serous crime about which I, of course, had not any knowledge. It was not known to any body else either, other than my friend himself. Under this circumstance, I took his birth-chart to Babubhai[3] (Bhrugu Shastri) on the request of the friend and came to know the full details of my friend's crime. Of course, his Naadi book did not contain the information (Prediction) of his crime before it was committed. We had approached Babubhai with the friend's birth-chart in the month of January. There was no mention at that time in his book about the crime he was going to commit in future (In the month of November). But I came across the information of my friend's crime he had committed about two months previously (In the month of November).When I had approached, Babubhai about one year later (In the month of January). This wonderful example, in my opinion, gives a hint that the CID and the police department can make use of this science for investigation crimes in the society". (Page 146) ...

Now the question arises: how did Giriraj come to know of his friend's crime after it was committed (In January, about a year later), which he had not come across in his friend's Naadi book before it was committed (In November)? No matter how he came to know of it. (Giriraj had not elaborated this point) It is abundantly clear that the plan (of the sages) seems to be that man should know the past but should not know the future. If his friend had come to know of the crime he was going to commit in future, (From his Naadi) he would not have committed it at all. But it was his destiny (and the desire of the sages) that he should commit the crime. Now suppose that the sages had written about his future crime in such a way that he knew it before hand. Then he would have avoided it. And the prediction of the Naadi would have thus been proved wrong! Thus it would have proved the sages' intention that the man should know his past correctly but should know the future wrongly. In other words, the above conclusion that the future

---

3. Well-known as Chhayashstri, who uses to measure the shade of the person to take out exact leaf for the person. His children are running the centre in Mumbai. For the latest addressee see List of Naadi centres at the last section.

should remain unknown to the man, which is nature's or (God's) plan, would be again vindicated! But of course, it was in the destiny of his friend that he should not know of his future crime from the Naadi and should commit it in accordance with the famous adage that 'Man's past Karma determines his present will or the man will obey the dictates of his past Karma (cqf) dekZuqlkfj.kh) that he should know of his crime from Naadi only after he commits it. That was his destiny and the sages also wanted that his destiny should prevail.

Giriraj says that police department can use Naadi for investigating crimes. It means that the Naadi reading should be undertaken only when it serves the purpose and should not form a habit of man; and this exactly is the purpose of the sages in writing Naadi books.[4] In this way, many eternal truths are revealed to man by the Naadi. That is why Giriraj finally says that Naadi phenomena of India should serve to throw light on thousands of ill-understood phenomena...

Naadi Predictions and Karma theory

The above mentioned case reports prove that human efforts are completely governed by Karma and can not be other than what they are as result of its prevalence. And when Karma prevails the predictions about the events take place after the person consults his Naadi are found to be invariably correct. Here are few samples to illustrate the point.[5]

The sage Bhrugu declared about the frustrated married life of lady that she had to suffer the consequences of her past Karma. Shukra, his disciple, thereupon tries to intervene on her behalf by pleading that he should suggest some spiritual

---

4. Naadi is useful to man during a crisis only and hence it should be consulted during a crisis only.

5. The reader is advised to read for more details the cases of Shi. Gore, Ajgaonkar, India-Pak conflict of 1965, premature death of Indian scientist Bhabha etc. given on pages 166-167 of the Marathi book ßukMh xaBk,dvH;kl&cS- 'kadjevBoyeP

remedy to alleviate her suffering. Bhrugu replied that though he had sympathy for her, he was helpless... in the course of this conversation, a correct prediction about India-Pak conflict was heard to have been made by Bhrugu, and it took place as predicted accurately...

Bhrugu also made a skilful reference to Bhabha's achievements (In the atomic field) and later his sad demise. Four months after this prediction was read Bhabha dies suddenly in an aeroplane accident, proving the accuracy of Bhrugu's prediction.

This shows that the sages are helpless before all powerful Karma. The prediction and its fulfilment itself testify their helplessness.

The duty of the sages' is to see that the law of Karma prevails. Naadi books are not written to predict future as commonly believed but to bring about the results of Karma in accordance with law of retributive justice which Karma stands for. This is accomplished by even making wrong predictions wherever necessary, as was done in the case of Talekar. Or by refusing to predict the future as was done in case of the millionaire or by pleading helplessness as was done in the case of the unfortunate lady (of frustrated married life) or as was done in the case of Bhabha's death, or India-Pakistan conflict, or as is always seen to take place in respect of natural events, as is proved by the following example:

"Shukra said to Bhrugu, (Because there was no rains) 'A plan is afoot to evacuate the people from this city of temptation (Mumbai) because of scarcity of water', Bhrugu said, ' listen Shukra, definitely there will be rains on the day specified by us and thereafter rains will continue to pour 21 days without break. Then the people who prayed for the rains to come will pray for rains to stop.'

... Last year, the citizens of Mumbai did have the salutary experience of this predictions which Bhrugu had made using the pretext of the Japanese machine of Achutbhai. There was absolutely no sign of rains till 22nd July. That night the Chief Minister of Maharashtra gave a call on the radio to the citizens of Mumbai to go back to their native places so that the city could tide over the water crisis. The rains started correctly in the early morning at 4a.m. on 23rd July as predicted by Bhurgu and that too heavily. It is well known fact that the rains continued to pour incessantly for next 21 days. Thus Bhrugu's prediction came true, in the literal sense."(Page 164-165)…

The above case (and other cases cited previously) proves that not only individual Karma but collective Karma (future) of humanity also is already determined and the accuracy of the predictions of the sages prove that they are omniscient that is, they know all, the future events correctly unless they were predetermined , that is preordained. These pre-ordained events include of those persons consulting their Naadi Putties (Leaves) are written by them. Those self-styled rationalists who seek to prove that the Naadi books are a fraud on the basis of the practical impossibility of writing of future of every person on the earth, are thus exposed as rank ignoramuses. That they know the hollowness of their own rationalist argument is proved by their unwillingness to have first hand experience of Naadi. They obviously do not have it for fear of being thus exposed. ❏

Atri Jeeva Naadi

DYNAMIC PREDICTIONS FROM MAHARSHI ATRI AND HIS CONSORT ANUSUYA

Jeeva Naadi is dynamic, vibrant and live Naadi predictions, wherein the Maharshi reacts to the needs or problems of a person, as if he himself is present before the seeker. He is reacting to the situation of the happenings on the spot. Thus, it is a very special and precise method.

Introduction

By now the readers of 'Naadi guru on web.org' web site are aware of the Naadi Predictions. They are astonishing divinations of the ancient sages written on the palm leaf like Agasthya, Vashista, Bhrugu, Shukar, Kak Bhujanda and many whose names we read only in scriptures of Indian literature.

What is Jeeva Naadi?

Jeeva Naadi is dynamic, vibrant and live Naadi predictions, wherein the Maharshi reacts to the needs or problems of a person, as if he himself is present before the seeker. He is reacting to the situation of the happenings on the spot. Thus, it is a very special and precise method.

The present standard system of Naadi predictions is that, the seeker gives the thumb impression as per the gender (who tries to reach the leaf) and tries to reach out to the exact leaf which matches to the description of the seeker. In this system, there are chances that one may be lucky to pinpoint the pertinent palm leaf in matter of minutes or some times after hectic search of many hours, one has to go empty handed to try for the next time or to forget it as a bad joke.

"Jeeva or Dynamic Naadi" apparently looks similar in its appearance. But the contents and the method of reaching to the exact matter on leaf differs to a great extent.

There is a Jeeva Naadi of Maharshi Atri or Atreya and his consort Mahasati Anusuya. Many may not be aware about these personalities as per *Puranic* legends. Atri and Anusuya, were the famous couple, for their penance and powers they had gained by severe *Yoga Sadhana*. They were tested by the three personalities who were supposed to be the creators Brahma, Vishnu the saviour and Shiva the destroyer. In disguise as hungry and tired pilgrims, the trio made a firm demand for mid-day meals immediately; putting a strange and queer condition; that, Anusuya should serve them without clothes, without waiting for the host Atri, who was yet to return from morning rituals, (Anusuya should serve them without clothes.)

Realising that this is a façade to test her, she complied the demand. Not only she turned the trio into infants but also breast fed them. Maharshi Atri was delighted to see the strange sight on return. His wife Anusuya, very fond of children was blessed with three extraordinary children. The trio asked Atri Maharshi to relieve them. However, the couple converted them in an *Avatar* called *Dattatreyaa. Datta* means given or presented, *traya* means trio , *Atreya* means *to Atri family.* In short, Avatar of the trio presented to Atri and his consort Anusuya for the betterment of the worldly affairs. The *Dattatreya Avatar* later on was treated to be the initiator of the *Nava Nath - Sampradaya* commune of nine Siddhas, Aadi *Nath* - Primal being Shiva.

The present day person could seek the counsel of Maharshi Atri and Anusuya from three packets of palm leaves. The seeker starts getting ready and instant written answers narrated by the Naadi reader as if the couple is present opposite the seeker.

The procedure

The seeker gets an appointment for the day and time. When called in, the seeker prays for the blessings of the Maharshi. The 12 conches or cowries are thrown for getting the exact leaf. There is another method of arriving to the exact leaf for those who are not physically present and wish to seek the blessings of Maharshi. The person has to tell, any random number from 1 to 108. Based on that number, the reader will reach to the leaf and start narrating the matter pertaining to the question / query. On one occasion in reply to a specific query, Atri Maharshi had suggested this method to get him from far off places in future. The seeker loudly narrates the query, question or requests in his language. The reader understands it with the help of the translator, if needed. After turning requisite palm leaves based on the number of cowries falling overturn position, the reading starts.

After reading some sentences from the leaf the reader starts narrating what Maharshi has to say on the posed question. The meaning is narrated in the required language. When the narration is over the seeker could ask next point, if needed. Maximum of five questions or points are replied in one session.

The points in written format help to be precise and easy for comprehension. On many occasions, it is observed that the point is further elaborated by the way of discussion between the couple. On occasions on behalf of the seeker, *Maata* - Mother - Anusuya elaborates the question or some times persuades to (remove) her spouse to provide the solution or remedy out of her concern for the seeker.

While in the session the atmosphere gets surcharged with emotions. It changes in jiffy. Some times laughter occupies the light mood, smile appears on the receiving best compliments from Maharshi. When scolding appears through the reading for the mistakes committed, face becomes gloomy; the tears roll out for regrettable the plight; on finding solutions to come out of the grim future the heart beats return to normal pace. On some occasions Maharshi himself, with his spouse gets choked up with emotions. They plead for grace of the Almighty - *Param Shiva* - to pull out the deplorable state of his seeker. The seeker feels overjoyed when Maharshi himself assures that he will start penance on his behalf. The heart fills with gratitude that in times of difficulties one is not alone. There is some great power to protect us, guide us if sincerely reach out for the assistance in time. What is the meaning of this sentence.. Heart filled emotions, tears in eyes, when all - seeker along with reader and translator - come out, every one goes into exhilarated state of mind for a long long time.

This is only the outline of what happens inside the reading room. One (had) has to witness it, experience it to get the divine blessings and guidance of spiritually enlightened souls. With the hands folded for prayers, head bowed down with reverence, if one goes to seek blessings, why will he not get the best of the supreme divine?

❑

Sarva Dharma Temple

Agasthya Statue installation in Sarva Dharma Temple
at B' lore Cantt Railway Station and
creation of Saibaba Temple
at H. Nizamuddin Railway Station

(Gp Capt Rakesh Nanda showing his palmleaf before
Agasthya's statue)

In an interview of Gp Capt Rakesh Nanda by Wg Cdr Shashikant Oak, he narrates how this temple has taken shape. How wonders like Honey dropping, Appearance of Holy ash on Naadi leaf and materialized Golden coin on 23rd Feb 2012, took place. Saintly temple has gained reputation of place of fulfilling of rightful desires. (इच्छापुर्ती मंदिर)

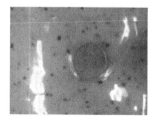

Naadi Maharishi Agasthya statue was installed on 29th March 2012. B'lore Cantt Railway Station complex, in 160 MCO's office peremises, Sarva Dharma Temple, to pay homage for his contribution of Naadi literature in Tamil, under supervision of Shri Ananth Raman great devotee of Saibaba of Shirdi.

Rakesh says his outlook towards life underwent change after getting blessings and readings by many Naadi Maharishis.

(Gp Capt Rakesh Nanda praying to Saibaba in his new temple made in Oct 2012 in Nizamuddin Railway Station office premise)

❑

It was written...

Gp Capt Rakesh Nanda's firsthand experience of finding his Brahma Sookshma Naadi Palm Leaf is another example supporting the strong belief that 'everything is written'.

(Gp Capt Rakesh Nanda in his full medals)

"Pranam, Sir; I am on the way to Pune." Wing Commander (the then) Rakesh Nanda, my best friend opened up the conversation on an early morning phone call. It was impromptu and without notice. His voice was not cheering as usual, and therefore I happened to ask if everything was alright. He said, "Sorry to inform, Renu – my wife has lost her mother and hence we are on the way to Pune. I'll contact you upon reaching. Let's see if we can meet up."

At about 10:30 hrs, as I was getting ready by finishing the morning duties, Rakesh called up to intimate that he had dropped his wife at his in-law's place, and he had reached Pune Railway Station for booking the return tickets. "Where can we meet?" Rakesh asked. Imagining all the situations and considering the time schedules together, I said, "You are already half the way towards Koregaon Park. If you don't mind, we can meet up in Shiva's Naadi Center itself." Of course, it was comfortable for both of us to meet up at a Naadi Center in this situation. "No problem Sir, I shall be waiting for you at the Naadi Center," Rakesh replied even without giving a second thought.

By the time I reached, Rakesh had already given his thumb impression to the Chief Naadi astrologer Mr. Shiva Shanmugam. "Shiva informed me that he has packets of Brahma Sookshma Naadi written by Brahma Maharishi. I had heard about this before, but had never got a chance to check out my own predictions. Therefore, just out of curiosity, I've given my thumbprint," Rakesh explained.

After a while, Shiva brought out a sword sized packet of palm leaves holding in his both hands. It was unexpected to see palm leaves of that length (later we also measured it, which came out to be around 30 inches). I noticed that the leaf had three written columns on it, differing to one written column in other palm leaves. The rear side had a few lines scribbled starting from one end to the other without any break whatsoever.

"Let us start searching, Swamy!" Shiva exclaimed in his heavily Tamil accent, indicating us to move to his reading room. At first, around 10 to 15 leaves were discarded as they were not matching with Rakesh's information. Gradually, a leaf was found which contained almost all the details. Rakesh kept confirming the details by answering every question in affirmative. Finally, we knew that Rakesh's leaf had been found out.

We left Shiva to copy the contents from the leaf in modern Tamil script, as Naadi readers usually do. Sitting next to him, we started conversation with each other. His writing was going on, and we were also noticing it. While copying down the names from the palm leaf to the notebook, Shiva promptly stopped writing the notebook, turned to us and showed us how each of the names like 'Rakesh' (self), 'Surender' (father), 'Chanchal' (mother), and 'Renu'(wife) appear in the palm leaf written in ancient Tamil script. Thereafter, he continued writing and we continued our discussions.

Suddenly, at one place Shiva stopped writing and turning towards Rakesh he asked, "Swamy, there is a mention about your parents, which I find vague. I am not able to understand. Can you please throw some light on this?" Shiva pointed out that in the palm leaf, it is written: "The day (on which this Jaataka has come to consult this leaf) is significantly special for his parents." Shiva went on telling that a figure '50' also appears on the leaf, connection of which he was unable to understand. According to him, the nature of the verses and language was that intricate.

Rakesh almost jumped to say, "Yes! Actually today happens to be the day of 50th marriage anniversary for my parents. We were prepared to celebrate it in grand way at our hometown in Rajasthan, but due to the unfortunate demise of my mother-in-law, we've cancelled the celebrations and came down to Pune. My parents should also be reaching Pune this afternoon by flight for the last rites. But how do you know? Is it written there?"

Shiva could not hide his mischievous smile while nodding his head and saying, "Everything is written Swamy, everything is written!"

The writing was over, the tape-recording was ready. While handing over the notebook and the cassette, Shiva carried the original palm leaf in his hands and gifted it to Rakesh as a special token from his Naadi Center. Too much dose for a day, Rakesh could not believe that a leaf was awaiting for him so far from his place, in Pune, and within two hours he shall have to compulsorily salute the Naadi Maharishi imagining how could the Maharishis know that Rakesh will go for his reading despite the sad event in his close family?

Many people must have read the fantasies of 'Alice in Wonderland'. But very few have actually experienced something that is more amazing and true also! It is my honor and proud-privilege to present this real time incident occurred in Pune. The Brahma Sookshma Naadi means the palm leaf believed to be written by Brahma Maharishi, which is of a sword's length was patiently waiting in some corner of a Naadi Center in Pune, to be picked up on 7th May 2010 – the day which was Rakesh's parents' 50th wedding anniversary! Rakesh had to undergo chain of extraordinary occurrences, culminating into getting his leaf in most accidental manner!

Normally, Rakesh's trip to Pune was not planned one, at all. Secondly, Rakesh had come to Pune Railway Station for his personal work, and had not even thought of going to a Naadi Center. It was my casual request to him to meet up in Naadi Center. And for that matter, even I didn't know he would go for a reading! We could have met anywhere else! I had requested him merely calculating the distance involved for both of us to cover to meet up at a common place.

Lastly, contrary to the traditions, Shiva had gifted the sword sized palm leaf to Rakesh, asking him to undertake future research work on it.

Attached the photographs of the palm leaf, for the benefit of those who are curious to see it.

That all aptly confirms a saying that all human beings are bound by the chessboard of destiny. Doesn't it so?

This is the 75 Cm size palm leaf narrated by Wing Commander Shashikant Oak. Photo craft and worded by Haiyo Haiyaiyo:

Gp Capt Rakesh Nanda has uncanny knack of maintaining 4-5 mobiles for the benefit of Naadi related queries !! Presently they are: 08510011372; 08800104572; 9870142928; 09986447895; 09763276806….!!!

चतुर्भुजा मोबाइल धारी। गले पांचवा लटकता है।
Holds Mobiles in four hands and fifth one hangs around neck!

Life Changing Events narrated by some Naadi Lovers

In my earlier edition books, I have narrated how the predictions and actual happenings were true, word by word, as per 9th chapter of my Agasthya Naadi predictions.

It is very solemn duty to provide as much assistance in monitory or other methods, to Shankar Netralaya (Eye Hospital, Chennai) and the Netradaan (Eye Donation).

I remembered some cases in connection with eyesight and Shankar Netralaya in Chennai.

One of the staff member of my Accts section in Air Force station Tambaram office in Chennai had to rush to Shankar Netralaya for emergency case of his son. His son accidentally lost eyesight during Diwali crackers show. While the child was under treatment, he rushed to Nadi predictions to know the predicament of his son. As told, he performed the remedial measures. The hopeless case as per doctor was a success story. The child's eyesight was restored. His timely performing the remedial measures suggested by Maharishi was the reason for his miraculous recovery, so when my colleague thanked me I felt I got credit for nothing.

Also he narrated one amazing case of a lady who had unique eye sight problem. She used to become completely blind on no moon day! And use to regain full sight gradually by full moon!! She became a test case for ophthalmologists all over world!!!

In another story, I happened to attend a marriage in Nashik, some time back. Someone attending the ceremony was selling some perfumes. I liked the flavour. So I managed to go to his house which was very near from marriage hall. As I was about to leave his house, he came to know my name. Hearing my name, the person became immensely happy. He said that he could not believe this, that Wing Commander Oak personally coming to meet him in his house! He not only returned the money for the perfumes but narrated how frantically was he in search for me for so many years! He said, some 10-12 years back he was to go to Shankar Netralaya in Chennai with a close friend of him, who lost eyesight while working in a factory. Some particle had got stuck in the side the retina. The case was very delicate. The Hospital authorities had told that chances of recovery were almost nil! While this was on, the perfume seller who was the then co-worker of that injured person remembered an article written by me in Marathi and some controversy created by the rationalists etc. By merely remembering the name of the place 'Tambaram', somehow he found out the center and got the readings. He was told to do some remedies, for his friend's eyesight. And assured him that the eyesight will be restored so much that one day he will forget that he lost it. As predicted, the eyesight was restored. Because of this incident he had very much faith on Naadi Predictions. His friend did not lose the employment and is still in the same company honouring higher posts. Whereas his friend changed the line and shifted to the perfume business. All these years, he was trying to get my changing addresses due to my defense service. On this background, when I met him in his house, for him it was a very pleasant shock. Later I got the telephone number of his friend and got the story confirmed from his mouth. When contacted his friend, he could not immediately remember his hospitalization in Shankar Netralaya years back! Only after his friend's reference, he could promptly recollect the incidence. He also thanked the Naadi Maharishi!

Thus, life changing events do take place because of the guidance by the Maharishis.

❏

Astrology: Ever-ready Punching Bag!

Astrology is an easy target always to degrade at the slightest excuse, in the eyes of general public.

(Naadi opponents show victory sign by bashing Astrology as a punch bag; but Naadi Maharishis knock them out.)

It is somewhat like a nagging mother-in-law accuses her daughter-in-law for any sundry reason. If nothing could be found she faults her in the food preparation - lacking salt! This allegation she uses as punching bag to beat repeatedly. Similarly, rationalists and atheists use Astrology as punching bag. Media takes care of publishing their views promptly.

But soon the daughter-in-law skillfully wins her husband to control mother-in-law's loud mouth. Similarly, astrologers take help of Naadi Granths to shut hoarse voices of challengers. Actually, challengers have no excuse except repeated accusation, that Naadi readers extract information and pretend to tell predictions being read from palm leaves! They claim to have done research on Naadi Predictions. When confronted with questions like how the names are etched out on palm leaves, they put forth lame excuse of not getting Tamil language expert and evade the topic.

❑

The Qawwali Competition

Astrology is an ancient science   *Astrology is a fake science*

Qawwali is a type of singing wherein two or more parties put forth their view point in form of songs. They present it in competition forum, clapping on stubborn rhythm. One side says for example – 'Love' (मुहब्बत) is a great deal of useful thing (काम की चीज़) in life; other side counters by denouncing concept of love as 'name sake' (नाम की चीज़) affair in life. Likewise there is another controversial subject which generates arguments from both sides. It is 'Astrology' - (फलज्योतिष).

Whether the planets and stars do have an impact on human life – invites heated discuss. What appears to be, there is no direct impact of planetary positions on human life activity.

Take an example. Great deal of road traffic comes to grinding halt at the sight of Red signal. When it turns into Green, the vehicles start and rush off. It will appear for a person who is unaware of the traffic rules, as if there is some sort of strange power in form of waves or vibrations, in the red and green lights which regulates the vehicles. Once this argument is accepted then one has to bring forth various queer arguments to support the hypothesis. Is it supposed to be impact of any kind of supernatural power? It does not appear so; then what is the truth?

Road traffic management had developed a system based on coloured light coding. The rules of this traffic system governance regulate the movement of vehicles. The driver knows the rules of traffic system. Thus, the respective colours regulate the movement. Someone goes for morning walk listening the sirun at 6 O' Clock, does not mean that the sound waves of sirun have some special powers which force only to him to go for morning walk. It is the system devised by him to suit his need.

Can we not accept Astrology as a system devised to indicate life events? The life meter starts with birth of person. The position of stars at the time and place is charted in the form of horoscope. Similarly planatory position at the time of events affecting one's life are compared with birth horoscope of a person. Maharishis, with deep study of plantory positions, have propounded systematic equations or Sutras. Based on Sutras astrologer can indicate, if so and so star configuration takes place in one's horoscope, at certain year of one's life that may be favourable for good results.

In the above mentioned example, it is not necessary that all vehicles will cross the street square, when traffic light goes green. Some vehicles may get stuck in between, due to lack of fuel, or mechanical failure etc. In case some vehicle, after crossing indicator light, meets with an accident, the traffic signal system cannot be held responsible for the mishap. Similarly, even though favourable planetary positions may indicate events likely to happen but due to significant other factors they may not occur at all or happen with delay or lesser intensity. It may be noted that non occurrence cannot be counted as failure of divining system called Astrology.

Prin. Adwayanand Galatge in his monumental book titled, "Science and Miracle" (विज्ञान आणि चमत्कार) referred Yogi Arvinda's quote, "Many astrological predictions come true, quite a mass of them, if one takes all together. But it does not follow that the stars rule our destiny; the stars merely record the destiny that has already formed, they are hieroglyph, not a force.... Someone is there who has determined or something is there which is fate, let us say; the stars are only indicators."

Those who sing Qawwali of deploring the system of Astrology and feel proud in burning the horoscopes in public as publicity stunt; is there any Red light signal to stop them?

❑

Report on the First International Conference

(Held in Prague, Czech Republic in Central Europe, on 5th and 6th June 2010)

Prague received the honour of conducting First ever Conference on Naadi Palm Leaf libraries. Previously, in India, conferences on Naadi Palm Leaf were held in Pune and Vadodara in year 2007 and 2009 respectively. Pavel Krejci was the main person behind this initiative. At that time, no one had slightest idea that the next Conference will be held outside India, by enthusiastic Naadi lovers from a far off western country like Czech Republic.

First Day - 5th June 2010

On 5th June, 2010 Saturday, morning sharp at 10 O'clock conference commenced in the specious old town Hall complex. Before that right from 9 O'clock onwards enthusiastic crowd had started to assemble in queue to register their names for the meet. No hustle. Everything was very peaceful and in orderly manner.

Unlike in India there was no stage arrangement of floral decoration. No banners, no photos of invitees and chief guests etc. hung as back drop. Large table covered with white cloth and decorative chairs, crowd of volunteers running about for last minute preparations were missing. Though the initiation was not as per Indian tradition with lighting of Deepam, the photos

(Peaceful queue for registration of names)

of Maharishi Agasthya and Bhrugu were placed with honour and dignity.

Joseph Schrotter, a friend of Pavel Krejci, announced formal opening of the Conference, from stage of a foot height. He invited Maria and Pavel Krejci for an opening address. Looking at us, he welcomed guests from India. He outlined the program to the audience, and handed over the mike to Maria. She has been the main force of the gathering. She presented bouquets to Chief Naadi reader Shiva Shanmugam, Palanisamy, another Naadi reader, Ravi English translator and Shashikant Oak, expert on Naadi Palm Leaf astrology.

Before the start of the conference, Pavel told us that he doesn't approve of any conventional style of big decorative stage arrangements etc as previous communist regime used to follow. To him, everyone goes to stage and simply delivers his speech holding mike in hand.

We were seated in front row, along with Naadi lover Pavel, Maria, her mother Zdenka. Rodka, son of Joseph was narrating the happenings on the stage in English to us. The entire event was video recorded for future documentary film on Visit of Naadi Maharishi in Czech Republic. Crew members John, Misha, Jiri and others were accommodated by the side of the large Hall. We were told by Town Hall authorities that not more than 30-40 people had gathered for conferences on earlier occasions. They were astonished at the enthusiastic crowd of more than 120 strong Naadi lovers.

Joseph is a well-known astrologer. He possesses psychic powers. He is one of the experts on psychic's analyzer in Czech Republic. He delivered speech with the help of power point projection, on "Sixth Sense and Naadi Palm Leaf astrology". He received very worm enthusiastic response by the delegates.

Next speech was by Shashikant Oak. Continuing the thread of the topic, sixth sense by Joseph, he explained that Naadi palm leaf writings are of similar powers to sixth sense or intuition. The great Maharishis in ancient past possessed many supernatural powers. As many as 72, till now known MAHARISHIS or Great Sages had developed art of collecting wisdom from the Akashik Records available to their highly developed wisdom. They used most extraordinary powers of theirs for the welfare and goodness of the common people. They rendered the services irrespective of any barriers of language, religions, colour of skin, or national boundaries; that too without any monitory gains.

Earlier in his speech, Shashikant Oak outlined the purpose and significance of this conference. His speech was translated in Czech language by Rodic, Son of Joseph. From the occasional powerful clapping by the listeners it appeared that the address was well received.

Maria alias Mari, narrated her experience of Naadi reading pertaining to her own case. She explained the benefit she obtained from Naadi readings and how astonished she was to see her name and other details being shown to her from the palm leaf.

The attendees scattered for the lunch break. Everyone went

to nearby restaurants. There was no special arrangement of lunch by the organizers. Hence, there was no rush for early lunch eaters.

Indian delegates went to one good restaurant. With a mug of beer, they enjoyed Czech Lunch. There was no undue hurry to finish food. Yet we were in time to be in the hall. Second Session started with Shashikant Oak again. He narrated very interesting incidences happened with him. How the predictions of Naadi palm leaf came 100% true. How he met his Guru Yogi Ramsurath Kumar and had glimpse of Divinity in the Ashram of Arvinda in Pondicherry.

Next, Shiva was called on stage. He, in his very melodious voice sang the *Shiva stuti,* praise verses of Lord Shiva. They were followed by singing of praise of Maharishis by Palanisamy. Shashikant Oak was invited to narrate the composition of various chapters or kandams of Naadi Predictions in 12 different facets of life. He described his own shocking experience of 9th Kandam. That amused the gathering.

After Pavel spoke about his own experience, Shashikant Oak, in his third session, opened the topic of human body and development of psychic development of his many faculties by the performing of Yogic practices. They were described by great Sage Patanjali. Thus, the first day ended with "Omkar" singing by Shiva and Palanisamy. Energy level of everyone was ecstatic in the hall with resounding vibrations.

Second Day - 6th June 2010

Without wasting much time, the first session of the second day began with the speech by Shashikant Oak, by sharp 10 O'clock. He narrated the importance and necessity of performance of Shanti Deeksha, as per Naadi predictions. He also narrated many instances of those who performed these rituals as suggested and how they were benefitted from it. He requested the audience to perform as prescribed at the earliest, without fail. The results are obtained sometimes late but are always beneficial.

Shiva took the dais next. He narrated after learning of difficult script in Tamil, how he became expert Naadi reader at young age. Later on in span of 25 years, he had readings of thousands of Seekers, scattered from all round the world. The audience was thrilled to hear that in last 15 years, he had more than 10,000 readings of Japanese clients.

Later Palanisamy narrated how he grew in small village side in south of Chennai, capital city of Tamilnadu, India. After graduation in Science, he picked this art of reading as traditional and sacred duty. Shiva's disciple and distant relation Palani had acquired the status of expert Naadi reader in last 15 or more years.

Translator Ravi, short name of Ravi Golpalan, narrated his background. He was from Pondicherry. After his early struggle, he picked up this profession with the request of Palani. Ravi has the knack of translating the complex and intriguing Tamil poetic expression in simple and most appropriate English. It helps further translation easy, where the seeker belongs to different country/language. He politely stated that he has been serving the needy for more than ten years. He also thanks Maharishis for bestowing with expression power so that difficult and delicate Tamil translation work gives maximum satisfaction to the clients.

Before narrating his experiences Shiva started chanting *Omkar.* The other Indian delegates and entire audience followed him. The auditorium was chock with resounding vibrations of *Pranav Mantra,* for quite some time. It had everlasting impact on the emotionally charged audience.

Shiva narrated what were the predictions by Agasthya Maharishi about a lady who was seated in the first row, named

Zdenka, mother of Maria. He said Agasthya Maharishi had called her as divine incarnation of Mother of Jesus Christ, Mary. Agasthya Maharishi had a high regard for her affectionate eyesight as *Divya Drishti* - Divine Vision. Many amongst present who knew Zdenka, acknowledged with round of applause as a mark of respect.

In between lunch break, many persons wanted to converse with each one of us. But in absence of proper translator many crowded around English speaking persons. In the meanwhile, box kept for collection of queries and doubts was full. All needed to know more about this amazing predictive method.

Shiva, Palani presented memento of Dancing form of Lord Shiva – Nataraja to Joseph, Maria and Zdenka. Shashikant Oak honoured Pavel Krejci and others with Shawl and presented him an abstract painting of Lord Ganesha.

In the end, Shiva sang the praising verses for Agasthya, Vasistha, Shuka, Kak-Bhujander and Koushika and many other Maharishis. The auditorium surcharged once again with very high positive energy.

Joseph Schrotter announced the end of conference, after Pavel Krejci made thanks-giving speech. Thus, the first ever conference in the capital city of Czech Republic concluded with enthusiasm and expectations.

In the next three weeks, more than one hundred Naadi palm leaves were searched out successfully. Video shooting was conducted for everyone. Some paid extra to get recording from the opening of first packet first palm leaf. Everyone was requested to bring own translator for Czech language.

In the concluding days of the stay, the report on this conference was published in July issue of REGENERACE Magazine.

Ladies everywhere!!

Maximum crowd of the conference was of colourful ladies. Youngsters were in tight modern dresses. Some ladies were from affluent society. Many were elderly, above 50 types. Some ladies were acquainted with Indian terms like *Pranaayan, Yoga*. Gents mostly appeared to have arrived to please their spouse. Some gentlemen were attentive and sharp. They were expert in Astrology Energy levels,

Hugs and kisses!!

Greeting pattern in the western world was completely unusual and strange to all of us. A gentle hug and brief lip touching on both sides of cheeks was so rampant that we were flooded with it.

At one time Palanisamy said in jest, "Aiyya (Sir), I have exceeded the number of hugs and kisses till now with my wife in this single day!"

❏

And Holy Ash Appeared on the Leaf…!!!

(Maharshi Bhrigu's Divination in the presence of Shukracharya and other disciples in his gurukul)
Conceived by – Wing Commander Shashikant Oak
Art work by – Sri Hiremath, Pune. (22ⁿᵈ Nov. 2012)

It was Tripurari Purnima (Full moon day) on November 28, 2012 . Place – Hoshiarpur, Bhrigu Vihar, 3rd lane of Birbal Nagar on Una Road. Guru Nanak Jayanti was being celebrated by cutting a cake. Pandit Shyamacharan Tiwari, Bhrigu reader (Vachak) was surrounded by Sardarjis and some women. I too found place near to the reading dais, keeping video recording equipment ready for shoot. Before that I presented above picture of Maharshi Bhrigu and Shukra Maharaj with their disciples divining about people present, in his Gurukul to Pandit Shyama Chanran ji. A copy of Special Diwali issue published in Marathi, focused on Naadi Granths was also presented to him. Around four o'clock in the afternoon, Pt. Shamacharan ji opened old manuscript pages of Brigu Kathan (Phal) from neatly wrapped in Satin like cloth.

Some handful of pages, may be about 40-50 were picked and distributed to 5-6 people by him. A bit surprised, I asked, "What am I supposed to do?" A woman sitting next to me (later I found her name to be Neeru Bhatia) said, "Keep turning these pages one by one. Whichever page appears with Vibhuti (Holy Ash) will be the one on which divination will be read for the day." Everyone began to turn the pages. Someone from behind shouted, "Wait, I have something." Like in the game of Houji - Houji or popularly known as Tambola, someone claims the stake, but that turns out to be a hoax call. Thus, finding the exact page continues. After turning some 12-15 pages, I was shocked at the sight of Holy Ash appearing on a page in my hands! "Look at this!!" I exclaimed with surprise! White ash was neatly spread over bogus yellowish old sheet of paper with some purposeful shape! Someone said, "Look, look, this is just a replica of the picture just presented to Pandit ji!" Everyone readily agreed looking at cryptic shape of Maharishi Bhrigu and Shukra Maharaj with disciples sitting opposite in semicircle!

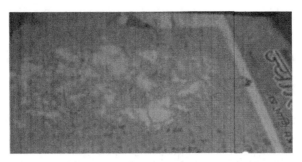

Holy ash appeared on this page

Soon reading started. After some reading about persons present there, Maharishi Bhrigu started narrating about me, which was as follows:-

"O Shukra,… Today, Shashikant – my devotee – is also within my sight. He shall continue to be engaged in studying many of my divine texts, especially the Naadi Granthas. He shall continue to publish the texts for the cause of social welfare. His work shall cause benefit to the needy souls. By the virtue of these deeds, he himself shall get good returns. He shall continue to receive the choicest blessings from many places.

O Shukra, in the ancient times he used to reside in my Ashrama and it is from the teachings of those times he remains eager to earn the choicest blessings through my voice. I too, derive pleasure while blessing him.

O Shukra, let be my choicest blessings on this auspicious celebration day. This day also forms the yoga of the destruction of the demon Tripura. Thus, by chanting Lord Tripurari Mahadeva's name shall bring good fortune to him by eradicating three disorders (mental demons) within him. In the coming times, he shall get to know many strange secrets and shall get the divine darshanas (visions) of many masters and sages. As the choicest blessings, I have transmitted this message of wisdom today. Time to time, in the future, he shall receive the divine orders from various places."

❑

Emergence of Bhrigu Divination on Blank Paper!

Pandit Madan Mohan reading from blank paper!

Place – Punjab – Jalandhar, Bhrigu Darbar of the Pt Madan Mohanji's residence Kothi 11, Prakash Vihar Enclave on Nakodar Road. On November 27, 2012, I was welcomed into his house early in the morning. On his suggestion, I took bath and had heavy breakfast of Punjabi stuffed parathas prepared by his wife Nirmalji.

Bhrigu Pandit Madan Mohanji is different person from other Bhrigu readers. He does not possess many old manuscripts bundles of Samhitas. In typical Punjabi mixed Hindi he narrates some experience of people visited him. He mentioned about USA based my friend Mr. Sanjay Aggrwalji, how did Maharishi Bhrigu blessed him to start divining his *wani* abroad etc. I informed him that Mr. Sanjay ji had created Bhrigu Ashram in California after divination given by Bhrigu and other Maharishis in India. These days he delivers Bhrugu Wani(Phal) to divotees.

Since last few days, Pandit Madan Mohan Ji said, he divines predictions and blessings holding in hand A4 size blank paper sprinkled with *kumkum*. Sometimes the matter appeared on a single page is equivalent to 15-20 hand written pages!

At my request, he allowed video recording* of divination for me. After divination was over as per the order of Maharishi the blank paper was held on oil lamp till it got converted into ashes.

Here is the sample of the divination: - ... "Shashikant (Namwale) named son, what more question do you want to ask? If at all, anything left please ask. All types of blessings, especially the blessing of devotion (*Bhakti*)is bestowed upon you. All your work by the power of devotion be fulfilled. Be fulfilled. Be fulfilled. Let good *Karmas* be performed through your hands. Even more tasks are expected to be performed by you to enhance the name and fame of these divine writings. Let your tongue be residence of my divine words. Whatever you utter be fulfilled completely. With these blessings my soul will return to.... Vishnulok . *Shubham Bhavatu.*"

After reading this paper, (O Bhrigu) reader should hand over to the flame.

(***Author's note:** Interested readers could view many video clips available on 'You tube Ac :shashikantoak and get connected to Blogs in Marathi, Hindi and English through my email: shashioak @gmail.com for the latest study work on Naadi.)

❑

In search of Bhrigu
Patras - Nepal Pilgrimage

Nepal Segment Part 1
Report by Vivek Chaudhari (Mo:72760300020)

Dear Naadi Lovers,

We are coming to you with photos and other information on the completion of our Pilgrimage to Nepal and Pratapgadh (UP) 23rd March to 02nd April 2015.

Early morning Wing Commander Shashikant Oak boarded in Goa Exp later I, Vivek Chaudhari joined at Jalgaon and our pilgrimage started in real sense. Before leaving Delhi International

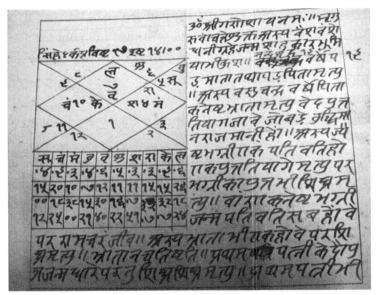

Oak Sir carried a sample of Bhrigu Samhita from his possession.
It proved very little to impress many viewers and Bhrigu Shastra later!

Airport lounge with a huge statue of an old age queen? We were on Tribhuvan Airport Kathmandu by indigo E6031 10.55h

On reaching the airport we were surprised to get greeted by Ms Sanu Thapa Madam. Oak Sir told us that it was just one day before he got the information that she will receive us! We thus were taken care of by divine power to guide the path ahead, in an alien land! She took us to Marwari Samaj Dharamshala. The AC room was suitable for our comfort and purse! Later, one Maharashtrian couple - Mr and Mrs Karmarkar came to meet us in a hotel. For 4-5 generations they were residing in Kathmandu. Yet they spoke very decent Marathi! 'Thanks to my Mrs', said Jagdishji, 'she being from Kashi, she speaks very good Marathi. But now we were worried to get a suitable bridegroom from Maharashtra mainland or from outside places like Varanasi, Gwalior, Jhanshi who could speak fluent Marathi'. They suggested meeting someone called 'Janardan Ghimire', some other press and TV media people so that the message of our search could reach many concerned local people. Ms Sanu told us that she had already tied up with Janardan Ghimire ji, who will conduct a live program on FM radio Channel. It was a surprise for us!

Post lunch, we reached the main Palace called Hanuman dhoka (gate). Drizzle was following us. Met a lady Managing Director of Museum, Smt Saraswathi Singh! She did like the idea of Bhrigu Samhita Patras being in the private hands in Nepal. She said, 'But we are not in a position to do much in this respect. However, we will be on watch in this manuscript. But this type of work is conducted by the National Archive. Collecting her Visiting card we returned from the Royal Palace area. Impressive tall multi-storied monument in intricately carved wooden structure proved how in olden days the royal families used to stay. Hanuman Ji's statue and pair of white painted animals were greeted to go inside the Ministry of Federal Affairs and Hanuman Dhoka Durbar Museum Development Committee.

*Figure 2 : Impressive tall multi-storied monument
in an intricately carved wooden structure*

Figure 3 : Entrance of white-painted animals.

Figure 4 : Oak Sir watching the palace details

On 24th March Ms Sanu Thapa came to the hotel to take us to Raj Jyotish Dr Madhav Bhatarai. We went to meet him by Taxi. The taxi fare used to be Nepali Rs 300 (Rs 200 approx.) The exchange rate being India Rs 1 = Nepali Rs 1.60!

But before that, we went for stroll on the nearby streets. There, we bumped into the Nepal India Library. An inquiry found that a very vast collection of books on many subjects are supplied through the Indian Embassy channel. We got the address and name of the high official to be contacted as Abhay Kumar, PCI.

On reaching his office after gruelling long-distance walk due to some road construction works. We were greeted by strong tea and Jaggery! While getting introduced, Ms Sanu said, she is Sadhika. She left the job and joined Ashram at Goa. On instructions by Pujya Param Guru, she had come to her motherland, Nepal. Since 6 months she has devoted herself for social service Ms Sanu Thapa Madam with Vivek Chaudhari and Sadhana.

'Who is your Guru?' probably because of the spoiled image of saffron-clad Sadhus etc, Abhay Kumar Ji asked mockingly. What Ms Sanu said in a firm yet polite voice, was an eye-opener for all of us. Our Param Guru is Dr Jayant Athawale. He established an institute called 'Sanatan Sanstha'. Though I am Nepali, I was born in Hongkong. Later because of my father's transfers I was brought up in different countries. I was serving in Hong kong. Later I came in contact with Ashram and found myself in mental peace with Sadhana. I was told by Paramguru Dr Athawale to go to Nepal, where her services are required. Thus I am here in Kathmandu. I am accompanying Shashikant Oak ji and Vivekji as per instructions by Param Guruji.

Soon on the introduction of the topic of Bhrugu Samhita and Naadi Predictions, I handed over Oak sir's Hindi Book for his perusal. Going through the book he said, 'Seems very interesting subject'. Looking at the letter by Oak sir, which he had prepared in the meanwhile, requesting his English and Hindi books on Naadi Predictions may be acquired from Delhi based Diamond Pocket Book publication directly.

Mr Abhay Kumar said, 'Well, it is not completely in my hand, but I will strongly recommend to include publications in next year's demand list so that it will be supplied to not only Nepal based Bharat library but also in all libraries run in each embassy in all countries of the world! It was an unexpected assurance! Whether his efforts fetch results or not the time only will tell!

Figure 5 : Nepal - Bharat Library in Kathmandu

Figure 6 : At Dr Madhav Bhattarai's residence
he is being honoured with a shawl

On 24th March, Ms Sanu took us to meet at Dr Madhav Bhatarai's residence. Soon some 8-10 persons arrived as if they were invited along with us as planned! They all later on concluded to have a meeting of Astrologers followed by media reporters and TV channels! So that the people from far off places could get a message of our requirements, and contact Dr Madhav Bhattarai for further details, which impressed him most!

In the meeting, we gave a shawl and showed manuscripts of Bhrigu Samhita to all present.

On the 25th, we got up by 4 am and went to Kantipur studio in Pulchowk. On the way, we picked up Ms Sanu. In early morning show of Geerwan Bharathi (Sanskrit description and Indian culture-related topics)

This is Kantipur - FM Radio on 93.1. Suprabhat, ... Kathmandu and Nepali listeners, this early morning program is being presented by your favourite 'Janardan'. Today our guest is

Shashikant Oak from Pune, India. He was in the Air Force. Now retired and has come to Kathmandu in search of Bhrigu Samhita Granthas. Welcome Oak ji, taking Hindi book on Naadi Grantha Janardan asked, 'what is Naadi? What is the purpose of your visit and in short what is written in Naadi Predictions? Questions were in Nepali and Oak sir replied in Hindi. The same was translated in Nepali by anchor Janardan.

The interview ended with, 'How come Naadi Maharishis are better than Nostradamus?' This question remained unanswered because of the time limit! His appeal in Nepali dialect went to every corner of the Himalayan countryside! Without visiting any valley, mountain tops, villages, our message that whosoever owns Bhrigu Pothis, Patras, Tadpatras, Bhurj Patras are to contact Kantipura FM radio station proved very purposeful. For some time, we felt who would listen to the interview so early in the morning? Will anyone remember our message? Can it fetch any results? The answer we got on the next day when some Astrologers assembled for the meeting said, 'We listened to the interview. But your answer to Nostradamus's question remained unanswered! Why so?' We felt that our hunch was unfounded! Those who are concerned will get to know the requirement! It is a divine design! After that, Janardan Ghimire took to his office and discussed his mission of Sanskrit Gram Yojana! He said, 'We say English is a foreign language. But it is not so. English is nothing but a distorted form of Sanskrit. There is one Purushottam Nagesh Oak, whose writings impressed me most in my college days. After a further study on the subject, I confidently say, what Oak used to say is very correct. Say for example ... like that he narrated many words in English, which with a slight change of ascent to pronunciation means the same. For example, he said, word 'Exit'. It means to go out. Now see 'It' or 'Et' in Sanskrit go, Gaman, Ex means out. So Exit means outgo! Take another word, in Sanskrit, 'Gharma' means generate heat. This word transformed into English as 'Thermo', in Arebic language, it became 'Garam' – hot! In a very short time, he rolled out many English words which had as pr him Sanskrit origin! Smilingly Oak Sir said, 'P.N. Oak happened to be his Uncle!' He jumped from his seat! And said, 'What a surprise! Nice to know that you are close relatives of Oak Ji. I have very high regards for his work on linguistics research!'

Before leaving we visited Pashupati Nath Temple. Inside, there is Adi Shankarachrya Mutt. Before that Oak Sir had occurred Autowriting which indicated to visit the mutt to seek the blessings from the Adi Shankarachrya.

Pratapgadh Bhrigu Centers Segment

Bhrigu centres of Dr Anita Prakash ji Sadhana Surya Ji and Pandit Bipin Mishra ji. They possess the Bhurj Patra written in lipi.

Strange Experience of Lucknow Naadi center

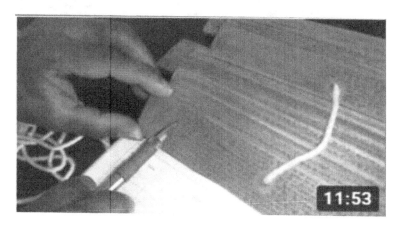

Please click here to know how the names are written in the Naadi palm leaf.

❏

Corona Pandemic and Naadi Predictions

As we are now undergoing the COVID 19 - second wave all over the world. It will be interesting to see what ancient sages had said about its spreading and letting it go. (Sep 26th 2020 situation:- Deaths in India - 93,319 and 9,89,502 in the world.)

Reading of Maharishi Atri and Mata Anusuya over mobile conversation with Eashwaranji

On 30th July 2020, Avadhani and his family contacted Eshwarji's Naadi centre to seek blessings from Maharshi Atri and mother Anusuya.

This the conversation occurred between Avadhani ji and Eshwaran ji the Naadi reader. When as per the process, 7 conches had fallen facing upwards. He requested Eshwaran ji to find out about the present situation in India and its effect on humanity in general. What we should do to avoid Corona for many Naadi lovers. What is going to be the future course of action to avoid getting affected by this pandemic? O Maharshi, could you please also bless us so that we have not affected by the disease.

In reply, after opening appropriate Naadi leaf from the packets of Jeeva Naadi possessed by him. Ishwaran ji started reading. He first narrated the significance of the day, 30th July 2020, saying this being Thursday, day of Lord Datta and Jeshtha Nakshatra and Rashi Vrushchik. Seven indicates in many ways towards Devi or Goddesses number. So I will speak to you. You have come here (contacted) after a long gap. You are feeling tired and mentally down.

Easwaran says after reading from the leaf in Tamil, that (Avadhani) your request for this humanity related question has reached to us while we were just coming out of the temple Dattatreya Temple. Anusuya Mata said that I would like to advise Avadhani and his wife. They are totally dedicated to the cause of Naadi reading and has spread the messages to the deserving souls. As previously granted, he has the power to save someone's life as per the divinities wish. Both of them have come with a request.

This coronavirus pandemic (It is for the first time the specific name has been mentioned from the leaves!... - the brackets are from Shashikant Oak) created a lot of loss of life throughout the world. As per our previous advice by many of Maharishis, at different times and places, we have told you that it is a man-made calamity and will have to be dealt with modern medicines and methods. Also, some of the herbal medicines and ancient practices will help to get cured. Please remember many of the messages about this virus has been explained with many faults by the readers as they were not fully conversant with the meanings of the wordings. Some interpreted as per their little understanding, so inaccuracies had cropped up. Yet the general meaning was conveyed correctly.

This situation slowly will ease-out, we are looking after fates of deserving Naadi lovers. This type of situation occurs once in a century. One should not get unnecessarily fearful. It is in as way a curse (अभिशाप) to humanity. It is a nexus of political and drugs manufacturing cartels, research labs lobbies all over the world. However many are conducting research and making vaccines with sincerity.

All are aware of the precautions to be taken suggested by governmental agencies yet some are neglectful. For some, it has become money (Mudra) making business.

Here Maharishi Atri intervenes to say to Anusuya Mata as it was her prerogative to communicate to the couple before them (on Thursday and with the number 7 occurred,) please tell them what is the present position of the vaccine being searched. She accepting the request says, "Yes the vaccine (word in the leaf is not 'Vaccine' but western medicine.) is ready but under rigorous checking so that it should pass all the conditions. It will that take another 4-5 months to get it for the use. But the spread is wide and fast, in the meanwhile don't get worried about, 8 out of 10 are not affected. Keep adopting the Indian way of life, medicines etc.

To you, wife and daughter I bless as usual. I and who had held my hand forever we take your leave.

Shubham.

The Great Naadi Lover - Kaustubh Butala

In the times of Corona pandemic, he has been instrumental in giving the required guidance to many politicians and Govt

Kaushubh Butala

officials. He gets the readings from Naadi Reader MS Ravi, Chembur and Harshad Bhai of Grant road, Mumbai of Surya Samhita. The recent readings he had shared on Naadi Lovers' WhatsApp group.

For the benefit of the reader, some posts are shared in parts.

In a car accident, he miraculously survived. After that his excerpted readings were presented by him on WhatsApp group. He had relentlessly taken part in saving Corona cases arranging hospitals and required emergency equipment in many ways. However, his mother was a victim of Corona.

Excerpts of his Naadi readings

Om Agastyeshay Namah! Om Namah Shivay.

I, Kaustubh Butala, say, always totally surrender without doubts and Maharshi's are very compassionate.

A few days back Lord Shiva said that fully surrender to your

Guru Agastya and selflessly serve the poor, this is the only remedy. More couple of incidents where some corrupt beings will collude to stop me while I try to be focussed on goals set for me. Your prayers will help me. I am sharing some portions...

O, dear Devi... Today, it is utmost necessary to keep him alive. It is also necessary to show him the right ways so as to help him live a meaningful and worthwhile life. And to be able to live a meaningful life, he needs to know some secrets about 'life' itself.

O, Devi... That time is now ripe; this is the right moment for me to reveal some deep secrets about 'life' before him. I shall reveal and describe some relevant facts in detail; which should make the situations clear to him. Please be known... In the recent past, few people who are extremely contemptuous and have a lack of respect for others in general; have been successful in certain vigorous and determined attempts. These people are spoiled and unfit themselves; and with their spoiled brains, they have diminished and destroyed the value and quality of certain situations...(...08)...

O, son...! Be cautious and alert to the dangers like penalties, litigation and imprisonment. The utter darkness of captivity makes anyone lose his vitality and such a person grows weak. Do you realize something, son? Utter selfish people who cannot think beyond themselves, are the ones who usually prosper in material life. If politicians sensibly wish, then they can serve the nation; they can make the nation prosperous. It is their duty also, but they don't do that. **In the company of such people; even the smallest mistake committed by you; shall cause you certain major problems; and shall put you in extremely unwelcome and harmful situations. Therefore, beware; and be your own guard. In the coming times; spend your time and energy for better things like saving the genuine,** righteous people by silently helping them during the anticipated dangerous and distressing situations… (…13)…

The ongoing times are extremely challenging; not only for you; but for everyone in the world. During these times you may have to face many difficulties. Unnecessary complications shall creep in your life during these times, even without you noticing. Even if there are no apparent problems; it is very much likely that you yourself shall invite problems into your life knowingly or unknowingly. To avoid all of this, you must spend your time in meditative sessions. Meditate concentrating upon the soul; and also chant hymns in the praise of Maharishi Agastya. You must do this daily and regularly, and must do it by yourself. Maharishi Agastya shall successfully penetrate into your mind and shall show you the right way ahead. He shall take you to an inner journey of self-exploration; where you'll learn about your ultimate goal in life. It shall help you in improving your own self… (…14)…

O, son… It is better for you to accept the absolute truth through my words than to learn hard lessons by the stroke of time. Meditation shall help you to thoroughly desaturate yourself; and shall make you able to accept the truth comprehensively. Right now it will be best for you to surrender to a right Guru. Therefore, like the right disciple; surrender to the right Guru at the right time and right place. Follow and accept Guru's directions without any doubt or protest; without crossing him or by putting your own decisions above his. O, son… When you lead such a way of life; you will be able to see through your own life. All your difficulties, sufferings and miseries shall disappear from your life. For your entire life, you shall be able to serve society without any obstacles. You shall achieve your goals, and a sense of satisfaction and fulfilment will be there in your life… (…15)…

Though still in very early stages; **the times of armed**

conflicts between different countries have already arrived. The ongoing war shall prolong; shall take a few more years to reach its midpoint. Please be known; towards the end of the Kaliyuga; the truest, self-created and self-manifested final incarnation shall arrive on the planet earth. It is His job to end the Adharma and reestablish the Dharmic order of the world. It is His job to turn the wheel of times. He shall save innocent people; He shall eliminate all brutal and vicious people. Due to His services; the golden age shall begin on planet earth. O child...! Have patience. However prolonged the present times of conflicts and confusions may be; they shall definitely end one fine day... and only after that, the higher era namely Satya Yuga shall bloom. In the Satya Yuga, only intense truth shall rule the planet earth with complete control.... (...17)...

O, child; it is not at all a bad thing to aim to protect the world. But it needs to be done very carefully and very systematically. You can definitely serve the world, aiming to protect it. But before attempting all that, you must identify the persons who are using you; persons who are taking your undue advantage. Because; right now you are surrounded with absolutely ungrateful people. Today they need you and therefore they are climbing upon your shoulders to ride upon you. But you should always remember one thing... That, in all possibilities these people shall be nothing but unthankful to you. By their own choice or by the absolute will of the mighty 'time' itself; these people shall conveniently destroy all your help and services. O, son... They'll just use you for their own political growth by pretending as if they've joined you in your larger cause... (...20)...

Part 2 End.

❑

Interview with Kalicharan Maharaj

Kalicharan Maharaj As narrated by Shashikant Oak

Kalicharan Maharaj

Due to the topic Naadi Granth, I keep getting introduced to many saints - Mahatma and many well-known people. Recently got introduced to Kalicharan Maharaj. I was very impressed by his medium height, fair complexion, melodious voice, scarlet colour, jatadhari (matted hair) hairstyle, the rudraksha mala (Rosary beads) Kirit on it, etc. The meeting for a few minutes turned into hours! Then I suggested that we run a workshop on

Naadi Granth. If you permit, we can present this conversation to the readers. He immediately agreed. Girishji who came with him and prepared the video shooting on his mobile phone. And without any prior preparation, the account of the influence of the Naadi texts of Maharishi in the life of Kalicharan Maharaj Ji is presented to you today. Naadi texts have been engaged in the service of humanity for so many centuries. Naadi Maharishi's Grantha treasure (Sampada) has been motivating us in many ways. When the holy scripture Bhavishya Kalicharan Maharaj proves to be a master and authority figure in his life as a guru, his acquainted, blessed disciples also encourage him to find solutions to the questions and problems present in his biography. What is the significance of human life? Which of our ancestors has caused us problems? How should we live the coming, remaining life so that we do not have to face difficulties in the future life? Ordinary people are confused today due to systematic answers to these questions and lack of proper proof of rebirth and Karma theory. Light on many aspects of Naadi Granth future, the answers to these questions are received from the Naadi granths! The experience of the reincarnation of persons like Kali Putra Kalicharan Maharaj is a living example of the Karma (Vipak) principle. The inspiration and guidance given to thousands of his disciples have brought both spiritual and physical changes in their lifestyles. His followers have experienced the initiation of peace initiation in the Naadi bar in their cohabitation, they are very Thankful to you. The episode of Kalicharan Maharaj ji is published exclusively in Hindi edition of the book "Naadi Grantha Bhavishya - Chouka Denewala Chamatkar". Hope that the readers of the country and abroad will enjoy reading this description and will get inspiration to see the future of Naadi Granth.

Kalicharan Maharaj Akola Interview Part 1-5

Kalicharan Maharaj talks about Naadi Granth future books

I used to call myself Kalicharan since childhood!

Acharya Naveen Kumarji

Acharya Naveen Kumarji is a unique personality. His horoscope matches with that of Bhagwan Gautam Buddha! Maharishis had asked the Naadi reader to do Puja and greet him with honour. His spiritual kandam is provided by him for the benefit of the readers.

Sri Mahaganapathi Thunai; SHIV GNANA

NA SUKSHAM: Perused for Sri Navinkumar:

Goddess Parvathi beseeches Lord Shiva:
Wearing the crescent moon on thy hair joyously, thou activate the human minds, I praise, praise! Just to save the celestials from

the evils of the demons, thou burnt Tripura, I praise, praise! Having given half of thy body to me to indwell magnanimously, thou established equality between male and female, I praise, praise! Having enacted thy cosmic dance at Chidambaram, thou reveal thy five-folded activities such as creation, preservation, destruction, concealment and eternal bliss, I praise, praise! My ceaseless search for beautiful sentences to praise thy glory has proved futile but I revealed a little above just to glorify thou, O Lord and beseech thou to describe proper ways and means to our beloved son to come up in spiritual life with reference to Gnana Chapter, O Lord!

Benedictory reply from Lord Shiva:

I am very much pleased with thy prayer my dear Devi, let me guide our son to come up in spiritual life, as he desires, as thou implored. He was born in Libra ascendant when the Moon was posited in Scorpio, Kethu was posited in Aquarius, Mars was posited in Gemini and all other planets are posited in Leo. As Kethu, the Gnana Karaka is posited in Kendra (5th) house to the Lagna and because of Purva Punya (impacts of spiritual activities that he had involved during the past births), it is sure, he will come up in spiritual life during this present birth endowed, as he desires. He is Naveen kumar; his parents are Nirmala and Krishnan. Jyoti is his wife. He refers to this holy script when Saturn is posited in Virgo and Jupiter is posited in Aries. Enriching his knowledge in various sastras; he will improve his thirst to enjoy further progress in the spiritual life and having engrossed Me (Lord Shiva) both in his mind and heart ever, by sharing his spiritual experiences to the deserved through effective writing, he will win wide popularity in the realm of yogic sciences like meditation.

I know him well and his intention too. I bless him to enjoy flourishing developments in the spiritual life and to get liberated at the end. Impressing high command over the wavering mind, sitting still, contemplating on me constantly, he is advised to involve wholeheartedly in transcendental meditation and for that yogasanas would also be more helpful. Impressing high command over the five motor organs, when he involves in transcendental meditation, he will be able to feel divine vibration and cosmic energy all over his body. Bringing his mind steadily on a horizontal line, he has to listen to the tintinnabulation of Pranava inside, concentrating much on the core centre point between the eyebrows. At this stage, slowly, he will be able to enjoy perfect perfection, embracing the light emerges inside.

Discharging the material duties and spiritual responsibilities vested in him properly, unveiling the curtains that conceal eternal reality, perceiving the truths hidden in eight directions, discriminating the souls that wander hither and thither, understanding the natures and features of Jeevatma (soul) and Paramatma (eternal reality), leaving glittering material clutches, he will be able to realize what Gnana is. Using various mudras properly, measuring the values of shrinking and spreading fingers, he has to grasp cosmic energy at the tip of the fingers and through which; he will be able to perceive the heat passes inside and outside. It would help him to understand proper ways to impress high command over the motor organs and the mind. Grasping spiritual energy at the tip of the fingers, sending the same inside gradually, he will start to operate kundalini inside the spine from Muladhara to Sahasrara.

At this stage, during the cycle, the sperm will become stronger and the body will perceive the heat and sweating inside will take him to reach the zenith. He will start to feel vacuum inside during the process and by oscillating this vacuum up to pass through the seven stages inside the spine and bringing down to pass through the seven stages, keeping his body like a mother, he will become motionless, impressing high command over the Panchabhutas prevail outside. In such transcendental meditation, tethering what withers inside, he will find some secrets on how to roll the chakra (wheel) which emits seven wonderful colours.

Using the light glitters inside, he will visualize himself between the eyebrows, unveiling the curtains conceal. Getting disconnected from the material world, balancing with the rolling of seven colours, he will get merged with the wheel that rolls just above his head, i.e. nothing but ME, Gnana, the ultimate.

For reaching this stage, leaving material clutches properly, he has to purify both inside and outside using various Sadhanas. Sharing the same to the victims of material clutches obviously, hiding nothing inside, he will become medicine or nectar to many devotee disciples. There will be many Monasteries of his. Revealing the top secrets implied in Vedas and Vedantas simply understandable to the deserved, keeping his mind and heart away from material dirt and dust like an infant, I bless him to exist beyond the material body. Convey these secrets to our beloved son, my dear Devi!

Shubham

Translated by P Babu Swami, Nasik.

❏

Conclusion

Astrology is a very interesting and deep subject. It depends on you as to how deep you want to go.

The purpose of this book is to mentally prepare the reader to seek Naadi-readings. Thousands of years ago under very difficult conditions and with deep meditative concentration our ancient sages made those Naadi predictions. Why not then benefit from them and avail of glimpses of your own future?

What will happen at the most? A few years after you have seen and read your Naadi if the events shape as predicted, you would certainly discuss the matter with your relatives and friends. If events do not turn out as predicted, you might drop the matter saying that the sages could not properly predict or there were shortcomings in the same.

Much more can be written about Naadi astrology. The Naadi literature is certainly very astonishing and an important cultural treasure of ancient India. About 200 years ago the heir of Chhatrapati Shivaji, viz. the Maharaja of Tanjavour, Vyankoji Raje Bhosale, made an attempt to preserve and rewrite lakhs of Naadi patties and has thus obliged mankind.

Why is it not possible for modern-day human beings to write out predictions about the future generations, if those predictions could be recorded in ancient times? There are a number of institutions engaged in ascertaining the truth on a scientific basis. They may examine this issue.

If Naadi Pattis record the name of an individual just from his or her thumb impression, is it not possible to make use of this for tracking unknown criminals from their thumb impressions available elsewhere? They could even be convicted on the basis of Naadi prediction evidence. It is also possible that the courts may accept the evidence of Naadi as proof.

It is also necessary to consider whether, instead of having to visit far-off places like Chennai, it is possible to establish Naadi Centres in all other parts of India. If some readers come forward with generosity and offer accommodation and if the problem of translations of Naadis into other Indian languages such as Marathi, Gujarathi, Bengali, Punjabi, Hindi and English etc. is solved, it is possible to propose to Naadi Shastris to setup their Centres in those respective regions of India and abroad. My appeal to Naadi Lovers to come forward to open Naadi Centers in different states of India has turned in to reality. List of such centers is glaring example.

This book has taken into account only such Naadi records which mention a person's name, the names of his parents, wife or husband, the birth date, day, month, year and Tithi are carved on the Patti and the predictions are made from the thumb impressions or from the horoscope. This writer does not recommend or take into account any published Samhita books, which claim to be 'authentic' based on Bhurjapatra etc. I do not condemn those books to be false either. The reader may take note of this.

A lot of research work is yet to be done to know about the history and scope of Naadi as also about the country's future and the possible holocaust of mankind in the future. In the quest, I made frequent visits to the Saraswathi Mahal Library, which is one of the oldest libraries in Asia. Saraswathi Mahal Library is located in Thanjavur, Tamil Nadu, India; and has on display a rare collection of Palm leaf manuscripts and paper written in Tamil, Hindi, English, Telugu, Marathi, and a few other languages indigenous to India. In the same quest, I further visited the institutes which mainly study the Indology; viz: The Institute of Asian Studies, and The French Institute in Pondicherry. During these visits, I got a chance to discuss the topic in length with the stalwarts, and the discussions have widely opened up the new avenues of study. The ancient Tamil language, and the *Koottezhuthu* script in the Naadi palm leaves is now the main topic of discussions of these stalwarts.

I must state that I have exhorted the expert linguists and authorities on the Tamil literature to critically examine the forms of poetry found in the Naadi palm leaves. It has been found out, to say it in short, that the poems in the Naadi are found composed in the style called 'Sindhupa'. It has been stated that the form of poetry is such an intricate one, that it would be the most difficult part for someone to just casually jot down the events in someone's lives in the said form. To give a helping hand to the persons who are studying and researching the Naadi palm leaves from these aspects, I hereby appeal to the readers to send your notebook's photocopies with your written consent, so as to study and use them for public presentation. I also appeal to the software programmers to come forward to program a databank management software which shall further help the researchers in the coming future. Also I request all readers of this book or those who have already obtained their Naadi-reading, to communicate to me their reaction, suggestion and experiences so they can be included in the future editions of this book.

❑

Please Remember

Wing Commander Shashikant Oak does not divine Naadi Predictions. Naadi Predictions are not based on thumb-impressions. Thumb—impressions are used only to trace out the relevant palm leaf of the individual. The predictions are etched out on narrow palm-leaf strips in cryptic Tamil language. Naadi-leaf packets of males are identified by means of their Right-hand thumb impressions, while those of females from their Left-hand thumb impressions.

These predictions are not available by post. To experience the miracle of Naadi predictions your personal visit to the Centre is a must.

To perform the rituals as advised in Shanti – deeksha kandam or not is entirely in your hands. However, if you wish to perform the same; supreme devotion and concentration is a must. You must perform your own rituals of visiting various temples, feeding the poor etc. In case of personal inability your blood-relation should perform the same in the advised sequence. In Deeksha Kandam one is required to pay some rupees on a per-day basis, which includes Puja materials like coconut, flower garland, sweets and the priest's honorarium etc.

Please do not make the advance payment for various kandams. It is my experience that due to tremendous pressure of work, Naadi-Centres do not respond to reminders through letters, or on telephones. Please finish all your Naadi business in your own presence, till then do not be in any hurry to return home.

Please do confirm from the Naadi-readers and available Tamil knowing persons as to how your and your relations' n ames and other details are inscribed in the Naadi-leaf. Please carry your horoscope along to match with the horoscope mentioned in the Naadi Pattis.

There are some individuals and organizations active in creating false propaganda about Naadi predictions. This is something for you to experience and benefit for yourself.

देवनागरी लिपी	ENGLISH	तमिल लिपी	कूट तमिल लिपी
श	SHA	ஷ	
शि	SHI	ஷி	
का	KA	கா	
(अनुस्वार) .	N	ந்	
त	THA	த	

(The Author's Name - SHASHIKANT-
in Devnagari, English, Tamil & Tamil Code Script)

Note: Kindly refer to Page No. 18, 141 & 147 of this book.

Please refer following Blogs and Websites for more information on Naadi Predictions. (click to get connected)

- **At A Glance 1- Shashikant Oak**
- **Workshops on Naadi Granthas**
- **YouTube Account - Naadi Lovers Center, Shashikant Oak,**
- **Wikipedia page for Wing Commander Shashikant Oak (Retd)**

For the information of the readers-

You can download something from the Android apps Google Playstore.

1. Comparison of Naadi Maharishi and world famous Astrologer Nostradamus.
2. Atri Jeeva Naadi - A unique experience.
3. Is Naadi Predictions - a hoax?
4. How to plan a visit to Nav Graha temples in Tamilnadu?
5. How do I get the addresses of Naadi centers?
6. Great Naadi Granth Lover - Group Captain Rakesh Nanda

❑

Acknowledgements

I am extremely happy to make available to English readers this book on "Naadi forecasts" which was originally written in Marathi and later published in Hindi and Tamil. All the publications - in Marathi (6th Edition), in Hindi (3rd Edition) and in Tamil (1st edition) have been highly appreciated.

My sincere thanks to Prof. Sudhakar Joshi who translated the book from Marathi version, in spite of his busy schedule. My special thanks are also due to Sri P. N. Oak, for his invaluable guidance in editing this version.

I also hereby express my gratitude to all admirers of Naadi-preditions who volunteered to convey me their experience of Naadi-Centres and permitted me to mention their   names, in this book.

The help that my family members extended to me in this endeavour also deserves special mention. They looked upon this project of mine as a duty I was rendering to the public in general.

I sincerely thanks **Mr Narender Kumar ji** for Publishing this book by **Fusion Books**, X-30, Okhla Industrial Area, Phase II, New Delhi 110020.

I also hereby acknowledge with thanks the help that the G.D.P. Computer Systems and some Air Force colleagues extended to me from time to time in readying the final version for printing.

Name & Addresses of the Naadi Centers
(Revised upto the year 2021)

The following is alphabetically arranged consolidated information for readers to know some of the places where Naadi Granthas are available at present. Please note that in the course of time some addressess will get added or deleted, phone nos. and fees charged will get changed. The easiest way to obtain date and time of appointment is to send a postcard or contact over telephone / mobile.

Andhra Pradesh / Telangana State

S. No.	Naadi Center	Address
1	Sri Agasthiya Maha Shiva Naadi Jyothishalayam	Door No 1-10-9, Railway Station Road, Bhanugudi Junction, Kakinada - 533003, Andhra Pradesh, Near Blue Bells School, Sri Ram Nagar Mob. : 9573406777, 9959734555, 9032124999 {9/20}
2	Thiru Karan Swamy Mahasiva Sukshma Thulya Naadi Jyothishya	28-16-2, SAI Bhavani Nilayam, Rama Mandiram, Chintavari Street, Eluru Road, Governerpet, Vijayawada – 520002 0886-6631253 Fees Rs 500/- and Rs 300/- (Monday Holiday)
3	Sri Maha Shiva Sukshma Vasishta Naadi	31-3-1A, Beside Masjid, chuttugunta BSNL office, Venkata Ramaiah Street, Maruthi Nagar, Vijayawada - 520004 Ph. : 8099045376 Fees Rs 500/- and Rs 300/- (Monday Holiday)
4	Agasthya Naadi	House No 2-2-647/185,Centre exercise colony, Street No 6, Amberpet, Nallakunta, Beside Lane of SBI, Hyderabad - 500044 Ph. : 40-33064291{5/16}

5	Thiru Dr. K Selva Muthu Kumaran Attri-Graha (Jeeva) Naadi	12/14-A, Thiruvadudhurai Madathu Street, Amberpet, Hyderabad Mob. : 9443986041.
6	Agasthya Naadi Nilayam .	Plot No. A3, MR Towers, Arravelli Enclave, Hasmathpet Road, Old Bowenpally-bowenpally, Hyderabad - 500011 Mob. : 9502238225. Near Pallavi Model School, Mano Vikas Nagar {New 4/16}
7	Sri Nilayam	Plot No.181, Sri Nilayam, 1st floor, S.S. Colony, Hydernagar, Katpally, Hyderabad - 500072 Ph. : 40-65137137 Mob. : 9703720037 {5/16}
8	Thiru A. Thiyagarajan Maha Shiv Vakya Thulya Naadi	H. No. 6/2, Qtr. No. 952/3 opp. Lane to Shahjahan Apartments, Khairatabad, Hyderabad - 560 004 Tel. : (040) 3321196, 23304548 Mob. : 9347146381 Fees not fixed {9/20} Near TV Tower, Saleem Nagar Colony, Malakpet, Hyderabad - 500036 {New} Mob. : 9908904977
9	Mahashiva Vakya Naadi	House No 6-4-321/1, Bholakpur Main road, Musheerabad, Hyderabad-500020 Ph. : 40-39513143 Beside Mallanna Temple, {New 5/16}
10	Sri Agasthiya Maha Siva Vakya Naadi Nilayam	Floor Plot No 22/631, Cm Nagar Vandiyur, Madurai, Tamil Nadu 625020 Phone: 040 27848435 , 040 27722777
11	Vasishtha Naadi	3-9-42, ADRM Hospital Lane Ramanthapur, Hyderabad-500013 Near Devi Sreerama Apartments Sharada Nagar Colony Tel. : 040-27031312 Mob. : 9963334337, 9346346956 {5/16}
12	Sri Agastya Maha Shiva Naadi Astrology Jyothishya Nilayam	1-8-701/3, First Floor, Padma Colony, VST Road, Nallakunta, Near IIT, Ramaiah Near Andhra Bank, Vidyanagar, New Nallakunta, Hyderabad-500044 Telangana Mob. : 8801741837

13	Sri Shiva Naadi Jyothisya Nilayam	MIG-658, 2nd Phase, ESI Dispensery, Ground Floor, Kukatpally Housing Board Colony, Kukatpally, Hyderabad-500072 Telangana Mob. : 99085 02671
14	Thiru Dr. K Selva Muthu Kumaran Attri-Graha (Jeeva) Naadi	Near Ayyappa temple road, Warangal-506 007 Andhra Pradesh Tel. : (0870) 2423363
15	Atri Maharishi Naadi Astrological Center	H.No:15-2-203,, Bhadrakali Temple Road, Warangal-506007 Telangana Tel No. :04364 276188

Delhi State and Noida

S. No.	Naadi Center	Address
1	Sri Agasthiya Mahashiva Tulliya	WZ-35, Janakpuri, Near Laxmi Narayan Mandir, Delhi – 110058 Tel: 9711357510, 9555732017
2	Pandit Jugal Joshi Arun Samhita	C/15-B, Jung Pura Extn., New Delhi -110014 Mob. : 8800804599 Fees Rs. 5000/-
3	Sri Agasthiyar Sughar Naadi Jyodhish Bhawan	65- A, DDA MIG Flats, 100 Yards Opp Qutab Hotel, Phase-1, Near Mother Dairy Booth, Katwariya Sarai, Delhi – 110016 Tel : 26515146, 26851833 Mob. : 9818234498 Fees Rs.1500/- General Kandam Rs. 600/- for rest. (Monday Holiday) {9/20}
4	Naadi Astrology	B-41,1st Floor, Behind Sandeep Vattika, Delhi Cantt, Near Allahabad Bank, main Kantinagar, Krishnanagar, Delhi – 110010 Mob. : 9582117444, 9582106111
5	Agashiya Naadi	E-1/209, Second Floor, Krishna Market-1, Lajpat Nagar, Delhi- 110024 Tel :(11)-29817280, 29813679 Mob:- 9968508239 Fees Rs.900/- General Kandam Rs. 500/- for rest. (Monday Holiday) {9/20}
6	Agastiyar Naadi Jyothish Kendra	J-19/30, St No.3, Vinod Nagar East, near Gurudwara, Mayur Vihar, Delhi 110091 Tel. : 011-2278 9926

7	Naadi Jothida Nilayam	Ch. Dhoopen Singh Marg, Humayunpur, Safdarjung Enclave, New Delhi - 110029 Tel. : 011 2610 5745
8	Thiru Kumaresan Agasthiya Tulya Naadi	2/44 , B Type Building 4 Old Rajender Nagar, N Delhi-60 Tel.: (011) 2582 0012 Fees Rs. 900/- General Kandam Rs. 600/- for rest (Monday Holiday)
9	Thiru R Jaya kumar Agasthiya Tulya Naadi	24/41, 1 & 2nd Floor, Near Madona Hotel, Old Rajender Nagar, New Delhi – 110060 Tel.: (011) 25810300, 25861543 Mob. 9868819221 Fees Rs. 900/- General Kandam Rs. 600/- for rest (Monday Holiday) {9/20}
10	Thiru A Siva Swamy Agasthiya Tulya Naadi	B-5/, Safdarjung Encl., Near Deer Dictrict park, New Delhi – 110067 Tel.: (011) 6105745 Fees Rs. 1500/- General Kandam Rs. 600/- for rest (Monday Holiday) (Temporariily closed) {7/16}
11	Thiru Siva Subramanium Agasthiya Tulya Naadi	A-2/162, Ground Floor, Safdarjung Encl., Near Singapur Pre School, Mary's School, New Delhi – 110029 Tel.: (011) 9910234551, 8860679998 Fees Rs. 2600/- General Kandam Rs.1600/- for rest. (Monday Holiday) {7/16}
12	Sri Agasthiyar Naadi Jyothish Bhawan	14A, D.D.A. M.I.G Flats, Phase 1, Katwaria Sarai, N. Delhi, 110016 Tel. : 98182 34498 Fees Rs. 1500/- General Kandam Rs. 600/- for rest (Monday Holiday)
13	Agasthiar Naadi Centre	C 8 /8667, Vasant Kunj, Near DPS Vasant Kunj, New Delhi-110070, Mob : 911010003 Fees Rs. 1500/- General Kandam Rs. 600/- for rest. (Monday Holiday) {9/20}
14	Delhi Naadi Astrology	14 DDA MIG Flats Gate No-1 Sumitra Hospital, Opp. Madipur, Delhi-110063
15	Naadi Astrological Centre Govi Jayraman	M-104, J S Aracde, Sector 18, Near Wave Silver Tower, Noida - 201301 Mob : 9899725288, 9810054700

16	Agasthya Naadi Jythidam	C-22, 1st Floor, Sector 39, Noida- 201301 Tel : 0120 6414802 Mob. : 9810054700, 9899725288 Landmark: Near New Saleem Golf Course Fees Rs. 900/- General Kandam Rs. 600/- for rest (Monday Holiday)
17	Naadi Astrological Centre Govi Jayaraman	C 41, 1st Floor, Sector 40, Near Mohan Mandir, Noida – 2013010. Tel : 120-6560124, 6560125
18	Thiru J Shivshankar Agasthiya Tulya Naadi	Sector 18, J S Archet building, Shop no-102,1st Floor, Near Bikaner, Noida-201301 Te.: (120) 5346670 Mob:98100 54700 Fees Rs. 900/- General Kandam Rs. 600/- for rest. (Monday Holiday)

Gujarat and Rajasthan State

S. No	Naadi Center	Address
1	Thiru S. Murthy	206, Block 18, Karnavati Flats, Opp Gupta Nagar, Ganapathi Mandir Sec. Ahmedabad- 26 Mob : 98982 27728, 9898461230 Fees: 350 for General 300 for rest. (Monday Closed)
2	Thiru R. Kumarvel Agasthya Maha Siva Vakiya Naadi	J/106 Shree Nand Nagar, Part 4, Torrent Power Road, Vejalpur, Ahmedabad - 380051 Mob. : 9408292508, 9974028551, 9714107446 Near Sonal Cinema {New 5/16}
4	Thiru U. Shivraj Agasthya Maha Siva Vakiya Naadi	Eladge Apartment, Next to Kantilal Shivlal's Shop, Khokhara, Memnabad Ahmedabad-18. Mobile : 09824566449 Fees : 350 for General 300/- for rest. (Monday Closed)
5	Agasthya Maha Siva Vakiya Naadi	55, Hari Colony, Near Railway Colony, Near Shitla Mataji Temple, Maninagar East, Ahmedabad - 380008 Mob. : 9824566449 Fees : 550 for General 300 for Rest. Monday Closed {9/20}

6	Thiru Kaushikan Agasthya Maha Siva Vakiya Naadi	5 /2 Floor, above Indian Bank Mukhi Corner flats, Opp Siddhi Vinayak Temple, PT College road, Narayan Nagar Paldi, Ahmedabad-38007 Mob : 9825008455 Fees Rs. 500/- for Rest Kandam Rs.300/- EnglishTranslator available. {New 4/16}
7	Thiru R. Kumarvel Agasthya Maha Siva Vakiya Naadi	Periya Road, Opp. Amrapali Police Station, Vaishali Nagar, Rajkot-4 Tel. : 0281-2474726 Mob. : 98225 43343 Fees : 350 for General 300 for rest. Monday Closed (Temporarily Closed)
8	M Nagrajan Augusthya Naadi Center	C 13 Purminima Soc Zoomed Galli, Near Rameshwar Temple, Ghod Dod Road, Surat-395007 Tel : 0251 3916043 Mob : 09998398891
9	N. R. Raman Agasthya Maha Siva Vakiya Naadi	Flat No 8, Nilkamal Society, Opp Gelani Petrol Pump, Nizam Pura, Vadodra. Tel : (0265)2782734, 3256284 Mob : 9898270318, 9998287218 Fees: Rs 350/- for General Rs 250/- for Rest. (Monday Closed)
10	Thiru Sakthivel Agasthya Mahashiv Jyotida Nilayam	No. 25, F Floor, Prabhunagar Soc, Part 2, Opp. Bhumi Complex road, Surat - 395009 Mob : 9925849695
11	Thiru Satyamurthy Agasthya Maha Siva Vakiya Naadi Center and Vastu consultant.	79/84 Shipra Path Off Aravali marg. Mansarovar, Near Dr Talwar Hospital, Jaipur. Mob : 09636740066, 9636252302 Fees: General Kandam Rs. 2500/- for Rest Kandam Rs. 1400/- Hindi, English Translator Available. {7/16}
12	Guruji VSG Nanda ji Agasthy Mahasiva Naadi	G5, D Block 30, AR Aprts Radha Vihar, New Sanganer Road, No 80 Pillar, Opposite Lane, 2nd right last building, Entrance from basement side, Jaipur-302006. Mob: 9829331959, 9928778421 Email:vsgnanda@gmail.com Fees: Geneal Kandam 1500/- Rest Kandam 500/- (Monday Holiday)

13	Thiru Ashok Kumar	8/17, LIG Flats, Near Subzi mandi, Vidyadhar Nagar Bus-stop, Jaipur. Mob. : 9829139566 Fees: General Kandam Rs. 500/- for Rest. Kandam Rs. 400/- English Translator Available (Temporarily closed for last some years) {7/16}
14	Sri M. Ramesh Naadi Jyothisya Nilayam	Sri M. Ramesh Naadi Jyothisya Nilayam, Flat No. 363, First floor, near Jal-Vayu Vihar area, 7th Sec, Vidyadhar nagar, Jaipur. 01412- 339429, 9982345902 {7/16}
15	Bhrugu Vakta Pt. Abhishek S/o Pt. Gopal Lal	S/o Hiralal ji Vyas Bhrugu Samhita Village- Karoi, on Bhilwara - Udaipur highway, Rajasthan. Tel : 0142 -284709. Mob : 9461206047 (Pt. Abhishek), 9414040788 (Pt. Gopal Lal) No Specific fees.
16	Bhrigu Vakta - Pandit Nathu Lal Vyas	(01482294605 - for appointment) Adjacent to each other of Pt. Abhishek S/o Pt . Gopal lal S/o Hiralal ji Vyas Bhrigu Samhita Village- Karoi, on Bhilwara- Udaipur highway, Rajasthan. Tel : 0142 -284709. Mob : 9461206047 (Pt. Abhishek), 9414040788 (Pt. Gopal Lal) No Specific fees.
17	Thiru Ganesh Swami Agasthya Naadi	Flat no. 102, Classic Tower, Ambamata Road, Opp. MMBM College, Udaipur Mob : 098281 98678 fees – Rs. 500 General Kandam Rs.300/- Rest Kandam (Monday closed)

Karnataka State

S. No	Naadi Center	Address
1	Thiru Manivasakam	Agasthya Mahashiv Naadi, 2nd Cross, Bhavani Nagar, Opp. Chandrodaya Kalyan Mandapam, Bannerghata Road, Bangalore - 560 029 Tel. (080) 6441169

2	Agasthiya Mahashivanadi Jothisham	Bommanahalli, Bangalore - 560068 Mob : 80-23465710
3	Thiru Nathan MR Agasthiya Naadi	Naadi Gruha 33, 5th Main Road, Chamrajapet, Bangalore - 560 018 Tel. : (080) 26601971 {9/20}
4	Naadi Astrologer Room	No 1, 2nd Floor, Pushpagiri Complex, Chikmagalur - 577160, K G N Auto Circle Mob : 9480233173, 8266260123
5	Shree Brahmi Naadi	Astros No.18, Devasandra, Near Ramiah Hospital Signal, Bangalore - 560012 Mob. : 8095461665, 7795490023
6	Thiru T Mari Muthu Agasthya Mahashiv Vakya Naadi	7 -1 Dhuler, Mapussa, Goa - 403001 Tel.: (0832) 2225905, 6525628, Fees - Genl Kandam Rs. 700/- Rest. Kandams Rs. 300/- Translator in Marathi not available.
7	Shri Agasthiyar Shiva Vakkiya Naadi Jothishalayam	No. 666, Janani Building, 2nd Main Road, Coffee Board Layout, Hebbal Kempapura, Hebbal, Bangalore - 560024 Near Families Super Market {9/20}
8	Agasthya Naadi Nilayam	No 50, 3rd Cross, Kuvempu Road, Hebbal, Bangalore - 560024, Near Sindhi College. {5/16} Mob : -9894861786, 9360155005
9	Thiru Damodaran Navagraha Naadi	No.16, BH FMC, 3rd Main, 3rd Cross, Hoysalangar, Ramamurth Nagar, Bangalore – 560016 Tel : 080-66499351. Fees: Gen Kandam Rs. 350/- Rest Kandam Rs 250/- {9/20}
10	Agasthiya Mahashiva Naadi Jyothidham	No. 618, Behind FMC, 3rd Main, 12th Cross, Hoysala Nagar, Ramamurthy Nagar, Near Ganesha Temple, Bangalore - 560016 Ph. : (80)-65343699 Mob. : 9900466450, 8792346712 {9/20} Fees Rs 1500/- and Rs 1000/- (Monday Holiday)
11	Agastya Naadi Jyotishya Kendra	Shop No. 28, Vivekananda Corner, Desai Cross, Club Road Hubli, Hubli - 580029, Near LIC Office, Mob. : 9591931818

12	Sri Agasthia Mahashiva Vakkiya Thulliya Naadi	No. 3695, 1st Floor, 9th Cross, 13th D Main, Hal 2nd STG, Service Road, Indiranagar, Bangalore – 560038 Ph. : 80-49609041, 65951246 Mob. : 9844166538 Wood stock Restaurant, Bhangani opposite, Muneshewara Temple. {9/20}
13	D.S.K. Nayanar Ashok Kumar Agastya Sri Kousika Naadi Jothidam	No. 312, Behind Trishul School, 8th Cross, 35th Main, 6th Phase, J PNagar, Bangalore - 78 Mob : 93433 63181 Tel : (80)-26656000 Fees Rs 500/- and Rs 300/- (Monday Holiday) {9/20}
14	Agasthya Muni Ashram	No.160, 17th C Main, 5th Block, Koramangala, Bangalore - 560095 Near Canara Bank Mob : 9845929101 {9/20}
15	Agasthya Jyotishakaya	No. 161, 1st Floor, 7th Main, 4th Cross, Nagendra Block, Bangalore - 560026 Mob : 9448770665 Seetha Circle Bus Stop {New 4/16}
16	Agasthya Naadi Nilayam	No. 36, Sri. Nanjundeshwara Nilaya Lakshmi Sagara Layout, Mahadevapura,Bangalore-560048 Behind MTB School Mob. : 9425286033 {5/16}
17	SRI Agasthya Naadi Jyotishyalaya	No.917,1st Floor, 6th Main, WOC Road, 2nd Stage, Mahalakshmipuram Layout Bangalore - 560086 Near Modi Hospital Mob. : 9448770665
18	Sri Kousika Agasthya Maharshi Naadi Jyothisha Nilayam	8/A, 14th Cross, V. V. Mohalla, Mysore - 570002 Fees Rs 500/- and Rs300/- (Monday Holiday)
19	Agasthya Naadi Astrology	No:618,12th Cross, 3rd Main Road, Near Ganesha Temple, Hoysala Nagar, Ramamurthy Nagar Extn, Bengaluru - 560016 Mob. : - 8792346712

20	Sri Kousika Agasthya Maharshi Naadi Jyothisha Nilayam	Astrology No 45/2, Bangalore City, Bangalore - 560002, Opposite Railway Station Agasthya Mahashiv Naadi Center, Main Road, Bazaar Street, Ulsoor, Bangalore - 560008 {New 4/16}
21	Sri Agasthya Mahasiva Naadi Jyothishya Nilaya	Main Road, Bazaar Street, Ulsoor, Bangalore - 560008 Mob : 9611227898 Tel : 32469293

Kerala State

S. No	Naadi Center	Address
1	Naadi Center	Aroor Sreedharapanicke Memorial Byepass, Opp. Aroor Church, Aroor Church Bus Stop, Aroor - 688534 Alappuzha District, Kerala Ph. : 0478 2876618 Mob : 98463 15900 Fees Rs. 350 for General Kandam Rs. 250/- for Rest Kandam. English Translator available.
2	Bhrighu Naadi Astrologer Aroor	Sreedharapanicker Memorial Pradeep Maekkara Near Karthyayani Temple, Railway Station Road, (Karthika Hospital) Aroor-688534 Alappuzha, Kerala Ph: 0478 2875536 Mob : 94471 75536 Fees Rs. 350 for General Kandam, Rs. 250/- for Rest Kandam. English Translator Available.
3	Sri Maha Siva Tulya Sukshma Naadi Jyothishalayam	29-25-39, Vemurivari Street, Eluru Road, Near Anjaneyaswamy Temple Kothavantena Centre, Arundelpet – 520002. Kerala Mob. : 9440119626, Ph. : 863-2436183
4	Agastya Sri Naadi Jyothisha Nilayam	7 Asariyathu house, Sampthripthi lane, Cheruparambathu Road, Kadavantra. Ph. : 2321622, 2316190 Mob. : 9895035535 Fees Rs. 350/-for General Kandam. Rs. 250/- for Rest Kandam. English Translator available.

5	Siva Vakkya Naadi Jyothisham	Ponoth Radd, Kathrikadavu, Kaloor, Kochi-682017 Kerala Mob. : 94971 88953
6	Vashishta Naadi Jotisham	Aroor gram panchayat, Kochi, 688534 Kerala Mob. : 94471 75536
7	Naadi Reader Jothisha Thilakam	C. Saravana Swamy DCH, Tech, MISTE 41/5, Kavukutty Bhavan, Mullassery Canal Road, Near KSRTC Bus Stand, Kochi - 11, Kerala. Ph. : 0484 2372110 Mob. : 98951 04551 E-mail: naadinilayam@hotmail.com Fees Rs. 350/- for General Kandam. Rs. 250/- for Rest Kandam. English Translator Available.
8	Siva Mayam Naadi Jyothisham	Souhrdha Colony, Kunathurmedu, Palakkad-678013 Kerala Mob. : 98473 60740
9	Naadi Astrology	TC 25/776, M.S.R Lane, near New Theatres Thampanoor, Thampanoor, Thiruvananthapuram-695014 Kerala Mob. : 99941 60913
10	Thiru Shiva Mangalam Agathiya Naadi	43/646, Kozhempil Junction, Valiyaveedu Lane, Kamaleshwaram, Manacaud, Thiruvananthpuram-695 009 Tel. : (0471) 2450708 Fees Rs. 350/- for General Kandam. Rs. 250/- for Rest Kandam. English Translator Available.
11	Thiru K. Subburaya Agathiya Mahashiva Naadi	Opp.Sreekanteshwaram, Thiruvananthpuram-695 023 Tel. : (0471) 2474068 Mob. : 9865548459 Email:k.subburaya@yahoo.com Fees Rs.500/- for Locals, Rs 1500/- for North Indians, Foreigners. Rs 5000/- Gen. Kandam. English Translator Available
12	Sri Agastya Naadi Jyothishanilayam	1 Km from Trichur Swaraj Round, Trichur. Ph. : 0487 2306244 Mob. : 9447706244 Fees Rs. 350/- for General Kandam. Rs. 250/- for Rest Kandam. English Translator Available.

Maharashtra 1 Western Rly Side

S. No.	Naadi Center	Address
1	Surya Samhita Chhaya shastri	Acharya - Harshad Bhai, Rajni Bhai, Anil Bhai, Kamlesh Bhai Joshi, Chhaya Shastry S/o. Late Babu Joshi Surya & Bhrigu Samhita, Details : 418, Rawal Building, 2nd Floor, Near YMCA Building Dr. Bhadkamkar Road, Mumbai - 400 004 Tel. : (022) 2382 1916, 2382 6988
2	Sri Bhokhar Agasthya Naadi Astrological Center	Room No 6, 1st Floor, Ajantha Building, Veera Desai Road, Andheri West, Opp Sri Ganesh Iyengar Bakery Or Near Axis Bank, Mumbai– 400058 Fees Rs. 750/- for General Kandam, for Rest Kandams Rs.500/- English & Hindi translator available Mob. : 9324444575, 9867466443
3	Shree Mahashiv Vashista Naadi Shashtra	Flat No B/719, 7th Floor, S R A Cooperative Society Ltd, Dutta Guru Nagar, Amboli, Casesar Road, Andheri West, Mumbai – 400058 Mob. : 9224942726, 9322613201, 9022161629, 9076037248 Hindi Translator available. {9/20}
4	Jay Suresh & Senthi Sri Agasthya Naadi	House No A-3, Om Pushpanjali Building, Veera Desai Road, Opp Purple Gym, Andheri (West), Mumbai - 400058 Mob. : 9324444575, 9833510306, Hindi translator available. {9/20}
5	Guruji Sakthivel Agasthya Sugar Naad	Building 13/304, Oshiwara Utsav Society, Mhada, Near Shreeji Hotel, Andheri (W) Mumbai 400053 Mob: 09702143488, 8879325543, Monday closed), Near Oshiwara Police Station. {9/20}
6	Agasthiya Mahashiva Naadi Shastraa	D-01, SAI Sadan, Four Bunglows, Ratna Nagar, Andheri West, Mumbai - 400053, Mob. : 22-32423839, 9769618677, 9821942960 Hindi Translator available. {9/20}

7	Shri Vashista Naadi Centre S. Rajendran	Flat No 2704, Building No 61, M H Colony, Gandhi Nagar, Opposite Bank of Maharashtra, Kherwadi Signal, Bandra East, Mumbai - 400051 Mob. : 9702602246, 9322612256, 9833141367 Fees Rs. 750/- for General Kandam for Rest Kandam Rs.500/- English & Hindi Translator available
8	Thiru.Tankmani And Jaipal Shree Mahashiv Vashista Naadi Shashtra	Building 63/2773, MHB Colony, Gandhi Nagar, Near Mig Cricket Club, Bandra East Mumbai 400051. Ph. :022-64408945, 26434707 Mob : 90042844230, 9790968974 English & Hindi Translator available {9/20}
9	Shree Sughar Naadi Astrology Centre	Room No. 1205, Ruby Tower, Plot No. 15, Rsc No. 25, Charkop, Sector 8, Mumbai - 400067 Mob. : 9820715567, 9172278693, 9820915373, 9167794237 {9/20}
10	Thiru Raja Prakash Agasthiya Naadi (Murugan Translator)	9, Sreejee Apartments, Near College road Vadkun C/o Shri Pradip C. Patel Sagar Lodge, Dahanu Road-401602 Tel. : (02528) 222525 Mob. : 9822687648, 9764604415 (Murugan) Fees Rs. 750/- for General Kandam Rs.-350/- for Rest Kandam
11	Guruji C Balakrishan	Flat No 101, Shivranjani Aprt Ramabainagar, Opp. IIT gate and Hiranandani Hospital, Powai, Mumbai-400079. Mob. : 9920232525, 9444237181 Fees Rs. 750/- for General Kandam for Rest Kandams Rs.500/- English & Hindi translator available.
12	Vasishta Naadi Center	18/ 141, Ground Floor, Old Anand Nagar, Santacruz East, Mumbai - 400055 Mob. : 98210 81022 Near Ganpati Temple, Vakola Bridge {9/20}
13	Shree Kaushika Naadi Astrology Centre	Flat No. 25/195, Nehru Road, Santacruz East, Near Vakola Bridge, Anand Nagar, Mumbai-55. Translator in Marathi not available Tel. : 98676 63250

14	Thiru K R Murugeshan Vashishth Mahashiv Naadi	19/151, 1st Floor, Old Anand Nagar, Vakola Bridge, Santacruz East, Mumbai- 400055 Ph. : 022 26681023 , 022 26681642 Mob. : 9821081022 , 9821193529 Fees Rs. 750/- for General Kandam for Rest Kandams Rs.500/- English & Hindi translator available.{9/20}
15	Thiru B.Subhash Shri Koushika Vashishta Naadi Astrology Centre	25/200, Vakola Bridge, Anand Nagar, Santacruz East, Mumbai- 400055 Ph. : 022 65396680 Mob. : 9869180325, 9867663250 Landmark: Behind Om Estate Fees Rs. 700/- for General Kandam Rs. 300/- for rest Kandams. Translator in Marathi not available.

Maharashtra 2 C Rly and New Mumbai

S. No.	Naadi Center	Address
1	Agasthya Naadi Nilayam	Madrasipada, Ulhasnagar No. 4, Thane - 421004, Opp Ulhasnagar Motor Driving School Near Station Mob. : +(91)-9860270774 {9/20}
2	Agasthya Naadi cente	Flat No. A/ 4, 2nd Floor, Plot No. 453/ A, Gayatri Apartment, Monora Road, Opposite Sant Nirankari Samagam, Collectors Colony, Near Chembur Camp, Fertilizer Township, Chembur East, Mumbai-74 Ph.. : 22-38584408 {9/20}
3	Sri Agasthiyar Vasishtar Naadi Jothida Nilayam	Building No. 134, Flat No. 4673, Om Shiv Sai Mandir Road, Chembur West, Opp Tilak Nagar Rly Stn Rail view HSG Soc, Mumbai – 400089 Fees Rs. 750/- for General Kandam Rs.-350/- for Rest Kandam Ph. : 22-25272568 Mob. : 9920991052, 9870087973 {9/20}

4	Thiru M.R.Ravi Agasthiya Naadi	453/A, Gayatri Apartments, 2nd Floor Chembur Camp, Chembur East, Mumbai- 400074 Ph. : 022 25546300, 45201073 Mob. : 9867105909, 9322918119 Landmark: Above South Indian Bank Fees Rs. 750/- for General Kandam Rs. 500/- for rest Kandams. Special Family Chapter Rs. 3000/- Translator in Hindi available.
5	Sri Agastiyar Saptharishi Naadi Jothida Nilayam	Flat No. 1811, 1st Floor, Puskaraj Society Building No. 53, Govandi Railway Station Road, Chembur East, Opposite Muktanand School Subhash Nagar, Mumbai - 400071 Mob. +(91)-8655973788, 8286671237 Tel. : 22-25201115, 25216882 Fees Rs. 750/- for General Kandam for Rest Kandams Rs.500/- English Hindi translator available.
6	Thiru G. Kripanand Agasthiya Mahashiv Tulya Naadi	Room No 1, Ground Floor, Mayura Apartments, Model English Road, Ramchandranagar, (Pandurangwadi), Dombivali (East) Tel. : (0251) 244 3036, Mob: 93733 20923 Fees Rs. 1501/- for Full Kandams Translator in Marathi available {9/20}
7	Thiru A. N. Murugesan Agasthiya Mahashiva Naadi Operating since 1995 onwards.	Flat No.: 301 & 401, Toral Building. Shastri Nagar Dombivali (West) Pin - 421201 Tel. (0251) 2212396 (Residence) Mob. : 98213 07193, 9820872834 Fees for General Kandam for Rs.300/- other Kandams Rs. 300/- Hindi Translator available
8	Thiru A. N. Murugesan Agasthiya Mahashiva	Flat No: 1-2, Dheeraj Apartment Compound, Odhadbhai Lane, Near Puja Hotel, M.G. Road Ghatkopar (East), Mumbai- 400077 Mob. : 9930501995, 9321241631, 9323738109 Hindi Translator available. Office No. 1, Hare krishna building, Jawahar Road, Ghatkopar East, Mumbai-400075, Opp. Railway station {9/20}

9	Naadi Jyothish Kendra	281, Khanbande Buldg, Near Jama Masjid Kalwa, Thane-400605 Mob. : +(91)-9967609145, 9172681625 Fees for General Kandam Rs.500/- other Kandams Rs, 300/- Hindi. Translator available {9/20}
10	S K Amarnath Swami Shree Mahashiv Vashista Naadi Shashtra	Room No. 03, A wing, 2nd Floor, Heena Nivas Building, Bhakti Mandir Road, Near Bhanusagar Theatre, Bhanu Nagar, Kalyan West, Mumbai- 421301 Mob. : 9833755687, 9324465778, 9930031128 Ph. : 251-3212979, 2310546 Hindi translator available. {9/20}
11	Agasthya Mahashiv Naadi	S.R.S. Vivekanand Rajyog, Plot No. 65/30, Sec. 12, Opp. Gokhale school, Near Ganesh Mandir, Kharghar Navi Mumbai-410210 Mob: 9890420681, 9890730722, 993073397, 9920229567 Fees: General Kandam Rs. 1000/- Rest Kandam Rs. 500/- Full Sukshma Rs. 2500 {9/20}
12	Appu Rathnam, Sri Agasthya Sugar Naadi Jothida Nilayam	104, R.N. Cosmos Chs., C-Wing, Beverly, Near Kanakia Police Station, Beverly Park, Mira Road (E), Thane-401107 Mob :987078801, 9320802235 Ph. : 022 6448263 Translator in Marathi not available. {9/20}
13	Thiru R.K. Manirajan Agasthiya Mahashiv Naadi	Flat No. 101, First Floor, Mahavir Darshan, LT Road, Near Mulund (East), Mumbai - 400006 Tel. : (022) 64126031, 21636546 Mob. : 98213 82314, 98721942960 Fees Rs. 700/- for General Kandam Rs. 500/- for rest Kandams. Translator in Hindi & English available. Fees refunded if predictions do not occur after performance of Shanti Deeksha.
14	Thiru Vijay kumar Swamy Agasthiya, Saptarshi Naadi	Vijay Kumar Swamy, House no. 4225, Deeplakshmi, next to Sita bhavan, Panchvati -16 Mob: 07588702219 (Main Office in Nashik) Fees-Gen Rs. 500/- for full life

15	Agasthiya Naadi	Thiru Bala, Plot No. 19, Flat No. A/3, Sector 17, Ramtanu Society, Opp White House, Nerul East, New Mumbai. Tel. : 022 – 27717395 Mob. : 98220 09334. Fees Rs. 525/- for General Kandam Rs. 300/- for other Kandams. Translator in Marathi Not available. {9/20} Monday Closed
16	Thiru Kartik Kumar Agasthiya Mahashiv Naadi	Bld No. C-1/A Room No. 2, Sec- 8, Suryoday Society. Near Mahatma school, Khanda Colony, New Panvel, Navi Mumbai. Mob. : 9867257509, 9769157011 Gen Kandam Rs 700/- Rest Kandam Rs.500/- (Monday closed)
17	Agasthiyar Shree Sukar Maharishree Naadi	G-1, E Wing, Sion Kamgar Co Operative Housing Society Ltd, Opp Croma Showroom, 29th Road, Sion, Mumbai-400022 Or Room No 2, Kishorbaiya Chawl, Sion Trombay Road, Sion, Opposite Runwal Omkar, Behind Fish Market, Joglekar Wadi, Mumbai - 400022 Mob. : 9768824167, 8286838155, 8286838151 Ph. : 24098607 Fees-Genl Kandam Rs. 700/- Rest Kandams. Rs. 500/- Translator in Marathi not available {9/20}
18	Thiru V. G. Selvakumar & Thiru N. Balaji	201, Osho Ashta Vinayak Soc. Shivaji Nagar, near 'B' Cabin Road, 2nd floor (2 minutes walk from Platform No. 1) Naupada, Thane (West) - 400 602 Mob. : 98213 72864 (Balaji) 98921 54976 (Selvakumar) Fees for General Kandam Rs.500/- For other Kandam Rs. 500/- Family (Kutumb) Kandam Hindi & Marathi translator available.
19	Thiru Kumaresan Agasthiya Naadi	Type B. Bldg. No. 4, Room No. 6, Sector - 6, Washi, New Mumbai - 400 703 Tel. : (02272) 27820100 Mob : 9821204346 Fees Rs. 525/- for General Kandam Rs. 300/- for other Kandams. Translator in Marathi not available.

Maharashtra 3 Pune - Pimpri - Chinchwad

S. No.	Naadi Center	Address
1	Thiru G Mahendran swami	Flat No. 11, 2nd Floor, B Wing Ganesh Angan Building, Sambhaji Chowk Pradhikaran, Akurdi, Nigdi, Pune-411044 Mob. : 9764614574, 9075615728
2	Thiru Sarveshwaran & Thiru Ashok Kumar Agasthiya Naadi	Flat No. A/13, First Floor, Akshya Apartments, Lane Opp. Hero Honda Showroom, Anand Nagar, Vadgaon Bk., Sinhagad Road, Pune - 411 051 Tel.: (020) 2435 3018 Mob. : 9890726698 Fees Rs. 400/- for General Kandam Rs. 300/- for Rest Kandam Time:10 a.m. to 6 p.m. Monday closed, Translator in Hindi {9/20}
3	Thiru Kannan Saptrshi Mahashiv Sukshma Naadi Nilayam	Shop No. 250/5, First floor, Sankalp Park, Behind Shashwat Hospital, Nr. DAV School Aunth, Pune-411007 Ph.: - 020 27297755 Mob. : 9923468969, 8625052505 shrisaptharishinaadi@yahoo.com Fees: Rs 525/- for General, Rs 350/- for Rest. Marathi translation facility Monday Closed. {5/16}
4	Thiru V. Sadashivam and Arvinda Swamy Agasthiya & Vasishthar Naadi	A 6, Aniket Society No.1, Near Vasant bag Bus stop, Ground Floor, Bibwe Wadi, Pune-411037 Tel.: (020) 24215554 Mob. : 98409 22230, 9422042350 (Velu) Translator in Marathi not available. Monday Closed {New 4/16}
5	Thiru C M Pandian Shukar Naadi Nilayam	4, Giriraj Residency, C/o Dr. Sonawane, near Shahu Darsden, Vishveshar Temple, Chinchwad area, Pune. Mob. : 9404238973, 8055506745 Fees Rs. 500/- for General Kandam Rs. 300/- for Rest Kandam Translator in Hindi, Time:10 a.m. to 6 p.m. Monday Closed
6	Naadi Lovers Center	A4/404, Ganga Hamlet Society, near Corporation Bank, Pune - 411014 Mob. : +(91)-9657086957 {9/20}

7	Thiru Eashwaran Agasthiya Naadi	Laxmi Tara Complex Thergoan, Dange Chowk, 2nd Floor, Above Abhyuday Co-Op Bank, Chinchwad, Pune-411 033. Tel : (020) 27274742 Mob. : 94225 78099 (Eashwaran) Fees General Kandam Rs.750/- for Rest Kandam Rs. 500/- Translator in Marathi available Sunday half day & Monday full day closed. Also you can consult Maharshi Atri Jeeva Naadi & Hanuman Vastu Jeeva Naadi. Ask up to 5 Q's. No thumbprint needed. Instant answers available. Fees Rs 200/- per Q. {9/20}
8	Thiru Murali Agasthiya Naadi	Flat No. 101, A Wing, Shree Ram Empire Soc, Near Kamal marriage party lawns, (4 Kms from Alandi Vishrant wadi chowk), Dhanori, Vishrant Wadi, Pune-411 015 Tel. : (020)27171919 Mob. : 9423247477 Fees Rs. 350/- for General Kandam Rs. 250/- for Rest. Tuesday closed
9	Thiru Shiv Veeramani	Bld 41, Flat No 9, Harmes Paras, Near Adlab Kalyani nagar, Pune Tel. : 30464342 Mob. : 9822766139 Fees Rs. 750/- for General Kandam Rs. 500/- for Rest Kandam Translator in Hindi Time:10 a.m. to 6 p.m. (Monday Closed)
10	Thiru. Vinod Kumar, Agasthiya Mahashiv Sookshma Naadi	Row house 7, Shubhankar Residency, Near Reliance fresh, Opp.Amrapali Buiding, Behind Bharathi Vidyapeeth, Datta Nagar road, Ambegaon Katraj Pune 411046 Mo: 09766798035, Fees Agastya General Kandam Rs. 1500/- for Rest Kandam. Mahashiv Sokshma Naadi available. Rs 3500/- Translator in Hindi, Monday Closed. Time:10 a.m. to 6 p.m. {9/20}
11	Shri Agasthiya Mahashiv Naadi Astrology	Flat no. 11/A, Vaishnavi Apartment, Plot No. 68, Lane Number 8, Opp. Chandrika Apartments, Dahanukar Colony, Kothrud, Pune-411038 Mob No- 93227 90839
12	Mallika Meera-Rishi's Naadi Centre	Flat No. E-303, Surobhi Township,Vishrantwadi, Pune-411015 Mob. : 7218579254, 7218541660

13	Thiru Eashwaran Agasthiya Naadi	Flat No.11/A, 4th Floor, 8th Lane, Vaishnavi Apartments, Dahanukar Colony, Kothrud, Pune-4110 53, (Monday Closed) Tel. : 020 - 25395949 Mob. : (Mudliyar) 98232 28855 (Eashwaran) 9322790839, 9422578099 Tel.: (020) 5455949 Fees General Kandam Rs.750/- for Rest Kandam Rs. 500/- Time : 10 a.m. to 6 p.m. Translator in Marathi available Sunday half day & Monday full Closed. You can consult Maharshi Atri Jeeva Naadi & Hanuman Vas
14	Thiru Shiva Shanmugam Agasthya Tulya Naadi	Flat No 7, Rajnigandha Aprt, End of 5th Lane, South Main Road, Koregaon Park, Pune - 411001 Mob.: 98230 75938 (Sarvanan) Fees Gen Kandam Rs. 625/- Rest Kandam Rs. 300/- Translator in Marathi Not available. (Ravan, Bhrigu, Brahma, Kak Bhuander, Pathanjali, Yama, Garud, Nandi, Kak bhujander, rare Naadis available on demamd with Extra fees.)
15	Shri Veeramani Agasthya Mahashiv Naadi Nilayam	Flat No. 1, F.Floor, Sarthak Tower, Opp. Yahashavantrao Chavan Natya Grah, Kothrud Ph. : 020-65000275, 25382375 Mob. : 9850826667 Fees Rs. 500/- for General Kandam Rs. 350/- for Rest Kandam (Monday Closed) Translator in Hindi Time:10 a.m. to 6 p.m.
16	Thiru Muthu Swamy	Paud Road, Virendra Complex, 2nd Floor, Flat No. 3, Back Side Subway, opposite Cosmos Bank, Maharashtra-411038 Mob. : 9637148341
17	Thiru MP Bala Agasthiya Naadi	3rd Floor, 14 Hrishikesh Dham No. 2 DP Road, Parihar Chauk, Aundh, Pune-40007 (Monday Ciosed) Tel. : 020-25897784 Mob. : 9822009334. Fees Rs. 525/- for General Kandam Rs. 300/- for other Kandams. Translator in Marathi not available.

18	Thiru A N Muthu Swamy Agasthiya Naadi	Shankar Nagari Hsg. Soc. J' Bldg. Flat No. 19, 4th Floor, Next to Cosmos Bank, Paud Road, near Vanaz factory, Kothrud, Pune-29. Time : 10 a.m. to 6 p.m. Ph. : 20-65002403, 25396696 Mob. : 9637148341, 9823097002 {9/20}
19	Thiru T.R. Vaithyanathan Agasthiya Bohar Mahashiv Naadi	Flat No 101, A3/4, Yogi Society, Ajmera Complex, U Sector, Pimpri, Pune-411018 Mob. : 9960923879, 9423242279 Fees Rs. 500/- for General Kandam Rs. 300/- for other Kandams. Translator in Marathi Not available. (You can consult Maharshi Atri Jeeva Naadi. Ask upto 5 Q's. No thumbprint needed. Instant answers available. Fees Rs 100 per Q.)
20	Thiru Muthu Agasthya Mahashiv Naadi	26 Mittal Society, Flat No. 2, G.F., Pratik nagar, Near Siddhi Vinayak Mandir, Vishrantwadi, Pune-411006. Mob. : 09560084292, 9420152569 Fees Rs. 500/- for General Kandam Rs. 300/- for Rest Kandam (Monday Closed) Translator in Hindi, Time:10 a.m. to 6 p.m.

Maharashtra 4 Rest of Maharashtra
Akola/Aurangabad/Dhule/Goa/Jalgaon/
Kolhapur/Nagpur/Nashik/Sangli

S. No.	Naadi Center	Address
1	Thiru Balaswamy Agasthya Naadi	Chikte bunglow, Opp. Tukaram Akola-444001 Ph. : (0724) 6555524 Mob. : 9890851838 Fees General Kandam Rs.500/- for Rest Kandam Rs. 250/- Time : 10 a.m. to 6 p.m.
2	Naadi Jyotiba Nilayam	Bhandara Road, Nagpur-400008. Mob. : (91)-9421705980 {9/20}

3	Thiru G.M. Kumarasaami, Agasthya Mahashiv Naadi Center	N-5 Shreelok Appt, Near Lokmat Bhavan, CIDCO, Aurangabad-431003 Mob. : 9762918003 Ph. : 02406501855. Fees General Kandam Rs.500/- for Rest Kandam Rs. 250/- Time : 10 a.m. to 6 p.m. {6/16}
4	Thiru Kannan Swamy Agasthiya Naadi	Govind Apartments, Third Floor, near Indira Garden, MSEB circle Office, Dhule. Ph. : 02562-220716 Mob. : 98900 28073. (Kannan) General Kandam Rs.500/- For rest Kandams 400/-
5	Thiru T Mari Muthu Agasthya Mahashiv Vakya Naadi	7-1 Dhuler, Mapussa, Goa-403001 Tel.: (0832) 2225905, 6525628, Fees - Genl Kandam Rs. 700/- Rest Kandams. Rs. 300/- Translator in Marathi not available.
6	Thiru Kannan Swamy Agasthiya Naadi	2, Sai Plaza, 3rd floor, Near Mahabal bus stop, Jalgaon. Mob. : 9890028073 General Kandam Rs.700/- For rest Kandam 500/- Available from 1st to 15th of every month.
7	Thiru Sunderji Agasthya Naadi Nilayam	13/1, Manisha Colony, Behind Shubh Mangal Karyalaya, Ganpati Nagar, Jalgaon-425001 Ph. : 0257-2236634 Mob. : 9890967636 General Kandam Rs.700/- For rest Kandam 500/-
8	C Vadyanathan Agasthya Bohar Mahashiv Naadi	Flat No. 7, Saraswati Complex, 10th Galli, Rajaram Puri, Main road Crossing, Kolhapur-416008, Mob :. 09421849393 Fees Rs 700/- Gen kandam Rest Kandam Rs 500/- Rs 500/- for Jeeva Naadi for 5 Q's.
9	Tiru Jayasurya Agasthiya Mahashiv Naadi	Vasantleela Sadan, Mandlik Park,13th Lane Rajaram Puri, Kolhapur-416001. Ph. : (0231) 2520315, 2524361 Mob. : 9960620623,9370194214 Fees General Kandam Rs.350/- for Rest Kandam Rs. 250/- Time : 10 a.m. to 6 p.m.
10	Shri Vashista Jevaa Naadi Jyotish S P K Vijayan	Flat No. F1 Digvijay Appartment, 5th Lane Rajaram Puri, C.S. No. 1830/2, Eward, Kolhapur Mob. : 9960051843 Fees Rs 700/- Gen Kandam, Rest Kandam Rs 500/-

11	Thiru Babu Swamy Mahashive Sukshama Naadi	Flat No. P 3-4, Atharva Apartment, Opp Vrundavan Park, Near Kirti Automobile, Gangapur Road, Nashik-442013 Tel. : 0253-2596925 Mob. : 0880076869, 9373905534 Fees Agasthya Gen Kandam Rs. 500/- Mahashiv Gen. Rs.1000/- Shiv Sukshma Rs. 2000/- Param Ati Sukshma Shiva Rs. 5000/- (Thrusday Holiday)
12	Thiru Sarvanan Agasthya Vashishtha Naadi Center	Flat No 7, 3rd Floor, Suyojana Aprt, Vise mala, Opp. Patil Plaza, Canada Corner, Nashik. Ph. : 0253-6057111, Mob. : 9860180972 Fees General Kandam Rs. 600/- Rs. 300/-for rest Kandams, For Full Sukshma Kandam Rs. 2000/- (Temporarily Closed) {7/16}
13	Thiru Jo Kumar Agasthya Mahashiv Naadi	Bunglow No. 17, Opposite Topavan Road, Kathe Galli, Ganesh Nagar, Near Trikoni Garden, Nashik-422007 Mob. : (91) 9970682291, 9890290564 Fees General Kandam Rs. 1300/- Rs. 2500/- for rest Kandams For Full Sukshma Kandam Rs. 2000/- {9/20}
14	Thiru MP Kirti AM Shanmugam Agasthya Mahashiv Naadi	4 Villa, Rowhouse No 2, Behind Essar Petrol pump, near cricket ground, Mahatmanagar, Gangapur Road, Nashik-422013 Ph. : (0253) 6513207 Mob. : 9860596910 Fees General Kandam Rs. 500/- Rs. 300/- for rest Kandams
15	Thiru Vijay kumar Swamy Agasthiya, Saptarshi Naadi	4255/A, Pujari wada, Near Kartikeya Temple, Shani Chouk, Panchvati, Nashik. Tel. : (0253) 2621534, 2629129. Mob. : 9850150461, 9271267202 Fees Gen Rs. 500/- for full life.
16	Thiru Purushottaman Agasthiya Mahashiv Tulaya Naadi	303, J.P. House, Near Ravi Nagar Chowk, Nagpur-440010 Tel. : (0712) 6576022 Mob. : 9226760223, 7709000895 Fees- Gen Kandam Rs. 600/- Rest Kandam Rs. 300/- Time : 10 a.m. to 6 p.m. Marathi Translation not Available. Monday Holiday. {9/20}

17	Thiru Sachidanand Swamy Makarandhan Agasthiya Naadi	A/20, Vastushilp Colony, Near Friends Colony, Katol Road, Nagpur - 444013 Tel. : (0712) 2574200 Mob : 97665 22379 Fees- Gen Kandam Rs.500/- Rest Kandam Rs. 350/- Time : 10 a.m. to 6 p.m. Marathi Translation not Available. Monday Holiday.
18	Thiru R. Ishwar Agasthiya Naadi	110, Telecom Nagar, Nagpur-440022. Mob. : 9373114999 Fees Gen Kandam Rs. 400/- Rest Kandam Rs. 300/- Time : 10 a.m. to 6 p.m. Hindi Translation Available. Monday Holiday.
19	Thiru MS Tamrai Selvan	Flat No. 9, PL Apartments, Opp. Mansure Classes, Viveknagar, Nanded. Mob. : 8830483689, 7350263137
20	Thiru U. Babu Swami Agasthiya Mahashiva Naadi	Utkarsh Banglow, Behind Podar International School, Veer Shaiva Mali Mangal Karyala, Sharada Nagar, Kupwad Road, Vishram Bag, Sangali-416416. Mob. : 9766798035, 9561416304 Fees Rs. 700/- for Agastya General Kandam Rs. 300/- for Rest Kandam. Mahashiv Sokshma Naadi available Rs 1500/- Monday Closed, Translator in Hindi Time:10 a.m. to 6 p.m.

Punjab and Haryana States

S. No.	Naadi Center	Address
1	K. S. Krishnan Shri Agasthya Nahashiv Vakya Tulya naadi Nilayam	House No. 171, Sector 21C, Back Side of Manav Rachna International Primary School, Faridabad-121001 (Haryana) Ph. : 129-2426934, 2426972 Mob. : 9910343365, 9716988891 Fees Gen Kandam. Rs 700/- Rest Kandam Rs 500/- Monday Closed {9/20}

2	Naadi Astrology Sri Agastiya Maha Siva Vakkiya Tuliya	H.No, 171, Sector 21C, Behind Manavrachana School, Faridabad-121001 (Haryana) Tel. : 0129 2426934
3	Thiru V S A Arul Muthu Kumaara Swamy Agasthiya Naadi	1131/Sector 17-B, IFFCO Colony, Near Maruti Udyog, Gurgaon-122001 Tel.: (011) 6343387 Mob.: 9810246999 Fees Rs. 1,250/- for General Kandam Rs. 1,000/- for rest
4	Naadi Astrology	G-2, House No.-643, Sec-31, (Gurgaon) Gurugram-122001 Mob. : 9810246908, 9810246999, 9868123999 Ph. : 124-2384111, 2380222 Near Chopra Diagnostic center {9/20}
5	Sri Agasthiya Mahasiva Sukshma Naadi Astrological Centre	No: 643,Shivashram, Sector 31, Gurugram-122003 (Haryana) Tel. : 0124 2384111
6	Pandit Suresh Jaidev Shastry Bhrigu Samhita	Opp. Civil Hospital, Hoshiarpur -146001. Tel. : (01882) 252193, Mob. : 09923468969 Fees Rs. 150/- and above for Prashna & Rs. 500/- for life reading Time : 9 a.m. to 5 p.m.
7	Pandit Lal Dev Sharma Ravan Samhita Shatri	Near Bagad godown, Deep nagar, Phagwada road, Hoshiarpur-146001 Tel.: (01882) 229974 Mob. : 98140 96437 Fees Rs. 150/- and above for Prashna & Rs. 500/- for life reading Time : 9 a.m. to 5 p.m.
8	Pandit Vishal S/o late Mahashiv Bhrigu Samhita	S/o. Ved Prakash 369, Jallandhar Road, Mohalla Gokul Nagar, Hoshiarpur-146001 Tel.: (01882) 251008 Fees Rs. 150/- and above for Prashna & Rs. 500/- for life reading, Time : 9 a.m. to 5 p.m.
9	Pandit Hari Dev Sharma Bhrigu Samhita	Jallandhar Road, Industrial area, near Gokul Nagar, Hoshiarpur-146001 Tel.: (01882) 253547 Fees Rs. 150/- and above for Prashna & Rs. 500/- for life reading, Time : 9 a.m. to 5 p.m.

10	Dr. Ratish Mohan Bhrigu Samhita Bhrigu Dham	Railway Mandi Hoshiarpur-146001. Tel.: (01882) 252114 Fees Rs. 150/- and above for Prashna & Rs. 500/- for life reading, Time : 9 a.m. to 5 p.m.
11	T. Ramanuj Sharma Bhrigu Samhita Bhrigu Dham	68, Railway Mandi Road, Hoshiarpur-146 001 Tel.: (01882) 252825 Fees Rs. 150/- and above for Prashna & Rs. 500/- for life reading, Time : 9 a.m. to 5 p.m.
12	Smt. Sneh Amrit Anand Bhrigu Samhita Sunder Sadan	Rambaug Railway Mandi, Hoshiarpur-146 001 Tel.: (01882) 252342 Fees Rs. 150/- and above for Prashna &Rs. 500/- for life reading, Time : 9 a.m. to 5 p.m.
13	Late Pandit Ram Kumar Sharma Bhrigu Samhita	98, Railway Mandi Road, Hoshiarpur-146 001 Tel.: (01882) 252342 Fees Rs. 150/- and above for Prashna & Rs. 500/- for life reading, Time : 9 a.m. to 5 p.m.
14	Pandit Shamacharan Trivedi S/o Late Jagannathji	Bhrigu Vihar, near Rosemary Nursary Una road, Hoshiarpur–146001. Tel.: (01882) 233223 Fees Rs. 150/- and above for Prashna & Rs. 500/- for life reading, Time : 9 a.m. to 5 p.m.
15	Pandit Madan Mohanji, Bhrugu Samhita	1. Dashsmesh Nagar Amritsar road Gali No.10, House No. 1962 Moga, Punjab Mob. : 9815098472 2. Nakodar road, near TV tower Prakash vihar Enclave Phase II kothi no 11, Jalandhar, Punjab Fees 111/- and above Sat, Sun Mon at Jalandhar (Monday closed). Reads from Akshya Patra. Instant Readings.
16	Pandit Shamacharan Trivedi	S/o Late Jagannathji, Bhrigu Dham 122 , Dayalsingh Colony Karnal –132 001, Haryana. Tel.: (0184) 272797 Optional Fees Rs. 150/- and above for Prashna & Rs. 500/- for life reading, Time : 9 a.m. to 5 p.m.
17	Thiru Selvaraj Samy Agasthiya Naadi	122/ "I" Block, Sarabha nagar, Ludhiana-141 001, Punjab Tel.: (0161) 25050864 Mob.: 98151 12381 Fees Rs. 500/- for General Kandam Rs. 300/- for rest

18	Bhrigu Pandit	5, Jalandhar City, Guru Amardas Nagar, Near Verka Milk Plant, Jalandhar - 144001 Mob. : 9872665529
19	Naadi Astrology Sri Agastiya Shiv	Govt. School, Balaji Niwas, House No. 524, Near Sec-25 Market Opposite, Panchkula -134112 (Haryana) Ph. : 0172 2565864
20	V. R. Muthuswami Maha Siva Vakiya Naadi	House No. 712, Sector 8, Panchkula-09 Ph. : 0172-565864 Fees: Gen Rs. 1000/- Rest Rs. 600 (Monday Closed)
21	Sri Abhay Kumar Sri Agasthya Mahasiva Naadi	House No. 45, Sector 2, Panchkula-134109 (Haryana) Fees Gen Rs. 1000/- Rest Rs. 600 (Monday Closed)
22	Pandit Mukesh Pathak Bhrugu Darbar	Near Bharmal Mandir. Sultanpur Lodhi, 60 Km from Jalandhar 30 kms from Kapurthala Mob. : 9417224838 Fees Rs. 150/- and above for Prashna & Rs. 500/- for life reading, Time : 9 a.m. to 5 p.m.

Tamilnadu 1 Chennai

S. No.	Naadi Center	Address
1	Thiru Suburathinam D Agasthiya Naadi	36, New State Bank Colony, Behind Philips Hospital, Tambaram (W) Chennai-600045 Tel. : (044) 22366264, 22264497 Mob. : (Mr. Manu) 9884429149, 9384045677, 9444032777 Fees in most of centers of Tamilnadu are in three tier. 1. For Tamilians Gen Kandam Rs. 450/- For rest Kandam Rs. 350/- 2.For Non-Tamil Indians. Rs. Gen Kandam 1000/- Rest Kandam Rs.800/- 3. Foreigners Gen. Rs.2000/-
2	Thiru Ramani Guruji Kak Bhujandar Jeeva Naadi	18, Alamellu Puram Opp. Bharat Engineering College, Selaiyur, Tambaram-East, Chennai-73 Ph. : (044) 22290595 No fees, Questions are answered by throwing Cowries. Reading Morning and Evening 7 to 9. May carry flowers and fruits.

3	Thiru S. Kumar, Sukar Markandeya Jeeva Naadi	New No. 8/ Old No 22, Arulambal street, T Nagar. Landmark: (Kanada Sangh School) Chennai - 600 017. Tel. : (044) 28342483 No specific fees. Sunday Morning Time 5 to 8 p.m., 8 to 11 other days (Tuesday Holiday). Preferably visit if your and Kark -- Wed, Simha and Makara –Saturday. Treatment on any day. And now a days reads from wooden stump like.
4	Shri Agastya Bohar Naadi M. Selva Ramesh	New No. 27, 1st floor, 37th Street, O Block, Ganapathy Colony, Anna Nagar East, Chennai-600102. Mob. : 9791166381, 9884532333 Ph. : 044-26222769 Fees in most of centers of Tamilnadu are in three tier. 1.For Tamilians Gen Kandam Rs. 400/- For rest Kandam Rs. 300/- 2.For Non-Tamil Indians. Gen Kandam Rs. 1000/- Rest Kandam Rs.800/- 3. Foreigners Gen. 1500/- Rest Kandam. Rs. 1000/- Hindi/English translator available.
5	Thiru Arun MS Saptarishi Naadi	3-13, Pancharatnan Flats, Welcome Colony, Thirumangalam Anna Nagar West, Chennai - 1 Tel. : (044) 26219145, Fees in most of centers of Tamilnadu are in three tier. 1.For Tamilians Gen Kandam Rs. 400/- For rest Kandam Rs. 300/- 2.For Non-Tamil Indians. Gen Kandam Rs. 1000/- Rest Kandam Rs.800/- 3.Foreigners Gen. 1500/- Rest Kandam. Rs. 1000/- Hindi/English translator available.
6	Sri Agathiya Maha Siva Sukshama Naadi Jothidalayam	R-9, Water Tank Road, MMDA Colony, Arumbakkam, Chennai- 600106 Ph. : 044 23631793 Landmark: Near Murali Krishna Marriage Hall Fees in most of the centers of Tamilnadu are in three tier. 1.For Tamilians Gen Kandam Rs. 400/- For rest Kandam Rs. 300/- 2.For Non-Tamil Indians. For Gen Kandam 1000/- Rest Kandam Rs.800/- 3.Foreigners Gen. 1500/- Rest Kandam. Rs. 1000/- Hindi/English translator available. {9/20}

7	Dr. Om Ulaganathan Errattai Naadi	F-28, Vasanth Apartments, 100 Feet Road, MMDA stop Arumbakkam, Chennai 600 106.Tel.(044) 24750246 . 24753450 Mobile : 98440 36196 Minimum Rs.2500 Hindi, English translator Available. Shastriji often busy with eminent and wealthy persons. {9/20} Ph. : 44-39974644 G 2 No. 1/26 Parasakthi Apartment, Jai Nagar 1st Main Road, Arumbakkam, Chennai - 600106, Opposite CMDT.
8	Tiru Mathiyazhagan Bhrugu & Agasthiya Naadi	841, Kala flat, 53rd street 9th avenue , Ashok nagar, Chennai- 600083 Tel :- (044)-24746919, 24749198 Fees in most of centers of Tamilnadu are in three tier. 1.For Tamilians Gen Kandam Rs. 400/- For rest Kandam Rs. 300/- 2. For Non-Tamil Indians. For Gen Kandam 1000/- Rest Kandam Rs.800/- 3.Foreigners Gen. 1500/- Rest Kandam. Rs. 1000/- Hindi/English translator available.
9	Thiru Kalyana sunderashwara Agasthya, Kaushika, Mahashiv Naadi	New 15 (Old 37), Second Street, Oppo.Hero Honda Show room, Indira Nagar, Adyar, Chennai-600 020 Mob. : 9840546464 Fees in most of the centers of Tamilnadu are in three tier. 1.For Tamilians Gen Kandam Rs. 400/- For rest Kandam Rs. 300/- 2.For Non-Tamil Indians. For Gen Kandam 1000/- Rest Kandam Rs.800/- 3.Foreigners Gen. 1500/- Rest Kandam. Rs. 1000/- Hindi/English translator available.
10	Sri Koushiha Agasthiya Mahasiva Naadi Jodhidam	129/313 Paper Mills Road, Jawahar Nagar, Chennai- 600082 Ph. : 044 26703311 Landmark: Near - Kamaraj Statue Fees in most of the centers of Tamilnadu are in three tier. 1.For Tamilians Gen Kandam Rs. 400/- For rest Kandam Rs. 300/- 2.For Non-Tamil Indians. For Gen Kandam 1000/- Rest Kandam Rs.800/- 3.Foreigners Gen. 1500/- Rest Kandam. Rs. 1000/- Hindi/English translator available.

11	Sri Vaithiswara Agasthiya Koushiha Naadi Jothida Nilayam	46, 1st Street, Mandapam Road, Kilpauk, Chennai- 600010 Mob. : 9442256853 Ph. : 044 26479463, 65640503, Landmark: Near Regina Hospital Fees in most of the centers of Tamilnadu are in three tier. 1.For Tamilians Gen Kandam Rs. 400/- For rest Kandam Rs. 300/- 2.For Non-Tamil Indians. For Gen Kandam 1000/- Rest Kandam Rs.800/- 3.Foreigners Gen. 1500/- Rest Kandam. Rs. 1000/- Hindi/English translator available.
12	Naadi Jothidar Rajendran	16/41, 1st Street, Mandapam Road, Kilpauk, Chennai-600010 Ph. : 044 26479463 Landmark: Back Renuka Nurshing Home Fees in most of the centers of Tamilnadu are in three tier. 1.For Tamilians Gen Kandam Rs. 400/- For rest Kandam Rs. 300/- 2.For Non-Tamil Indians. For Gen Kandam 1000/- Rest Kandam Rs.800/- 3.Foreigners Gen. 1500/- Rest Kandam. Rs. 1000/- Hindi/English translator available.
13	Thiru J Sathyamurthy Agathiya Mahashiv Naadi	14, Sunderlal Nahatha Avenue, Near Mummy Daddy, Kilpauk Chennai-600 010 Tel: (044) -25327083 Fees in most of the centers of Tamilnadu are in three tier. 1.For Tamilians Gen Kandam Rs. 400/- For rest Kandam Rs. 300/- 2.For Non-Tamil Indians. For Gen Kandam 1000/- Rest Kandam Rs.800/- 3.Foreigners Gen. 1500/- Rest Kandam. Rs. 1000/- Hindi/English translator available.
14	Thiru R. Rajendran Agathiya Mahashiv Naadi	16, Mandapam Road 1st Street, Kilpauk Garden, Chennai-600010 Tel: (044)-2647 9463 Fees in most of the centers of Tamilnadu are in three tier. 1.For Tamilians Gen Kandam Rs. 400/- For rest Kandam Rs. 300/- 2.For Non-Tamil Indians. For Gen Kandam 1000/- Rest Kandam Rs.800/- 3.Foreigners Gen. 1500/- Rest Kandam. Rs. 1000/- Hindi/English translator available.

15	Thiru Darume Selvaraaj Kaushik Agathiya Mahashiv Naadi	11, Rukmani Street, Mambalam West, Near postal Colony, Chennai-600 033 Tel. : (044) 23710365 Fees in most of the centers of Tamilnadu are in three tier. 1.For Tamilians Gen Kandam Rs. 400/- For rest Kandam Rs. 300/- 2.For Non-Tamil Indians. For Gen Kandam 1000/- Rest Kandam Rs.800/- 3.Foreigners Gen. 1500/- Rest Kandam. Rs. 1000/- Hindi/English translator available.
16	Thiru EKM Kumaran and Vinayaka Naadi	50, Pugahazhenhi Street, Jayachandran MGR Nagar, Chennai-600073 Fees in most of the centers of Tamilnadu are in three tier. 1.For Tamilians Gen Kandam Rs. 400/- For rest Kandam Rs. 300/- 2.For Non-Tamil Indians. For Gen Kandam 1000/- Rest Kandam Rs.800/- 3.Foreigners Gen. 1500/- Rest Kandam. Rs. 1000/- Hindi translator available.
17	Prof. A.N.K Swamy Meenakshi Naadi	Old (83) , 169, Kutchery Road, Vinayaga Nagar, Myalapore, Chennai –600 004 Fees not fixed
18	Sri Agasthiya Mahasiva Naadi Jodhida Nilayam	6, Nattu Veerachi Street, Mylapore, Chennai-600004 Ph. : 044 24660474, 24460474 Mob. : 9841213532, 9444054264 Landmark: Near Mundakanniamman Koil Fees in most of the centers of Tamilnadu are in three tier. 1.For Tamilians Gen Kandam Rs. 400/- For rest Kandam Rs. 300/- 2.For Non-Tamil Indians. For Gen Kandam 1000/- Rest Kandam Rs.800/- 3.Foreigners Gen. 1500/- Rest Kandam. Rs. 1000/- Hindi/English translator available. {9/20}
19	Agasthya Naadi Center	Bhut Road, Guindy, Chennai - 600032, (Near Ganapati Temple) Mob. : 9963334337, 9290884764
20	Sri Agasthiyar Maha Siva Naadi Jothida Nilayam	No 2/3 1st Floor, Salai Street, Mylapore, Chennai - 600004, Near Nadu Street. Ph. : 44-39619773 {9/20}

21	Thiru Satyam Vasishthar Agathiya Naadi	82/A, Sullivan Garden St. Opp. Vivekanand College Mylapur, Chennai-600004 Tel. : (044) 2 661754 Fees in most of the centers of Tamilnadu are in three tier. 1.For Tamilians Gen Kandam Rs. 400/- For rest Kandam Rs. 300/- 2.For Non-Tamil Indians. For Gen Kandam 1000/- Rest Kandam Rs.800/- 3.Foreigners Gen. 1500/- Rest Kandam. Rs. 1000/- Hindi/English translator available.
22	Agasthya Naadi Center	36/21, 3rd Main Road, Nanganallur, Chennai - 600061. Ph.: 44-26479463, 26452613 Mob. : 9442256853, 9710205655 {5/16}
23	Agathya Sivavakiya Naadi Jothidam	G-3, Achyuthan Sriraj Apartments, 10, Kamatchi Puram, Mambalam West, Chennai- 600033 Ph. : 044 24746919, 24749198 Mob. : 9940391449, 9843365388 Landmark: Near Karur Vysya Bank Fees in most of the centers of Tamilnadu are in three tier. 1.For Tamilians Gen Kandam Rs. 400/- For rest Kandam Rs. 300/- 2.For Non-Tamil Indians. For Gen Kandam 1000/- Rest Kandam Rs.800/- 3.Foreigners Gen. 1500/- Rest Kandam. Rs. 1000/- Hindi/English translator available.
24	Thiru S. K. Aravindha Swamy Vasishthar Naadi	5/66, Near Indian Bank, Bajanai Koil Street, Pallavaram, Chennai - 600043 Ph. : (44)-22364286, 65392482 Mob. : 9444129774 Fees in most of the centers of Tamilnadu are in three tier. 1.For Tamilians Gen Kandam Rs. 400/- For rest Kandam Rs. 300/- 2.For Non-Tamil Indians. For Gen Kandam 1000/- Rest Kandam Rs.800/- 3.Foreigners Gen. 1500/- Rest Kandam. Rs. 1000/- Hindi/English translator available.
25	Naadi Astrology Center	No.21A, Ibrahim Street, Alandur, Chennai-600016, Tamil Nadu Mob. :89401 39779

26	21Sri Agasthiya Gowshigar Naadi Jodhida Nilayam	3/5, Vadamalai Pillai Street, Ponnan Lane, Purasavakkam, Chennai- 600007 Ph.: 044 26400157, M.: 9841962421 Landmark: Near Tana Street Fees in most of the centers of Tamilnadu are in three tier. 1.For Tamilians Gen Kandam Rs. 400/- For rest Kandam Rs. 300/- 2.For Non-Tamil Indians. For Gen Kandam 1000/- Rest Kandam Rs.800/- 3.Foreigners Gen. 1500/- Rest Kandam. Rs. 1000/- Hindi/English translator available.
27	Dr. A. Karunakaran Sugar, Budh, Shiva Naadi	13, (31 New) Mannar Reddy Street, Near Krishnaveni Theatre T. Nagar, Mambalam, Chennai - 600 017. Ph. : 044 24360244 Mob. : 9840415605, 9841026373, 9884016622 (9840255580 Kaushik speaks in English) Landmark: Near Krishnaveni Theatre Fees in most of the centers of Tamilnadu are in three tier. 1.For Tamilians Gen Kandam Rs. 400/- For rest Kandam Rs. 300/- 2. For Non-Tamil Indian
28	Guruji Bala Krishnan	8-B, 3rd street, irunuliar, Nitya Nandam Nagar Tambaram (W) Chennai-600045 Fees in most of the centers of Tamilnadu are in three tier. 1.For Tamilians Gen Kandam Rs. 400/- For rest Kandam Rs. 300/- 2.For Non-Tamil Indians. For Gen Kandam 1000/- Rest Kandam Rs.800/- 3.Foreigners Gen. 1500/- Rest Kandam. Rs. 1000/- Hindi/English translator available.
29	Sri Agathiya Maha Siva Sukshama Naadi Jothidalayam	B-2 Ground Floor Navajeevan Flats 100Feet Road, Thirumangalam, Chennai- 600040 Mob. : 9444652115 Landmark: Opposite Water Tank Fees in most of the centers of Tamilnadu are in three tier. 1.For Tamilians Gen Kandam Rs. 400/- For rest Kandam Rs. 300/- 2.For Non-Tamil Indians. For Gen Kandam 1000/- Rest Kandam Rs.800/- 3.Foreigners Gen. 1500/- Rest Kandam. Rs. 1000/- Hindi/English translator available.

30	Sri Kousiga Agastheeya Naadi Astrological Bureau	New-11, Old-116/2, Elango Nagar South, Virugambakkam, Chennai- 600092 Ph. : 044 23770370, 23775838 Mob. : 9884350188 Landmark: Behind National Theatre Fees in most of the centers of Tamilnadu are in three tier. 1.For Tamilians Gen Kandam Rs. 400/- For rest Kandam Rs. 300/- 2.For Non-Tamil Indians. For Gen Kandam 1000/- Rest Kandam Rs.800/- 3.Foreigners Gen. 1500/- Rest Kandam. Rs. 1000/- Hindi/English translator available.
31	Thiru K Vijay Pandyan Agasthiya Naadi	56, 2nd Street, Vankatesha Nagar, Virugambakkam, Opp. Shri Rajeshvari Temple, Chennai 600 092 Fees in most of the centers of Tamilnadu are in three tier. 1.For Tamilians Gen Kandam Rs. 400/- For rest Kandam Rs. 300/- 2.For Non-Tamil Indians. For Gen Kandam 1000/- Rest Kandam Rs.800/- 3.Foreigners Gen. 1500/- Rest Kandam. Rs. 1000/- Hindi/English translator available.
32	Shri Agasthiya Kowsika Naadi Astrological Centre	28-B, 1st Main Road, Shastri Nagar, Adyar, Chennai - 600020 Tamil Nadu Mob. : 9840546464

Tamilnadu 2 Vaideeshwaran Koil

S. No.	Naadi Center	Address
1	Thiru A Siva Samy Sachida Nathan Agasthiya Naadi	Shri Laxmi Dharma Illam, 18, Milladi Salai, Vaidheeshwaran, Koil-609 117 Tel. : (04364) 279463
2	Thiru R. Rajendrasamy Agastya Mahasiva Naadi	27-D, East car Street Vaidheeshwaran, Koil-609 117 Mob. : 9245620853, 98946 39137 East car Street

3	Sri Agathiya Mahasiva Naadi Jothida Nilayam	No. 1, Opp. Temple East Tower, Vettukula Street, East Car Street, Vaithiswaran, Koil - 609117 Mob. : 9578160500, 9176830999
4	Sri Agasthiya Mahasiva Naadi Jothida Nila...	No. 5, Devasthanam Building, Perumal East Car Street, Vaithiswarankoil- 609117 Tel . : (4364)-325535 Mob. 9894052454, 9787654540
5	Thiru V. Balaguru Agastya Mahasiva Naadi	East Kar Street Vaidheeshwaran Koil-609117 Tel. : (04364) 279040 Fees Rs. 350/-
6	Thiru s. Venkatesanan Agasthay Mahasiva Naadi	21/15, East Kar Street Vaidheeshwaran, Koil- 609117 Tel. : (04364) 279289 East Kar Street
7	Sri Agasthiya Mahasiva Naadi Jothida Nilayam	No. 5, Devasthanam Building, Perumal, East Car Street, Vaithiswaran Koil-609117 Mob. : 984052454, Tel. : 04364-325535
8	Thiru K. Pichaimani Vyasar Bhrigu Naadi	Opp. Abhirami Hotel Vaidheeshwaran, Koil-609117 Tel. : (04364) 279116
9	Thiru Jemini Selvaraju Kakbhujandar Naadi Jyothida Bhavan	15/A, Kotta Street, 1st Floor, above Telephone Exchange Vaidheeshwaran Koil-609117 Tel: (04364) 279350 Fees Rs.200/- for Telephone Exchange
10	Thiru Govinda Raju Maha Siva Vakiya Naadi	Z- 48 Milk Depot Upstairs, Vaidheeshwaran Koil-609117 Tel. : (04364) 272664 Mob. : 9842380646 Fees Rs. 200/- for Milk Depot
11	Thiru S Thanikachalam Saptarishi Naadi	9, Milladi street, Vaidheeshwaran Koil- 609117 Tel. : (04364) 279350

12	Thiru VS Samy Sadasivam Kaushika Agasthay Naadi	Veda Bhavan 17/A, Milladi Street Vaidheeshwaran Koil-609117 Tel. : (04364) 279321 Milladi Street
13	Thiru S Sundara Moorthy Kaushika Thulya Naadi	22, Milladi Street, Vaidheeshwaran Koil-609117 Tel. : (04364) 279309, 279589 Milladi Street
14	Thiru N. Sivaraja Kaushika Agastya Mahasiva Naadi	1, Milladi Street, Vaidheeshwaran Koil-609 117 Tel. : (04364) 279407 Mob. : 93605 52946 Milladi Street
15	Thiru T. Ravi Agasthiya Naadi	22, Milladi Street, Vaidheeswaran Koil-609 117 Tel. : (04364) 279309
16	Thiru T. Mohansamy Kaushika Agastya Mahasiva Naadi	2, Milladi Street (Upstairs) Vaidheeshwaran Koil-609117 Tel. : (04364) 276174 Mob. : 98945 36840 Milladi Street
17	Thiru K. Ravi Kaushika Agastya Mahasiva Naadi	50, North Street, Vaidheeshwaran Koil-609117 Tel: (04364) 279581 North Street
18	Thiru N. R Selva Mani Arul Shiva Siddhas Navagraha Naadi	Nilayam Opp Hotel Sadabhishegam Vaidheeshwaran Koil-609117 Tel: (04364) 279239 Sadabhishegam
19	Thiru S. Saaminathan Mahasiva Thulya Shushma Naadi	9, Amman Sannathi Street, Near Thaila Lodge Vaidheeshwaran Koil-609117 Tel. : (04364) 279766 Mob : 94432 86032
20	Thiru Poosai Muthu Vasistha Naadi Nilayam	Sannathi Street, Vaideeshwaran Koil-609117 Tel. : (04364) 279 Fees Rs. 350 for Sannathi Street
21	Thiru K. V. Babusamy Agasthiya Mahasiva Naadi	Sannathi Street Vaidheeshwaran Koil-609 117 Tel: (04364) 279535 Mob : 94432 14785

22	Thiru A. P. Karunakaran Sri Agasthiya Naadi	23, Swami Sannathi Street Vaidheeshwaran Koil-609117 Tel: (04363) 279232, 279269
23	ThiruA.P. Babu A. P. Karunakaran Sri Agasthiya Naadi	24, Swami Sannathi Street Vaidheeshwaran Koil-609117 Tel. : (04363) 276033, 279269 Mob. : 93609 99914
24	Thiru Dr C Ravi Sri Bokar Vashishthar Naadi	Swami Sannathi Street Vaidheeshwaran Koil-609117 Tel: (04363) 279302 Swami Sannathi Street
25	Thiru Shiva Thilaga Sri Agasthiya Naadi	22/16, Swami Sannathi Street Vaidheeshwaran Koil-609117 Tel. : (04364) 320072 Mob : 93450 94482
26	Thiru M.R. Murthy. Thirumoolar Gnaneeswara Tulya Naadi	15/7, South Kar Street Vaidheeshwaran Koil-609 117 Tel: (04364) 276004 South Kar Street
27	Thiru Govi jayaraman Agasthiya koushika Mahasiva Naadi	West car Street, Opp Shanmugam Theatre Vaidheeshwaran, Koil-609117 Tel. : (04364) 279507 Mob : 94428 60666
28	Thiru Senthil Mahasiva Vakkiya, Agasthiya Naadi	32, West Kar Street Vaidheeshwaran Koil-609117 Tel. : (04364) 279195 West Kar Street
29	Thiru V.P.Anandh Mahasiva Vakkiya, Agasthiya Naadi	Near Theradi, West Kar Street Vaidheeshwaran Koil-609117 Mob. : 98942 01444 West Kar Street
30	Thiru G Selvaraj, Mega. Alexander Mahasiva Vakkiya, Agasthiya Naadi	51C, West Kar Street Vaidheeshwaran Koil-609117 Tel. : (04364) 279194 Mob. : 98650 32000 West Kar Street

31	Thiru D. M. Sivamani Sri korakar Naadi	45, West Kar Street Vaidheeshwaran Koil-609117 Mob. : 9443986044
32	Sri Paraasara Maharishi Naadi Jothidam	No. 13/3, Archana Hotel Upstairs, West Veedhi, Sirkali Taluk, Vaithiswarankoil-609117 Tel. : (4365)-279353
33	Surya Kumar Naadi Center	East Main Road, Perunchery, Mayiladuthurai Vaideeshwaran Koil Mob. : 9566952412 Tel. : 04336 4253393 {5/16}

Tamilnadu 3   Coimbatore/ Trichy

S. No.	Naadi Center	Address
1	Kovai Geetharamani Siva Jothida Nillayam	No. 45, Ramasamy Layout, Kumaran Medicals, Avarampalayam, Coimbatore- 641006 Mob. : 9790456788 Fees in most of the centers of Tamilnadu are in three tier. 1.For Tamilians Gen Kandam Rs. 450/- For rest Kandam Rs. 350/- 2.For Non-Tamil Indians. For Gen Kandam 1000/- Rest Kandam Rs.800/- 3. Foreigners Gen. Rs.2000/- Rest Kandam.Rs. 1000/- Hindi/English translator available.
2	SRI Bhrigu Kousikar Naadi Jothida Nilaya...	No. 1605, Opp To Joseph Convent, Trichy Main Road, Coimbatore Central, Coimbatore - 641018 Fees in most of the centers of Tamilnadu are in three tier. 1.For Tamilians Gen Kandam Rs. 450/- For rest Kandam Rs. 350/- 2.For Non-Tamil Indians. For Gen Kandam 1000/- Rest Kandam Rs.800/- 3. Foreigners Gen. Rs.2000/- Rest Kandam. Rs. 1000/- Hindi/English translator available. Mob. : 9444146009
3	Sri Agasthiyar Sugar Naadi Astrology Centre	No 51a, 4th Cross Road Vayallur Road, Tiruchirappalli East, Trichy - 620008, Opposite To Bishop Heber Coll Tel. : 431-2771868 Mob. : 9944851221, 9842420004

4	Siranjivi Kaaka Pujanda Mahasiva Naadi Jothida Nilayam	1373A, Jayasanthi Towers, 2nd Floor, Sathy Road, Ganapathy, Coimbatore- 641006 Mob. : 9360218678, 9843827587 Landmark: Near CMS Matriculation School Fees in most of the centers of Tamilnadu are in three tier. 1.For Tamilians Gen Kandam Rs. 450/- For rest Kandam Rs. 350/- 2.For Non-Tamil Indians. For Gen Kandam 1000/- Rest Kandam Rs.800/- 3. Foreigners Gen. Rs.2000/- Rest Kandam. Rs. 1000/- Hindi/English translator available.
5	Sri Shugar Naadi Jothida Nilayam	74, Sathy Road, Gandhipuram, Coimbatore-641012 Ph. : 0422 2494574 Landmark: Near GP Hospital Fees in most of the centers of Tamilnadu are in three tier. 1.For Tamilians Gen Kandam Rs. 450/- For rest Kandam Rs. 350/- 2.For Non-Tamil Indians. For Gen Kandam 1000/- Rest Kandam Rs.800/- 3. Foreigners Gen. Rs.2000/- Rest Kandam. Rs. 1000/- Hindi/English translator available.
6	Thiru Kannan Agasthiya Naadi	417, 6th Street (Exten) 100 Feet Road, Gandhpuram, Coimbatore - 641012 Tel. : (0422) 2436824 Fees in most of the centers of Tamilnadu are in three tier. 1.For Tamilians Gen Kandam Rs. 450/- For rest Kandam Rs. 350/- 2.For Non-Tamil Indians. For Gen Kandam 1000/- Rest Kandam Rs.800/- 3. Foreigners Gen. Rs.2000/- Rest Kandam. Rs. 1000/- Hindi/English translator available.
7	Sri Agathiyar Naadi Astrology Center	Maruthamalai Temple, 128, Maruthamalai Basement, Coimbatore-641045 Tel. : (422)-2426524 Fees in most of the centers of Tamilnadu are in three tier. 1.For Tamilians Gen Kandam Rs. 450/- For rest Kandam Rs. 350/- 2.For Non-Tamil Indians. For Gen Kandam 1000/- Rest Kandam Rs.800/- 3. Foreigners Gen. Rs.2000/- Rest Kandam. Rs. 1000/- Hindi/English translator available.

8	Sri Agasthiyar Naadi Jothida Nilayam	Old No. 239, New No 119, V G R Complex, Bharathiar Road, papanaickenpalayam, Coimbatore-641037 Mob. : 9843445444 Fees in most of the centers of Tamilnadu are in three tier. 1.For Tamilians Gen Kandam Rs. 450/- For rest Kandam Rs. 350/- 2. For Non-Tamil Indians. For Gen Kandam 1000/- Rest Kandam Rs.800/- 3. Foreigners Gen. Rs.2000/- Rest Kandam. Rs. 1000/- Hindi/English translator available.
9	Sri Akathiyar Maha Siva Naadi Jothida Nilayam	61, Siruvani Main Road, Perur Coimbatore-641010, Fees in most of the centers of Tamilnadu are in three tier. 1.For Tamilians Gen Kandam Rs. 450/- For rest Kandam Rs. 350/- 2.For Non-Tamil Indians. For Gen Kandam 1000/- Rest Kandam Rs.800/- 3. Foreigners Gen. Rs.2000/- Rest Kandam. Rs. 1000/- Hindi/English translator available.
10	Arul Nandhi Jeevaa Naadi	Tiruchirappalli Cantt, Trichy- 620001 Mob. 9840045217
11	Sri Sakthi Naadi Jothida Nilayam	New-21, Old-16, Sriram Layout, Sai Baba Colony, Coimbatore-641011 Ph. : 0422 2443681 Landmark: Near PNT Quarters Bus Stop Fees in most of the centers of Tamilnadu are in three tier. 1.For Tamilians Gen Kandam Rs. 450/- For rest Kandam Rs. 350/-2.For Non-Tamil Indians. For Gen Kandam 1000/- Rest Kandam Rs.800/- 3. Foreigners Gen. Rs.2000/- Rest Kandam. Rs. 1000/- Hindi/English translator available.
12	Sri Mahalakshmi Jothidanilayam & Vaasthumayam	No. 41, SBI Colony, 2nd Cross, Meena Estate, Sowripalayam, Coimbatore - 641028 Mob. : 914449915755
13	Sri Agasthiyar Naddi Jyothidam	No 8, 4th Cross VOC Street, Ladapuram, Trichy-621101, Kumaran Nagar Tel. 431-277057 M. : 9842472011

14	Sri Agathiyar Naadi Astrology Center	14-C, Government Hospital Back Side, Gopal Pillai Street, Sulur, Coimbatore - 641402 Fees in most of the centers of Tamilnadu are in three tier. 1.For Tamilians Gen Kandam Rs. 450/- For rest Kandam Rs. 350/- 2.For Non-Tamil Indians. For Gen Kandam 1000/- Rest Kandam Rs.800/- 3. Foreigners Gen. Rs.2000/- Rest Kandam. Rs. 1000/- Hindi/English translator available.
15	Sri Akathiar Naadi Jothida Nilaiyam	Vinayagar Temple, No. 1932 , R.K.V. Nagar, Kuthur, Trichy-621216 Tel. : (431)-2593334 Fees Rs. 400/- for General Kandam Rs.150/- for Additional Kandam
16	Sri Annai Meenakshi Jothida Nillyam	No 856, Vinayaga Complex, Mettupalayam Road, Flower Market, Town Hall, Coimbatore-641001 Tel. : 9894178562 Fees in most of the centers of Tamilnadu are in three tier. 1.For Tamilians Gen Kandam Rs. 450/- For rest Kandam Rs. 350/- 2. For Non-Tamil Indians. For Gen Kandam 1000/- Rest Kandam Rs.800/- 3. Foreigners Gen. Rs.2000/- Rest Kandam. Rs. 1000/- Hindi/English translator available.
17	Agasthya Naadi	No. 40/8, Balakrishna Nagar, Mannargudi HO, Mannargudi - 614001 Mob. : 9443475721, 9487841847
18	Thiru Jayashankar CP Agasthiya Naadi	101, Ganapathy Nagar Thiruvainai Koil Trichy-620 005 Tel.: (0431) 262190 Fees in most of the centers of Tamilnadu are in three tier. 1.For Tamilians Gen Kandam Rs. 450/- For rest Kandam Rs. 350/- 2.For Non-Tamil Indians. For Gen Kandam 1000/- Rest Kandam Rs.800/- 3. Foreigners Gen. Rs.2000/- Rest Kandam. Rs. 1000/- Hindi/English translator available.
19	Sri Agathiyar Sukar Naadi Astrology Center	No:15/3, Evr Road, Puthur, Puthur, Trichy-620017 Mob. : 9842420042 {9/20}

320 ———————————————————————— *Naadi Predictions*

20	Naadi Jothidam	2/C, M.M, Complex, Puthukottai Main Road, Tiruchirappalli HO, Trichy-620001, City Finance(Opp) TVS Tolgate M. 9965571837, 9842471837{9/20}
21	Late Thiru Dharani Balan Agasthiya Naadi	No6/9, Kumaran Nagar Bus Stop, South Ramalinga Nagar (Extn), 5th Cross, VI Road, Ramalinga Nagar, Trichy-620017 Tel. : 2770013 Fees in most of the centers of Tamilnadu are in three tier. 1.For Tamilians Gen Kandam Rs. 450/- For rest Kandam Rs. 350/- 2.For Non-Tamil Indians. For Gen Kandam 1000/- Rest Kandam Rs.800/-3. Foreigners Gen. Rs.2000/- Rest Kandam. Rs. 1000/- Hindi/English translator
22	Thiru A. Kalamegam	11/C, Varadachari Street, Ranga Nagar, Sri Rangan, Trichy-620 008. Tel.: 0431 - 2432566 Fees in most of the centers of Tamilnadu are in three tier. 1.For Tamilians Gen Kandam Rs. 450/- For rest Kandam Rs. 350/- 2.For Non-Tamil Indians. Rs. Gen Kandam 1000/- Rest Kandam Rs.800/- 3. Foreigners Gen. Rs.2000/- Rest Kandam. Rs. 1000/- Hindi/English translator available.
23	Thiru Dheivakanthan Agasthiya Naadi	Mumbai Salai, Srirangam, Trichy Tel : (431)-2433 169 Fees in most of the centers of Tamilnadu are in three tier. 1.For Tamilians Gen Kandam Rs. 450/- For rest Kandam Rs. 350/- 2.For Non-Tamil Indians. For Gen Kandam 1000/- Rest Kandam Rs.800/- 3. Foreigners Gen. Rs.2000/- Rest Kandam. Rs. 1000/- Hindi/English translator available.
24	Thiru S. Jayaraman Agasthya Naadi Jothida Nilayam	46, Thiruvadi Street Sri Rangam. Trichy-620006 Mob. : 9003583620, 9345124854. Just outside main Gopuram of main temple.
25	Sri Agasthiyar Sivavakkiya	No. 57, Sannathi Street, Thiruvanaikoil, Trichy- 620005 Near Hotel Mani Vilas Mob. : 9443986030 Tel. : 431-2231574 {9/20}

26	Sri Magarishi Naadi Jothidam	No. 12/8, Old Kaveri Bridge Road, Trichy Hotel, Trichy-620001 Tel. : 431-2433151. {9/20}
27	Sri Agathiya Maha Siva Thulliya naadi astrology centre in Trichy	Srirangam, Tiruchirappalli, Tamil Nadu-620006 Mob. : 919786776964

Tamilnadu 4 Rest of Tamil Nadu

S. No.	Naadi Center	Address
1	Naadi Astrology Online prediction	No. 148, Ground Floor, 3rd Street, AH Block, Shanthi Colony, Anna Nagar, Chennai-600040 (T.N.) Mob. : 9840517153
2	Sri Maharishi Thulliya Siva Sakthi Naadi Astrology	148, 3rd St, AH Block, Ishwarya Nagar, Shanthi Colony, Anna Nagar, Chennai-600040 (T. N.) Mob. : 9840517153
3	Siva Naadi Astrology Centre	No. 38/39, Valli Illam, Ainthu Kinatru Amman Kovil Backside, Cuddalore O T, Cuddalore O T, Pondicherry-607003 Mob. : 9600215686 Fees Rs. 500/- for General Kandam Rs.250/- for Additional Kandam
4	Sri Agasthiyar Naadi Jothida Nilayam	T.P.R Police Station, 24, II Cross Road, Vanktesan Nagar, T.P.R Cuddalore-607001 Tel. : (4142)-235734 Fees Rs. 500/- for General Kandam Rs.250/- for Additional Kandam
5	Sri Agasthiyar Maha Sivavakkiyar Naadi Jothida Nilayam	No 7, Tirupadiripuliyur, Venkateswara Nagar, Cuddalore - 607002 Tel : 4142-235734.
6	Dr. Om Ulaganathan Errattai Naadi	"630/A Jeevanatham Road Kulukadi Medu, Erode-638002 Tel. : (0424) 256313, 253499

7	Sri Siva Vaakiya Naadi Jothida Nilayam	No. 292/510, Skc Road, Surampatti, Erode-638009 Mob. : 9943400956 Fees Rs. 400/- for General Kandam Rs.150/- for Additional Kandam
8	Sri Akathiya Mahasiva Naadi Jothidam	70/1054, Koodudhurai Road, Bhavani, Erode-638301 Tel. : 4256-232075 Fees Rs. 400/- for General Kandam Rs.150/- for Additional Kandam
9	Sri Agathiar Jothida Nilayam	Chinnamuthu Street, Erode H. O., Erode-638001 Tel. :-2254887 Fees Rs. 400/- for General Kandam Rs.150/- for Additional Kandam
10	Vasishtha Naadi	Vasu Dandapani, Gobi Chettipalayam, Erode TN. {5/16}
11	Sri Agathiyar Sugar Naadi Astrology Center	24, Bagavathi Amman Kovil Back Side, Bharathiyar Street West, Jawahar Bazaar, Karur - 639001 Mob. : 9047515597 Fees Rs. 500/- for General Kandam Rs. 250/- for Additional Kandam
12	Thiru K Sakthivel & Selvam Agathiya Naadi	43, Step Colony, Near Nilgiries Bakery, Hosur - 600 092 Tele. : (04344) 278823 Fees in most of the centers of Tamilnadu are in three tier. 1.For Tamilians Gen Kandam Rs. 450/- For rest Kandam Rs. 350/- 2.For Non-Tamil Indians. For Gen Kandam 1000/- Rest Kandam Rs.800/- 3. Foreigners Gen. Rs.2000/- Rest Kandam. Rs. 1000/- Hindi/English translator available.
13	Thiru Sabhapathy Kaushika Agastya Mahasiva Naadi	Appuravoo Nagar, Thally Road, Hosur. Mob. 9362310588, 9443402684 Fees Rs. 500/- for General Kandam Rs.250/-for Additional Kandam
14	Sri Agathiya Maha Siva Naadi Jothida Nilayam	17, Thottam Mela Veethi, Nagapattinam - 7 Mob. : 9626569678, 9345906711 Fees Rs. 400/- for General Kandam Rs.150/-for Additional Kandam

15	Thiru Arul Shivram Sugar Naadi	35/C, Chengulpet Road, Chenna, Kanchipuram - 631503 Mob. : 9652655632 Fees in most of the centers of Tamilnadu are in three tier. 1.For Tamilians Gen Kandam Rs. 450/- For rest Kandam Rs. 350/- 2.For Non-Tamil Indians. For Gen Kandam 1000/- Rest Kandam Rs.800/- 3. Foreigners Gen. Rs. 2000/- Rest Kandam. Rs. 1000/- Hindi/English translator available.
16	Thiru P. M. Pandian Shri Kaushik Naadi	1, Nehru Nagar, Near State Bank, Colony (Toll Gate) Chingulpet Road, Kanchipuram-631 503 Tel. : (0411) 21062 Fees in most of the centers of Tamilnadu are in three tier. 1.For Tamilians Gen Kandam Rs. 450/- For rest Kandam Rs. 350/- 2.For Non-Tamil Indians. ForGen Kandam 1000/- Rest Kandam Rs.800/- 3. Foreigners Gen. Rs.2000/- Rest Kandam. Rs. 1000/- Hindi/English translator available.
17	Thiru Balasubramaniam Agasthiya Naadi	189, Periyar Nagar, Chinna, Kanchipuram-631503 Tel. : (04112) 269283 Fees in most of the centers of Tamilnadu are in three tier. 1.For Tamilians Gen Kandam Rs. 450/- For rest Kandam Rs. 350/- 2.For Non-Tamil Indians. For Gen Kandam 1000/- Rest Kandam Rs.800/- 3. Foreigners Gen. Rs.2000/- Rest Kandam. Rs. 1000/- Hindi/English translator available. (Tuesday Holiday)
18	Sree Agastiyar Naadi jodider Nilayam	PSS Complex, 2nd Floor, Vaiapurinagar, Karur-639002 Mob. : 9367123991 Fees Rs. 500/-for General Kandam Rs.250/- for Additional Kandam
19	Agasthya Bhrigu Naadi Nilayam	Aduthurai Road, Aduthurai, Kumbakonam - 612101, Govindhapuram Mob. : 9655263899, 9943021781 {9/20}

20	Agasthya Jyothisha	Thiruppuvanam Mani Road, Solan Nagar, Kumbakonam HO, Kumbakonam - 612001 Mob. : 9894906352
21	Sri Kousika Agasthiya Mahasiva Vakkiya Naadi	Jotihdam Bypass Road, Pasumpon Nagar, Palanganatham, Madurai – 625003. {9/20}
22	Sri Navagraha Jothida Nilayam	No 15, Opposite To Sudesi Cotton Mill, Kalaimagal Street 8th Cross, Pondicherry, H. O., Pondicherry 605001 Mob. : 9943837901 Fees Rs. 500/- for General Kandam Rs.250/- for Additional Kandam
23	Naadi Astrology Center Vaitheeswarankoil	Railway Station Road, Vaitheeswaran, Koil-609117 (Tamil Nadu) Mob. : 9963334337
24	Agastiya Naadi Jothida Nilayam	Plot No. 22/631 opposite Ambika Cinema Hall Arignan Anna Nagar Madurai-625 020 Ph. : 0452 2535010, 2521083 Mob. : 9443053313 Fees in most of the centers of Tamilnadu are in three tier. 1.For Tamilians Gen Kandam Rs. 450/- For rest Kandam Rs. 350/- 2.For Non-Tamil Indians. For Gen Kandam 1000/- Rest Kandam Rs.800/- 3. Foreigners Gen. Rs.2000/- Rest Kandam. Rs. 1000/- Hindi/English translator available.
25	Shri Agastya Kousika Mahasiva Naadi Jothida Nilayam	C-140/32 J Vairam Complex, Nehruji Street 4th stop Thirunagar Madurai-625006 Tel. : 0452 2483861 Mob. : 9345203660 Fees in most of the centers of Tamilnadu are in three tier. 1.For Tamilians Gen Kandam Rs. 450/- For rest Kandam Rs. 350/- 2.For Non-Tamil Indians. For Gen Kandam 1000/- Rest Kandam Rs.800/- 3. Foreigners Gen. Rs.2000/- Rest Kandam. Rs. 1000/- Hindi/English translator available. {9/20}
26	Sri Agasthiyar Maha Sivavakkiyar Naadi Jothida Nilayam	No. 2/311, Ammai Appan Illam, C M Nagar, Vandiyur, Yamunai Illam, Madurai H.O., Madurai- 625001, Kalamega Perumal Koyil. Mob. : 9600782121, 9443053313 {9/20}

27	Thiru S P Gurumoorty Kaushik Naadi	56, Thiruvalluvar, Kurukku Salai, Shanmugpuram,Palani-624601 Fees in most of the centers of Tamilnadu are in three tier. 1.For Tamilians Gen Kandam Rs. 450/- For rest Kandam Rs. 350/- 2.For Non-Tamil Indians. For Gen Kandam 1000/- Rest Kandam Rs.800/- 3. Foreigners Gen. Rs.2000/- Rest Kandam. Rs. 1000/- Hindi/English translator available.
28	Agasthya Maha Siva Naadi Astrology Centre	8th Cross St, Anugraha Satellite Township, Periyakattupalayan, Tamil Nadu - 607402 Mob. : 9042255527
29	Thiru Mathiyazhagan Bhrugu & Agasthiya Naadi	57, Brindavan Rd,Opp. Sarada College Fairlands, Murugan, Koil, Salem-636 016 Tel. : (0427) 2449397, Mob. : 94432 67089 Fees in most of the centers of Tamilnadu are in three tier. 1.For Tamilians Gen Kandam Rs. 450/- For rest Kandam Rs. 350/- 2.For Non-Tamil Indians. For Gen Kandam 1000/- Rest Kandam Rs.800/- 3. Foreigners Gen. Rs.2000/- Rest Kandam. Rs. 1000/- Hindi/English translator available.
30	Agathiyar Naadi Jothida Nilayam	No 172, Holy Flower School & Opp To New Bus Stand, Kannagi Street, Fair Lands, Salem-636004 Tel. : (427)-2445595 Fees Rs. 400/- for General Kandam Rs.150/- for Additional Kandam
31	Sri Agasthiya Mahasiva Thulliya Naadi Astrology Center	East Car Street Vaitheeswaran koil Vaitheeswaran Kovil, Sirkali - 609117 (Tamil Nadu) Mob. : 99527 93925
32	Agathiyar Naadi Jyothida Nilayam	No 1/D, Opp Sumathi Cinema Hall, Rangaswamy Nagar, Sriperumbudur- 5 Mob. : 9790944392 Fees Rs. 500/- for General Kandam Rs.250/- for Additional Kandam
33	Sri Agathiyar Naadi Jothidam/ Naadi Astrologer Vellore	Palani Rathinavel Street, Sainathapuram, RV Nagar, Vellore-632001 (Tamil Nadu) Mob. : 94437 35867

34	Agasthya Jeeva Naadi Shri Ganeshan	Dr. Vanitha, No. 33, 2nd Street, Kooturavu Colony Bus Stop Opposite, Thanjavur - 7 Mob. : 094434 21627 For Spiritual Jeeva Naadi Reading. Contact person & English translator- Mr J Kumar Mob. : 09944194218.
35	Thiru K.S. Krishnan Agathiya Mahashiv Naadi	23/8, Ammani amman Koil street Tiruvannamalai-600 010 Tel. : (04175) 250336 Fees in most of the centers of Tamilnadu are in three tier. 1.For Tamilians Gen Kandam Rs. 450/- For rest Kandam Rs. 350/- 2. For Non-Tamil Indians. For Gen Kandam 1000/- Rest Kandam Rs.800/- 3. Foreigners Gen. Rs.2000/- Rest Kandam. Rs. 1000/- Hindi/English translator available.
36	Naadi Astrology Centre	Agasthiya Maha Siva Naadi Jothida Nilayam, Swamy Sannathi Street, Vaitheeswaran, Koil-609117 (Tamil Nadu) Mob. : 999406913
37	A.Sivasamy, Sivanadi Astrology Centre	18, Milladi Street, Railway station road, Opp. Indian Bank, Vaitheeswaran, Koil-609117 (T.N.) Tel. : 4364-279 463
38	Naadi Astrology Centre	Agasthiya Maha Siva Naadi Jothida Nilayam, Swamy Sannathi Street, Vaitheeswaran, Koil-609117 (Tamil Nadu) Mob : 99941 06913
39	Thiru Varagabalan GT Agasthiya Naadi	1499, Cross 20 Phase - II, Sathhuvachari, Vellore-632 009 Tel. : (0416) 253949, 255848 Fees in most of the centers of Tamilnadu are in three tier. 1.For Tamilians Gen Kandam Rs. 450/- For rest Kandam Rs. 350/- 2.For Non-Tamil Indians. For Gen Kandam 1000/- Rest Kandam Rs.800/- 3. Foreigners Gen. Rs.2000/- Rest Kandam. Rs. 1000/- Hindi/English translator available.
40	Naadi Vaitheeswarankoil	No.45/2, opposite Railway Station, Vaitheeswaran, Koil-609117 (Tamil Nadu) Tel : 99943 64838

MP/UP/Uttrakhand/Bihar/Jharkhand/ C Garh/Odisha/W Bengal States

S. No.	Naadi Center	Address
1	Thiru SSP Raja Agasthiya Kausik Naadi	404 Chandan Deep, Apartments Jagdev Road, Bailey Road, Near IGMS building, Patna-800014. Tel.: (01882) 253547 Fees Rs. 150/- for Prashna and Rs. 500/- for life reading Time : 9 a.m. to 5 p.m.
2	Shri Shiva Naadi Astrology Centre	No. 11, Anand Nagar, Near Radha-Swami satsang, Raipur-492007 (Chhattisgarh) Tel. : 771-2422681 M. : 9425286033 fees Rs. 500/- Gen Kandam, Rs.300 Rest Kandam (Monday closed)
3	Naadi Jyotish Kendra Naadi Jyotish Kendra	Ananthpur, Ranchi, Near Overbridge Doranda, Jharkhand Ranchi-834002 Mob. : 966188246, 9835533647 {9/20}
4	Naadi Astrology India Shri Agasthiyar Mahashiva Naadi Jyotish Bhawan Divine Culture of India. The Ancient Vedic Naadi Astrology	No.3/17, MK Electrical 2,nd Floor Patrakar Puram Crossing Road Near Aryan Restaurant and Patrakar Puram Circle, Patrakar Puram, Vinay Khand 3, Gomti Nagar, Lucknow-226010 U. P. Mob. : 9721215463, Gomti Nagar, Lucknow, U. P. Mob. : 8840605945
5	Naadi Astrology, Meerut, Naadi Jyotish Kendra	RTO Road, Sector 3, Shastri Nagar, Meerut-250004 (U. P.) Mob. : 81265 64111
6	Shri Agasthiya Mahashiv Naadi Jyotish Kendra	5/18, Bairagarh, Near Jain Mandir, Behind Bus Stand , Swami Lilasha Colony, Bhopal-462030 (M.P.) {9/20}
7	Thiru Kantru Swami, Agasthya Maha Siva Vakiya Naadi	136/G - 1/32, Mayur Nagar Thatipur Gwalior - 474 011 (M.P.) Tel. : 0751-5081918 fees Rs. 500/- Gen Kandam Rs.300/- Rest Kandam Monday closed

8	Pundit Amareswar Mishra Tâmrapothi and Roupyapothi	Mahapurusha Achyutananda Kakatpur, 20 Kms from Bhubneswar, Odisa. Fees: as per wish (except Wednesday, eclipse-days, and Garoi function days)
9	Naadi Astrology Jharkhand	287, Ashok Nagar Road, Ranchi, Jharkhand. Mob. : 8940139779
10	Naadi Jothida Nilayam	71 D, Swinhoe Lane, Kasba, Kolkata - 42 Mob. : 09831896846, 9831896937 {9/20}
11	K. S. Krishnan Shri Agasthya Nahashiv Vakya Tulya naadi Nilayam	Agasthya, Kaushika, House No. 1A Lane No. 3, Kali Mandir Enclave, Opp. Khadi Gramodyog, GMS road, Dehradun. Ph. : 0135-3290072 Mob. : 9897461267 Fees Gen kandam. Rs 700/- Rest kandam Rs 500/- (Monday Closed)
12	Pt. Raghvendra Tripathi, Pratap Garhwale,	8th Generation. 254 /GF, Bhartiya Jyotish Sansthan, Sahara Trade center, Faijabad road, Indira Nagar, Lucknow-226016 Mob . : 9415023006 Fees 2100/- Send detailed horoscope by post, when leaf found, will be called by appointment.
13	Ravan Samhita	Ravan Samhita Guruwalia, Balia, Near Gorakhpur. Fees 500/- Mob.: 98388 26171
14	Mahashiv Naadi 3rd Reading	3/114, 2 nd floor Vinay khand Vidayakpuram, Gomati nagar, Lucknow-10 Ph. : 052-26453087 Mob. : 9721215463, 9369955690 Fees Gen kandam. Rs 700/- Rest kandam Rs 500/- (Monday Closed)
15	Pt. Vipin Dixit. Bhrugu Samhita Grand son of late Shivkumar Dixit.	421, Near Budhana gate, Meerut. U.P. Tel. : 0121) – 2523099, 2530935 Mob. : 9837066263 Fees 1000 /- and above as per the case. Send detailed horoscope by post, when leaf found, will be called by appointment.
16	Bhrigu Samhita Vachak	Dr. Anita Prakash : Station Road, Pratapgarh. Mob. :09935343825 8604864279

17	Bhrigu Samhita Vachak	Dr. Sadhana Surya : Sitaram lane, Station road, Pratapgarh. Mob.: 09450185962. Tel. : 05342 222258.
18	Bhrigu Samhita Vachak	Dr. Bipin Mishra: Bhagwa Nivas Station road Pratapgarh. Mob. : 9450187726 Tel. : 05342-222217.
19	Saharapnur - Kedarnath Prabhakar Ramtirth Kendra,	Ambala road, near Darpan Chinmay Jyotishya Anusandhan, Saharanpur-247001 (U.P.) Mob.09897780544. - (It is not Bhrigu Samhita Center. But Bhrigu Patras are available for study purpose).
20	Pt. Bhrhamadutta Dwivedi	Civil Lines, Pratapgarh bhriguji4u@gmail.com
21	Pt. Bhagvandas Chunnilal	Bhrigu Samhita Bhavan D-15/21, Man Mandir, Dashwamedh, Varanasi.
22	Guruji K. Arul Senthil ji Agasthy Mahasiva Naadi	Indranil Apart, 184, Rajganga Navapalli, Kolkata -700086 Ph. : 033-65693720 Mob. : 09830830424. Fees Gen Kandam Rs 700/- Rest Kandam Rs 350/- (Monday closed).
23	Thiru Sridhar Pandit Agasthy Mahasiva Naadi	39, Janak Road, Sarat Bose Road, Near Lake Market, Kolkata – 700029 Fees Gen Kandam Rs 700/- Rest Kandam Rs 350/- (Monday closed){9/20}
24	Shri Agasti Naadi Jyotishalaya	113A,1st Floor, Flat No. 3, M G Road, Haridevpur, Near Karunamoyee Kali Mandir, Kolkata – 700082 Mob. 9331723939, 9007420069 {9/20}
25	Naadi Jothida Nilayam	9, Lansdowne Terrace, Near National Girls High School, Near Deshopriya Park, Kolkata - 700029 Mob. : 9894861695 Ph. : 33-64556752, 24197076, 64531778, 24198885 {9/20}
26	Naadi Jothida Nilayam	187,Subarnarekha Apartment.4th flood room no.4A, Rajdanga Nabapally, Eastern Metropolitan Bypass, Nr Kasba Ruby Park State Bank, Kolkata - 700107 Tel. : 33-65693723, 9830830424, 9051910696 {9/20}